STALIN'S BRITISH VICTIMS

FRANCIS BECKETT

SUTTON PUBLISHING

First Published in the United Kingdom in 2004 by
Sutton Publishing Limited · Phoenix Mill
Thrupp · Stroud · Gloucestershire · GL5 2BU

British Library Cataloguing in Publication Data
A catalogue record for this book is available from the British
Library.

ISBN 0-7509-3223-6

Typeset in Sabon 11/14.5pt.
Typesetting and origination by
Sutton Publishing Limited.
Printed and bound in England by
J.H. Haynes & Co. Ltd, Sparkford.

Contents

	Introduction	vii
One	Daughter of a Revolutionary	1
Two	The Promised Land	15
Three	The Knock on the Door	45
Four	From Which No Traveller Returns	73
Five	Rosa in Kazakhstan	99
Six	Rosa in London	119
Seven	1956: The Prisons Yield up their Secrets	129
Eight	Rosa in Redcar	159
Nine	Shadows in a World after Communism	167
Ten	The Persecution Gene	187
	Source References	195
	Further Reading	199
	Index	201

Introduction

This book tells the stories of four remarkable British women whose lives were scorched by Stalin's purges. One was shot as a spy; one nearly died as a slave labourer in Kazakhstan; and two saw their husbands taken away to the gulag and had to spirit their small children out of the country.

We in Britain think of the horrors of the middle of the twentieth century – the Holocaust in Central Europe, the purges in the Soviet Union – as something foreign: terrible, but remote, like famine in Africa. But Rosa Rust, Rose Cohen, Freda Utley and Pearl Rimel were all Londoners, as English as fish and chips, as familiar in our capital as Piccadilly Circus. Like hundreds of young, idealistic Britons in the 1930s, they looked to the Soviet Union for inspiration, for a way in which society could be run better, without the exploitation and poverty that unrestrained capitalism had created in Britain. They were less fortunate than most of us: they saw their dream fulfilled.

This book does not pretend to be a history of the purges, nor even a history of Britons in the purges. Dozens, perhaps hundreds, of Britons joined the millions of Russians who suffered under Stalin – the KGB holds files on 1,500 British citizens. You will find something about some of the others in Chapter Seven.

But I became fascinated with these four women, and wanted to discover what sort of people they were and what motivated them, what their families and husbands and children were like, and what they felt when their dream disintegrated and turned to poison in front of them. I went in search of everything it was possible to find out about them, talking to their surviving relatives, looking at their surviving letters, and finding out what I could from the archives of the Communist International in Moscow.

I discovered more than enough to admire all four of them, and to draw a picture of four human beings who had little in common apart from courage, intelligence, originality and idealism, which all four had in abundance; and to explain how they coped with events which would have crushed many of us.

This book tells the dramatic stories of their lives. It tries to put those lives in context: in Moscow and London in the 1920s and 1930s, and in New York, Los Angeles, London and Redcar during the second half of the twentieth century.

The years immediately after the First World War and the 1917 Revolution in Russia were years of hope and optimism, when the British generation that had fought in the war vowed that their friends had not died in order to return to the same old unfair society they had known before 1914. This book is not just the story of four women. It is also the story of how those high hopes turned to dust and ashes in the years between the two world wars.

There are two views of Stalin's purges in 1936–8, in which millions were judicially murdered. One, articulated by Nikita Khrushchev in his exposé of Stalin in 1956, was that these events were simply the result of Stalin himself, a pot of poison at the heart of an otherwise benevolent social system. The other is that they were an integral part of the Soviet system inaugurated by Lenin in the 1917 Bolshevik Revolution. This second view was most neatly summed up by Robert Conquest:

> There was a great Marxist called Lenin
> Who did two or three million men in.
> That's a lot to have done in
> But where he did one in
> That grand Marxist Stalin did ten in.

If pressed I incline to the Khrushchev view. Conquest is less than fair to Lenin. Communism did not have to be the murderous, viciously petty-minded, sectarian and vindictive thing my four principal characters found in the Soviet Union. In theory, communism is a generous and fair-minded creed, which rejects, for good reason, the poverty amid plenty which is the hallmark of capitalism. There's a case for saying that it was simply hijacked by a cold-blooded mass murderer. But for that to be possible, the fault line had to be there. And the fault line was there. The seeds for the Stalin terror were there; but they needed a monster like Stalin to nurture them. The fault line was the sectarian intolerance and the lack of feeling for individual human beings which Russian communists took to be virtues.

Russian communists trained communist parties all over the world, including the Communist Party of Great Britain, to see these things as virtues too. One of the oddest and most fascinating parts of the stories of Rosa Rust, Rose Cohen, Freda Utley and Pearl Rimel is how Britain's communist leaders reacted to what they knew, and how they coped with their regular visits to Moscow, knowing what was happening to their friends there. This book examines how and why men and women who started out with genuine idealism and a rage against injustice ended by abandoning their friends and comrades when they needed them most, and continuing to praise and to obey the man who was responsible for their torment.

This book came about from my research for a previous book, a history of British communism from the creation of the Communist Party of Great Britain in 1920 to its dissolution in 1991, the year that saw the collapse of communism worldwide. That book, *Enemy Within*, was published by John Murray in 1995, and a paperback was published by Merlin Press in 1998. While writing it I came across two of these stories, and knew that I wanted to investigate them much more deeply.

A note about footnotes. None of my previous books has contained any footnotes at all, not just out of laziness, but because, as a reader, I get irritated with the academic habit of littering footnotes about the text like confetti. If you write a doctoral thesis, these are demanded of you, but I don't want a doctorate. However, I found that putting in no footnotes at all can sometimes lead to frustration for a reader, and worse, moments of embarrassment for me. This was brought home to me quite forcibly by one of Professor Peter Hennessy's PhD students who wrote asking for the source of a piece of new information in my biography of Clement Attlee. I had no record of where I got it from, and I could not remember. So I've compromised. Where a source might be important to some readers, and it is not clear from the context, you will find a word or two in brackets and italics. Look up the word in the section at the back of the book headed 'Source References'. There, for example, you will find that (*Morgan*) means that I got the quotes, or some of the information, from Kevin Morgan's excellent biography of British communist leader Harry Pollitt.

Kevin Morgan is also one of the historians I have to thank for his constant and unfailing help and guidance, without which many errors might not have been avoided. Another crucial guide has been Alison Macleod, who went to work as a journalist on the Communist Party newspaper the *Daily Worker* in 1944, and was still there when the storm of 1956 broke over the head of the Communist Party. Her luminous and illuminating book *The Death of Uncle Joe* is about how the *Daily Worker*, its editor and its staff reacted to the great events of 1956 – Khrushchev's revelations of the crimes of Stalin, the Soviet invasion of Hungary, and the British invasion of Suez. It was Alison who found Rosa Rust's address when I had failed to do so, and who originally alerted me to Pearl Rimel's story.

In Moscow, at the Russian Centre for the Preservation of Documents, I could have achieved little without my friend Pieta Monks, with her fluent Russian and her understanding of Moscow and its ways, gained from long study at Moscow University.

Other historians to whom I owe much are Monty Johnstone, doyen of communist historians, who has devoted much of his life to ensuring that the misdeeds of his comrades are not airbrushed from history; university academics Dr Francis King and Professor Colin Holmes, whose guidance on the files at the Russian Centre for the Preservation of Documents was invaluable; Dr David Turner, whose explorations into security matters nearly always produce something no one knew before, and whose continued exclusion from university academic life is a running scandal; David Burke of Cambridge and Westminster universities, a biographer of Theodore Rothstein, who was generous with his knowledge of aspects of communism; Stephen Bird, the always helpful and knowledgeable librarian at the Labour History Museum in Manchester, where the Communist Party's papers are stored; and Tish Collins, librarian at the Marx Memorial Library in London, who does not always like what I write, but always helps me find sources for it.

For the story of Pearl Rimel, my main debt is to Thijs Berman, Paris correspondent for Dutch Radio and the great-nephew of Pearl's ill-fated husband George Fles. He researched and wrote a book about the terrible fate of the great-uncle he never knew, which has been published in Holland but not in Britain, alas. Thijs has been generous with the fruits of his research, and has allowed me to use the excellent translation of his book made by Hanneke Klep.

Pearl's only surviving sister, Hetty Bower, at the age of ninety-seven, gave me a wonderfully clear and helpful two-hour interview, and allowed me to use her autobiographical notes. Other members of the Rimel family have also been generous with their time and knowledge: Diana Rimel, Mary Davis, Margaret Dolan and Delia Scales.

For Rosa Rust, my main debt is to Rosa herself; the day I spent listening to her was absorbing and exciting, and the reader will find out all about it. I also want to thank her husband George Thornton, her son David Thornton, and David's partner Harry Coen.

Rose Cohen's niece Joyce Rathbone was, to begin with, very helpful with information about Rose. Regrettably, she decided, for reasons I do not fully understand, not to carry on her co-operation when I came to write this book, but I have tried to make up the loss from other sources. Professor Chimen Abramsky helped me with information about Rose's husband Max Petrovsky.

Freda Utley's son Jon Basil Utley has answered all my (sometimes impertinent) questions about her, about him, and about their relationship, thoughtfully and patiently; and historian Douglas Farnie has put me right on several points.

But in the end, of course, if I have got anything wrong, it's my fault.

Francis Beckett
2004

ONE

Daughter of a Revolutionary

When his daughter was born on 26 April 1925, Bill Rust, 22-year-old leader of the Young Communist League, named her Rosa after the German communist leader Rosa Luxemburg, a martyr to the cause since her assassination in January 1919. He was sure that, long before she was a grown woman, the socialist revolution would have swept away the slums of London's East End in which he had grown up.

That weekend, Field Marshal von Hindenburg was elected President of Germany, and Rust, like all communists, saw that as the precursor to a right-wing dictatorship in Germany – the last gasp of a decaying capitalism, which must soon give way to a socialist paradise. He was half right: it was Hindenburg who, seven years later, was to appoint Adolf Hitler as Chancellor of Germany.

In Britain, a recent general election had given Prime Minister Stanley Baldwin a huge Conservative parliamentary majority, after the fall of the first short-lived Labour government of 1924. Nevertheless, Rust was sure that Baldwin represented not the future, but the past. The likes of Baldwin would give way, within Rust's lifetime, to a socialist future. Again, he was half right. Politicians of Baldwin's generation failed in their misguided attempt to recreate the world as it had been before the earthquake we call the First World War. But as for the socialist future, he was more dreadfully wrong than he would ever know. Rosa was to find out in the most

1

painful way just how wrong he was. When she died, seventy-five years later, she had seen, more graphically perhaps than any other person still living in Britain in the year 2000, just how badly her father's dream of a new and better society had gone wrong.

That weekend, Britain awaited the first budget which the new Conservative Chancellor, Winston Churchill, delivered two days after Rosa's birth. Informed speculation suggested he would return to the gold standard and cut income tax. He did, and communists like Bill Rust saw that as a policy which would lead to economic collapse, and eventually to the collapse of capitalism in Britain and the dawn of a brave new socialist era. Again, he was half right: the economic collapse, caused at least in part by Churchill's return to the gold standard, duly arrived five years later in 1931.

The man on the Clapham omnibus probably saw these things as part of the long, inevitable return to normality after the war, though there was to be no normality as those who had grown up in the pre-war years had known it. To most working people, but not to Bill Rust, that weekend was about Sheffield United beating Cardiff City 1–0 before a 90,000 crowd at Wembley Stadium, or the MCC, despite having Jack Hobbs and Herbert Sutcliffe in the team, returning from Australia without the Ashes. Noel Coward was appearing in his new play *The Vortex* at the Comedy, Sybil Thorndike was in *St Joan* at the Regent, and Gladys Cooper in Arthur Pinero's *Iris* at the Adelphi. Sir Arthur Conan Doyle, writer and spiritualist, gave a lecture to the Practical Psychology Club on 'The Proofs of Immortality'.

Newspapers were full of advertisements for cooks, maids, butlers, laundresses and gardeners, and announcements about the doings of the aristocracy. That weekend they breathlessly informed their readers that the king and queen were returning from Paris. A full half page of *The Times* was taken up with announcements from those aristocrats who wished society to know that they, too, were back in London, such as Lord and Lady Dunedin, who returned to 42 Lower Sloane Street from Monte Carlo two days after Rosa's birth. Harrods proudly announced that it was turning all 5 acres of its second floor over to furniture and that there would be an event, not a sale, for ten days. Two small Whistler drawings were sold for 560 and 360 guineas. No wonder Bill Rust, the working-class communist from London's East End, thought privilege and capitalism were bloated and ready to collapse.

Rust would have been busy encouraging the strike of London dairy roundsmen, who wanted a six-day instead of a seven-day week, a maximum working week of 48 hours, and a minimum wage of £4 a week. He would have paused for as short a time as possible from his hectic political activity to welcome his wife, Kathleen Louise Rust, née O'Donoghue, known as Kay, and his new daughter Rosa, home from Charing Cross Hospital.

Bill was a tall, stocky, grim but, to Kay, rather exciting former docker. He had a passion for motorbikes, and a militant atheism which had caused her Irish Catholic family to disown her for marrying him in a registry office. She was attracted too by his rather dangerous politics, the legacy of his harsh, undernourished childhood.

In Bill and Kay's home, politics were taken seriously. The Communist Party had been formed just five years earlier, in 1920, on the direct instructions of Lenin, the ruler of Russia since the 1917 Revolution. Lenin had carefully steered the warring British socialist groups into a merger, and continued secretly to provide the party with large sums of money, to take a personal interest in everything it did, and to send a permanent representative of the Communist International – the Comintern – to Britain to advise and mentor the infant party.

Lenin's optimism for the future of communism in Britain may seem odd in the light of history, but it seemed perfectly realistic at the time, not just to communism's friends but to its enemies too. The morning the party was formed in 1920, an editorial in the Labour-supporting *Daily Herald* said: 'The founders of the new Party believe – as most competent observers are coming to believe – that the capitalist system is collapsing.' The only question, it seemed to many of them, was whether the future belonged to the Communist Party; to the Labour Party, which was denounced by communists as hopelessly gradualist and reformist, and whose first government, which both came into office and fell in 1924, did nothing at all to inspire confidence that

Labour could change the world; or to the Independent Labour Party. The ILP, once the heart and engine room of the Labour Party, was by 1925 turning into Labour's turbulent left wing, furious at the failure of Labour's first government to do anything significant to help the poor, and at war with the Labour leadership.

Communists were sure they would triumph. And when the moment of communism's triumph came, few people had any doubt that Kay's husband would be one of its young stars, a man with a vital part to play in the affairs of his country and the world. Bill, to the end of his life, never doubted that his time would come. But there would be personal hardships along the way – that was the price of being a revolutionary leader – and Kay had hardly got her new daughter home when the police turned up and took her husband off to prison. It was October 1925, and the government was clearing the decks for the general strike which everyone knew was to come. As mine owners prepared to reduce the miners' already pitiful wages, and make them work longer hours, miners' union leader Arthur Cook tramped the country with a simple message: 'Not a penny off the pay, not a minute on the day.' The government was sure that communists would be at the forefront of agitation for a general strike to support the miners.

So twelve leading communists were arrested, tried swiftly for seditious libel and incitement to mutiny, and sentenced. Five of them, who had previous sentences, went to prison for twelve months, and Bill Rust was one of these. The others, declining an invitation from the judge to be let off with a caution if they renounced communism, went to prison for six months.

So it was that little Rosa took her first steps on the table which separated Rust from his wife when she visited him in Wandsworth Prison. And thus it was that Britain's five most important and effective communists were safely locked up and out of the way throughout the nine days of the general strike of May 1926.

The strike ended in humiliating defeat for the trade unions, which, so the communists claimed (with some justification), were betrayed by leaders who had never believed in the general strike as a weapon in the war for socialism. But for Bill Rust it was the loss of a battle, not of the war, and, as soon as he was free, he threw himself into the work of the Communist Party again. He already had the absolute faith in the Russian leaders of the revolution which was to last him a lifetime. One of his comrades once said that if you lost your faith in the Soviet Union, you were finished as a socialist and a revolutionary; and that summed up what Bill believed. The fierce loyalty he once gave to the leader of the revolution, Vladimir Ilyich Lenin, had been transferred to Joseph Stalin after Lenin's death in 1924. Bill did not know that Lenin died just before he was to denounce Stalin, and he believed all his life that this was one of the many Trotskyist lies.

So when, in 1928, Bill was offered a job with the Comintern in Moscow, he jumped eagerly at the chance to play his part in the shaping of the world socialist revolution. Kay and three-year-old Rosa went with him to Moscow, where Bill quickly became one of the Comintern's most loyal and energetic functionaries.

Bill Rust was a little grim. Few people saw him smile, or knew what made him tick, but he was a dedicated communist whose faith was rooted in the hardships and injustices of his childhood. He was able and alert, but not likeable, and seemed to those who knew him to have more than a streak of ruthless ambition. A close colleague later described him as 'round and pink and cold as ice', adding: 'If he remained in the leadership, it mattered little what indignities, what sacrifices might be demanded of him. Sooner or later communism would triumph and he would be one of the mighty. He would have power. He would have the chance of retribution.' (*Hyde*) If this estimate is correct, it may help to explain many of the episodes to be recounted in this book.

As Rust got older, he acquired the reputation of being the coldest Stalinist apparatchik Britain ever produced. Years later, when he edited the *Daily Worker*, one of the journalists who worked for him, Claud Cockburn, wrote: 'He had, besides a good head on his shoulders, a streak of the urchin and a bigger streak of the pirate. In other words, while as sometimes happened he was monstrously hypocritical, or lying horribly, he did those things with full consciousness, using the tricks as weapons.' Another communist who knew Rust well, Harry McShane, described him, correctly, as 'the man who wanted every little thing done just as Moscow said'. Some of his closest communist colleagues, including Britain's best-known communist and the country's communist leader from the end of the 1920s until 1956, Harry Pollitt, grew to dislike him intensely.

Born in Camberwell, south London, in April 1903, to a book-binder, there is no doubt that Rust had a harsh, difficult and prob-ably underfed childhood. He left school in 1917 when he was fourteen, worked first as a clerk, and all his life spoke like a London Cockney. He was a self-educated man, and owed his learning to the Young Communist League, the Communist Party and his spell in prison, where he seems to have started studying German, a language he later came to speak more or less fluently.

One early job was as a clerk at the Hulton Press Agency. While there, he found out that an engineering union leader was combining his union work with being a paid Labour correspondent for the agency, and revealed this – so he was fired. He joined the Labour Party at sixteen and the newly formed Communist Party in 1920 when he was seventeen. His first taste of prison was in 1922, when he served two months for wilful damage to property while he was resisting an eviction. By the following year he was the full-time secretary of the Young Communist League, and this meant that before he was twenty, Bill Rust had made the first of his many trips to Moscow to attend a meeting of the Communist International, the Comintern. He made it disciplined and utterly obedient to Comin-tern edicts. He wrote that, unlike other left-wing youth organisa-tions, the League was not 'an organisation of cultural faddists and intellectual idlers who spend their time building castles in the air' but a serious group dedicated to the overthrow of capitalism. He joined the party's Central Committee in 1923. (*Flinn*)

Working in party headquarters in King Street, an elegant building just off Covent Garden which Lenin had bought for the Communist Party, brought the party's young rising star into contact with Kay. She was a waitress in a local restaurant where the full-time communist leaders often used to have their lunch, and she started edging closer to what was obviously the most exciting conversation in the room.

At the Comintern Congress in Moscow in July 1928, just after he had moved there with his family, Bill Rust attacked his colleagues in the Communist Party of Great Britain (CPGB) for hesitating to obey the latest Comintern edict. The Comintern wanted them to adopt a new policy which it was imposing on communist Parties throughout the world, and which became known as 'Class against Class'. It meant no more overtures to the Labour Party, or to the Independent Labour Party, but unremitting hostility to them instead. Some senior British communists doubted the wisdom of the new policy, believing that the narrow doctrinal differences between socialists should not prevent them from working together. Moscow, with Bill Rust's enthusiastic support, forced them into line. The following year, after Trotsky had been exiled, Rust was one of those who led the denunciation of a man he had once revered.

It was an exciting time for Bill, but a miserable one for his small daughter. Three-year-old Rosa contracted scarlet fever as soon as she arrived in Moscow. She spent two weeks in hospital, in strict quarantine, which meant that her parents could not visit her, and no one in the hospital spoke any English. In later life she did not remember much about her hospital stay except that she was unhappy, but by the time her mother was allowed to visit, Rosa had forgotten her English and could speak only Russian. Until she was sixteen she spoke only Russian and some German, and then she had to relearn English. To the end of her life Russian was her first language, and she spoke her native tongue with a strong Russian accent, in a deep, clear voice full of great gusts of Russian-sounding laughter. In England she thought of herself as a foreigner.

She found herself translating in shops for her mother, whose Russian was never very good. (Her father's Russian, she said, was even worse, though fellow British communists thought it was rather good. Rosa was judging it by the standards of a native Russian speaker.) Shopping was very hard, and she had to show her mother how it was done: you queued for a ticket, took the ticket to a cash desk and queued again, then queued again to be given your purchases.

By 1929, the year when, at the Comintern Congress, Bill Rust condemned the leaders of Britain's Communist Party for lack of commitment to Comintern policy and to 'Class against Class', Rosa's parents' marriage was all but over. Bill, Rosa told me many years later, was 'very popular in Moscow, in demand everywhere, greatly admired, I am not sure why. To me he seemed a Mr Pickwick figure, balding, with a belly, never looked an attractive man to me, but many women thought him very attractive.' In fact, though the Communist Party hid it carefully, Bill seems all his life to have been something of a sexual predator, and he was then spending most of his time with a Russian woman called Tamara Kravets, whom he later married. His wife Kay's Catholic upbringing made it hard for her to admit to herself that her marriage had failed. (*Rust*)

Mother and daughter lived in a room at the Hotel Lux, on a corridor with twelve rooms and a communal kitchen. The Hotel Lux, where most foreign communists stayed when they were in Moscow, was in Gorky Street, now Tverskaia Street, conveniently close to the Comintern headquarters, Red Square and the Kremlin. It had five floors, a restaurant, and cooking facilities on each landing where most of its guests cooked their own food. Jack Murphy, the CPGB's permanent representative at the Comintern from 1926 to 1928, has left a description: 'The Lux was the most interesting hotel in which I have ever stayed; it had Arnold Bennett's Grand Babylon beaten to a frazzle, not in its efficient service and external and internal grandeur, but in the human material which flowed through it. The visitors came from the ends of the earth, workers, intellectuals, artists, ambitious politicians, revolutionaries, all vital, alive, intelligent, battling with ideas . . .'. (*Murphy*) It was conveniently just a few seconds' walk away from the Kremlin, and from the Comintern, where most of its residents spent most of their time, in a huge building with hundreds of offices and committee rooms.

Kay was working long hours as a junior reporter at the *Moscow Daily News*, the English language daily newspaper, and the increasingly important Bill Rust was seldom seen at the Lux. So little Rosa was desperately lonely, going only fitfully to school and spending much of her time on the Moscow streets, where she fell in with gangs of street children. 'I became a little hooligan, stealing things in shops for the excitement. It was better than sitting at home, alone.' She loved the gypsies she met, for they were always colourful and alive, and in later life it amused her to imagine how shocked her parents would have been if they had known who she was spending her time with. It was the start of a lifelong admiration for gypsies which was to serve her well in the most desperate time of her life.

An even more important lifelong love started on those streets. All her life Rosa loved the theatre – she was a talented actress, and given different breaks, could have been a great one, according to the actress Anna Calder-Marshall, who met Rosa more than six decades later. One day the small child found the Moscow theatre run by the great Constantin Stanislavsky. Somehow she got herself invited back to Stanislavsky's flat, and visited him and his theatre several times. She knew, I think, that this was what she wanted to do with her life. But fate dictated otherwise. (*Rust*)

In 1930 the Comintern decided that British communists should have their own daily newspaper – and that there was only one man they trusted to edit it: Bill Rust. Rust returned to London, but his wife and daughter stayed on in Moscow. Bill devoted much of 1931 to getting permission from the Soviet Union for Tamara to come to London to live with him, and getting the British authorities to let her in.

In London, Rust launched the *Daily Worker*. It must have been a busy and trying time even for this energetic, able loyalist. On top of all the other worries of the editor of a national daily newspaper, he had to cope with the fact that he had no journalistic experience, and neither his British comrades not his Soviet paymasters had any idea of what it took to make a daily paper work. The Soviets seemed to think that all it needed was to print, verbatim, every long and boring statement made by an important official. The rigid, humourless British party theoretician Rajani Palme Dutt denounced the inclusion of news about 'capitalist' sport, and especially the racing tips, which were hastily dropped – a sad early indication of the political correctness which was to ensure that the *Daily Worker* never, in the following decades, achieved a mass circulation.

The party General Secretary Harry Pollitt, desperate for more money to make the paper work, knew that the only way to get it was to do exactly what Moscow wanted, and asked the party's man in Moscow to sound out 'responsible comrades' on the paper's content and style. This request, of course, simply encouraged people who had never visited Britain and knew nothing about journalism to offer useless and ignorant advice on how to woo the British working class. The demands of a daily paper took most of the party's people and energy, leaving no one to revive the party's flagging fortunes elsewhere.

In June 1931, the Comintern appointed a British Commission to examine why the British party was making so little progress, and Rust had to go back to Moscow at the end of July to lead the team which would answer for himself and his colleagues, giving up the editorship of the *Daily Worker* in order to do so. Before a committee of Russian, Chinese, German and other communists, he asked for time to meet the objective of 5,000 new members by the end of the year (which he must have realised was not achievable). He was given a very rough ride. (*Thorpe*) It cannot have helped that he was being judged by people who knew a lot about Comintern politics and the pronouncements of Comrade Stalin, and virtually nothing about conditions in Britain. Bill Rust did not have much time to worry about his wife and daughter, even if he had the inclination.

Rust stayed in Moscow until 1934. That may have been why, in 1932, there was talk of sending Kay back to England – for by then their marriage was over and Bill Rust was openly living with his Russian future wife, Tamara Kravets. This complication, however, was not mentioned in the rather curious correspondence about Kay between Pollitt and the British party representative in Moscow, Robin Page Arnot.

Kay was not regarded as entirely reliable in Moscow, and Page Arnot wrote to Pollitt that she was to be sent to England, and Harry ought to find her party work to do, though that might be difficult: 'Quite a number of the Central Committee or other comrades who knew her [in England] regard her as not being a very responsible comrade and it is true that this impression was created here also. Added to this there was the affair of the Young Communist League nucleus here on two counts, one connected with her Party card, the

other on a more serious question.' This 'more serious question' was
that she had once been expelled from the YCL on the deadly charge
of 'Leftism'. Leftism was deadly because it had been condemned by
no less an authority than Lenin himself, his pamphlet *Left-wing
Communism: an Infantile Disorder*, written especially for the British
Communist Party. Lenin had wanted British Communists to seek
affiliation to the Labour Party. Leftists wanted to condemn the
Labour Party out of hand, a grievous sin until the line changed and
Stalin told them to condemn it. She appealed and her expulsion was
overturned, but the stain on her character seems to have been
indelible.

However, the letter continued, her deficient knowledge of
Marxism had now been partly rectified at Lenin School evening
classes. Page Arnot suggested she should be sent to Liverpool and
told to get a job as a typist. This might be difficult and 'her husband
will for some little time probably have to support her'. Page Arnot
added a personal appeal: 'Harry I think it is worth while if you can
manage it to take a little trouble to get Party work for Kathleen
which will develop her good qualities as a Party member and enable
any other qualities to wither away – for it is true that in the past
there has been some basis for the impression she had made on other
Party members, but I am sure that comrade Kathleen is anxious to
develop herself as a Communist Party member and is very seriously
facing up to her future work. So do the best you can.' (*Manchester*)

The unspoken subtext to all this, of course, was that Bill Rust no
longer wished to live with his wife – but the Communist Party
wanted to be seen as highly moral in personal matters, and Bill's
adultery was a closely guarded secret. So the return of Bill's wife to
England was a very delicate matter, the more so since she was, unlike
her husband, not considered ideologically reliable.

Perhaps, in the end, either Harry Pollitt or the Comintern decided
that on balance Kay was less of an embarrassment where she was.
Bill, who was planning to leave Moscow and bring Tamara to
London as soon as possible, may not have wanted the complication
of having his wife and daughter in England when he arrived there,
even in faraway Liverpool. Perhaps Kay was enjoying her work on

11

the *Moscow Daily News* – it was, after all, much better work than being a typist in Liverpool.

Whatever the reason, Kay stayed in Moscow, and that meant another hospital trauma for Rosa. This one proved far worse than her earlier two miserable weeks there with scarlet fever. Her mother was told that Rosa, at eight, must have her tonsils out. In Moscow in 1932, the practice was to remove your tonsils without an anaesthetic. Kay had flu and could not take her daughter to hospital. Bill was far too busy at important Comintern meetings. So Tamara was asked to take Rosa to hospital. Tamara disliked children, and Rosa loathed Tamara. Rosa also had some inkling of how unpleasant the operation was going to be.

'Tamara walked fast and kept turning an angry face to me and telling me to hurry up. She delivered me at the hospital and said "I'm going now." The nurse said: "Your little girl will need someone when it's all over", and Tamara said, "She's not my little girl", and left.'

Having your tonsils out without anaesthetic hurts just as much as it sounds it would. 'In the Soviet Union they just opened your mouth and out come your tonsils', she told me. 'Tonsils and adenoids. A big woman, she was like a Brunhilde, apron over her because of blood, she got me on her lap like that [she indicated arms firmly pinioned behind her] and held me. When they cut your flesh with a knife in a very sensitive part of your body, it hurts, I tell you, it hurts. I remember the pain. And the blood! There was so much blood.' And I shall never forget the hearty, full-throated, blood-curdling laugh she gave at the end of this horrible story. Rosa told me that when Kay heard the story, and how Tamara had refused to stay with the child, she went to Tamara's flat and hit her in the face, knocking her across the room.

But soon afterwards, things looked up for Rosa. Her father was sent back to England in 1934, taking Tamara with him, and became a full-time worker for the party in Lancashire. But his importance in a foreign Communist Party bought her admittance to a very splendid boarding school, Ivanovo-Vosnesensk. Ivanovo was a textile town and the place where the 1917 Revolution had started, and the school was originally built there to educate the children of those imprisoned by fascist governments, but it now educated the children of foreign luminaries like China's Communist leader Mao Tse-Tung, the Yugoslavian Marshal Tito, and Matyas Rakosi, then in prison in Hungary and later to become its ruler.

'It was the equivalent of a British public school, a very privileged education, we had everything', Rosa recalled. 'Lessons were run in two shifts and I had the afternoon shift, so I spent the mornings riding, skiing, skating, playing music, and doing my homework. I loved that school, it was the best thing that happened to me.' Although her schoolfellows included the children of important communists, the pupils seldom talked to each other about their famous parents – it was considered bad form – and Rosa was horribly embarrassed when her father came to address the school.

'I kept thinking, I wish he would go away. He was treated as a VIP. I hated being singled out in that way. He spoke and someone translated, his Russian was appalling.' Rosa liked Rakosi's children, but Tito's son, a little older than her, beat her up. 'He was nasty, nasty', she told me. 'The teacher made him go on his knees and beg my forgiveness. I saw him years later, he said, "Do you forgive me?" I said "No, you're still an arrogant bastard." He always had too much money and was always showing off.'

She loved poetry – her favourite poet was Pushkin. She loved music. She remembered the sights, smells and sensations of her schooldays all her life, as people do who have been happy at school. It was an idyll, and like all idylls, it could not last. You had to leave Ivanovo-Vosnesensk when you turned sixteen. So in 1941, just before the Soviet Union entered the war, Rosa was sent to Moscow. She was not to know it, but the darkest chapter of her life was about to start. (*Rust*)

TWO

The Promised Land

Rosa's parents were part of a growing community of communist idealists whose search for a better life and a better world took them to the cradle of the revolution, the Soviet Union. It was an excited and exciting expatriate community which believed, with all its youthful, passionate heart, that it was in at the birth of a new world order which would sweep aside the cruelties and injustices of the old.

Work and social life centred on four places. One was the Comintern. Another was the nearby office of the trade union international, the Red International of Labour Unions. The third was the Hotel Lux, where foreign representatives stayed during Comintern meetings, and whose longer-term residents included not just Rosa Rust and her mother, but also the permanent representatives of all the world's communist parties, in Moscow to ensure that the decisions of the Comintern were loyally conveyed to their home countries; and, to a limited extent, to help make those decisions. And the fourth was the International Lenin School, where most of them studied at some time.

The Lenin School provided intensive residential courses lasting from six months to three years for members of foreign communist parties. 'Rarely', write Gidon Cohen and Kevin Morgan, 'can there have been so systematic or effective an attempt to shape a generation of national political leaders from a single centre.' Its graduates included three of the men who were to govern Eastern Europe after

15

1945: Yugoslavia's Marshal Tito, Poland's Wladyslaw Gomulka and East Germany's Erich Honecker. They were to be Bill Rust's friends and colleagues in Moscow, and their children were little Rosa's schoolmates in the 1930s.

Its British alumni are naturally less well known, but about 150 British students passed through the school between 1926 and 1937, including some who were to become important figures in the labour movement in Britain. These included the Scottish and Welsh miners' leaders Alec Moffat and Will Paynter, as well as Allen Hutt who was to be a key staff journalist on the *Daily Worker* for many years, as well as president of the National Union of Journalists and founder editor of its magazine, the *Journalist*.

'The Lenin School', write Cohen and Morgan, 'was the most extreme of the intrusions by the Third International, the Comintern, into the history of the British left by the fashioning in Moscow of a trained, responsive and carefully vetted cohort of revolutionary activists. The contrast with the diverse, unsystematic and largely localised educational tradition of the British labour movement could hardly have been greater. Uprooted from their homes, housed in a single residential complex and deprived even of the use of their own names, the students – over a ten-year period at least 160 of them – came as near as any substantial body of British communists ever did to experiencing from the inside one of the Comintern's "total institutions".' (*Cohen and Morgan*)

Most members of the British community in Moscow were communist idealists like Bill Rust. Many of them had known each other in London, either in the upper reaches of the Communist Party (where their salaries had been paid by the Comintern), or working on the left-wing *Daily Herald*, or working for the Soviet embassy or the Soviet trade mission Arcos, or as researchers at the Labour Research Department (LRD).

Rose Cohen was one of those who came out of the LRD. She was born in 1894. Her older brother and sister had been born in Poland, near Lodz, where her father Morris worked as a tailor, but the family was forced to flee Polish anti-Semitism, and Rose and another brother and two sisters were born in London. They lived at first in extreme poverty, her mother Ada earning a farthing for each garment she made, until her father set up as a tailor in the East End of London. (*Rathbone*)

In those days, almost the only way for a working-class child from the East End to acquire an education beyond the 'three Rs' was through the Workers' Educational Association. Rose was a fast and hungry learner. The WEA gave her an extensive education in politics and economics as well as fluency in three languages. For a poor immigrant, and a woman at that, this was itself a remarkable achievement. It made her a welcome recruit, first on the staff of the London County Council, and then, towards the end of the First World War, at the Labour Research Department.

The Labour Research Department started as a Fabian body, the Fabian Research Department, founded by Sidney and Beatrice Webb, but its young Turks of Rose Cohen's generation resented the Webbs for their apparent meanness, and lampooned them for their moderation. The organisation moved away from the Webbs' control and into the orbit of the Communist Party, where Rose felt much more at home. Trade unions started to rely heavily on its research (and some still do, to this day).

It was a centre for young left-wing intellectual networks at the end of the First World War. These networks were described by Margaret Cole in her memoirs. They contained, she says, 'so far as I remember, nobody over thirty, and hardly any of its members had incomes of any size. As a result we had scarcely any personal ties . . . in effect we lived as well as worked together with our eyes on the job. . . . Being so dedicated, we were extraordinarily happy, so happy that we never realised it fully, but worked ourselves into states of tremendous agitation over minute differences in the philosophy of Guild Socialism. . . .' (*Cole*)

A satirical poem written by Margaret Cole and Alan Kaye gives a flavour of the political edginess between the Webb faction and the communists. It's modelled on a G.K. Chesterton poem. Chesterton had lampooned some hyperbole from F.E. Smith to the effect that a government bill to disestablish the Church in Wales would 'shock the conscience of every Christian community in Europe':

> Are they clinging to their crosses,
> > F.E. Smith
> Where the Breton boat fleet tosses
> > Are they, Smith?

Cole and Kaye's version was:

> In the Perfect Fabian State
> > Sidney Webb,
> Do they pay the Standard Rate
> > Webb, oh Webb?
> Where they read the Statesman's pages,
> And Miss Heiser's name is cursed
> For they dare not raise her wages,
> Lest the Petty Cash go burst;
> Does it matter if we rather
> Tend to underpay the Pleb,
> Since Miss Cohen has a father,
> > Sidney Webb?

Sadie Heiser was another LRD researcher, and the 'Statesman' is the *New Statesman* (another Webb creation). The reference to Rose Cohen's father suggests that his business had by then begun to prosper.

As the Fabian Research Department turned into the Communist-run (and, at the start, largely Soviet-financed) Labour Research Department, the Webbs broke away from it, Beatrice Webb complaining to her diary: 'The FRD – a promising child of ours – ends in a lunatic asylum. To take your livelihood from the Russian government, when millions of Russians are starving, for services which are obviously unreal or, at any rate, irrelevant to famine, is rather a poor business.' (*Morgan, Rose Cohen*)

Rose, writes Maurice Reckitt, who knew her well at that time, had 'great vivacity and charm' and 'was probably the most popular individual in our little movement. . . . With her ardent spirit, coupled with an absence of any national roots, it was natural that she should plunge into and swim with the Communist tide which flowed so strongly in 1920, and I have always believed that her love for the Russian ballet had not a little to do with her enthusiasm for the country (though not the regime) of its origin.' (*Reckitt*)

She was a founder member of the British Communist Party in 1920 and, from the start, part of the small circle of young communists which soon came to dominate the party, including its future leader, and the most important figure in British communist history, Harry Pollitt. She was, according to everyone who knew her, lively, intelligent, literate and hauntingly beautiful, with brown eyes and long dark hair. All the men who knew her talked of her smile, but say she was unaware of its magical quality. I have seen a packet of letters written to her during the 1920s which clearly indicate a large band of obsessed male admirers throughout the British left.

Perhaps the most obsessed of them all was Harry Pollitt himself. In 1926, the year of the general strike, Pollitt had already been identified by the Comintern as the man on whom the future of communism in Britain was going to depend, and the small group around him included Rose Cohen. Pollitt could not have guessed, in those bright days when the world seemed full of hope and optimism, that twenty years later he would be pleading with Stalin for Rose's life.

Born in 1890 in a tiny terraced house in the grim industrial town of Droylsden, between Manchester and Ashton-under-Lyne, Pollitt grew up in grinding poverty. His mother, like most working-class women, lost as many children in infancy as she brought up, for want of sufficient care, the right food, and enough time off from her exhausting job to look after herself and her babies – for without a second income the family would starve. When Harry was twelve, he went out to work with her, and he later wrote: 'Every time she put her shawl round me before going to the mill on very wet or very cold mornings, I swore that when I grew up, I would pay the bosses out for the hardships she suffered.' (*Pollitt*)

He became a skilled craftsman, a boilermaker. Short, heavily built, with a Lancashire accent, a ready laugh, a natural warmth that communicated itself to those around him, and a powerful platform presence in that Indian summer of political oratory between the two world wars, he quickly established himself as one of the key figures in the infant Communist Party.

He fell passionately in love with Rose Cohen. On the back of a picture of Rose taken in Moscow is an inscription in Pollitt's writing: 'Rose Cohen, who I am in love with, and who has rejected me 14 times.' But by 1925 he knew he had lost her, and he married a communist teacher, with whom he remained for the rest of his life, though his friends (as well, perhaps, as his wife) were sure he never got over his love for Rose. According to one of her friends, Harry said to her: 'Rose, all my life is yours, at any time you want it.' (*Carswell*)

He lost her to Max Petrovsky, whom Rose met in 1921 when the Soviets stepped in to guarantee contract work for the LRD to keep it alive after its links with the Labour Party were severed. Max had had an extraordinary life. A Ukrainian Jew, born in 1883 (or thereabouts – so much of his life was lived in secrecy that we cannot be sure of the exact date) in the Ukrainian city of Burdichev, he was the son of a wealthy merchant. His real name was David Lipetz, and at various times he used the names Petrovsky and Goldfarb. Leading Bolsheviks before the 1917 revolution generally had several names: it was how they stayed alive. He was an active member of the Jewish Socialist Bund, under the name Max Goldfarb. Forced into exile, 1907 found him at the London conference of the Russian Social Democratic Party, this time as Lipetz.

He took a doctorate in Brussels and went to the USA, where he was a leading political writer in the Yiddish socialist newspapers which flourished there. Returning to Russia after the 1917 revolution, in 1918 he was elected president of Burdichev, as well as leader of the city's Jewish community. He defended his city's Jews against the Bolsheviks and was twice sentenced to be executed, first by the Ukrainian army and then by the Soviet military command. He went to Moscow in 1919, now using the name Petrovsky, and became a key official in the Soviet Commission of Defence, as well as editing and publishing Lenin's works in Yiddish. (*Abramsky*)

In 1924 Petrovsky was sent to Britain as the Comintern representative, to be guide and mentor to the infant Communist Party of Great Britain. He took over from Mikhail Borodin, whose pseudonym of George Brown had been penetrated by the British police and who had served a thoroughly unpleasant six months in Scotland's grim Barlinnie prison as a result. He described Barlinnie as being colder than Siberia, and Borodin knew what he was talking about. Petrovsky, when in England, used the name Bennett. He managed to avoid the British police for five years – a remarkable feat which no subsequent Comintern representative ever equalled. His influence on the British Communist Party was huge. It's unlikely that any major decision was made without his approval, even though he soon added French communists to his brief and thereafter spent much of his time in Paris.

Life must have seemed like a wonderful adventure to the clever and beautiful young Rose Cohen in the 1920s. As a Comintern agent, she travelled the world, entrusted with secret missions and conveying not just messages but money and advice to communist parties everywhere. In 1922 and 1923 she spent long periods in the Soviet Union and travelled extensively, to Finland, Germany, Lithuania, Estonia, Latvia, Turkey, France, Norway, Sweden and Denmark, and we know that she was a Comintern courier and carried large sums of money to the communist parties in many of these countries. (*PRO KV2/1397*) She was back in London by 1924, dividing her time between work for the Soviet embassy and its trade department, and for her old Fabian colleague G.D.H. Cole. The next year, 1925, the year of Rosa Rust's birth, finds Rose Cohen spending several months in Paris on a secret mission for the Comintern, and handing over thousands of dollars to the French Communist Party.

In 1927 Rose and Max Petrovsky moved permanently to Moscow. Whether they were married in London first, or married in Moscow, we do not know for certain. In 1929 she spent six months travelling in China and Japan, and also visited Poland and Germany on missions for the Comintern, and 1930 finds her studying at the Lenin School before, in October, starting to work as a journalist on a weekly English language newspaper, the *Workers' News*, which later merged with another publication to become the *Moscow Daily News*. Rose's star rose with that of the *Moscow Daily News*. (Kay

Rust also worked for the paper, but in a much more junior capacity.) The editor was the American communist Anna Louise Strong. Meanwhile Rose's husband Max Petrovsky ran the agitation and propaganda department at the Comintern before becoming a member of the praesidium of the Supreme Soviet Economic Council. (*Morgan, Rose Cohen*)

'You will be amused', Rose wrote to a friend, Eva Reckitt, in August 1931, in a letter that was intercepted by the British security services, 'to hear that I am now working on the *Workers' News*, doing editing and writing up stuff. I rather enjoy it, but it is going to be difficult to combine with my studying. The other night we met Crowther and Julian Huxley at a house warming at the Fox's. . . . Crowther came down to the dacha the day after with Ralph and Madge. . . . I'm sorry Nellie [Rose's sister] is so upset about my not coming . . .' – for Rose had not been able to make her intended trip to London. (*PRO KV2/1397*) But the next month she was writing to another friend, Olive Parsons, that although she was finding the work interesting, 'I want to leave and continue studying, but they won't let me go.' (*PRO KV2/1397*)

Rose and Max were very happy. They were the golden couple of the expatriate community in Moscow, both had exciting, important and interesting jobs, and their son Alyosha was born in December 1929. They were devoted to him. They were sure, not only of their own future, but of the future of the great socialist revolution of which they felt privileged to be a part.

In 1930 they moved out of the Hotel Lux and into a flat – a rather splendid one by Moscow standards of the time. A letter of 1 June 1930 from Harry Pollitt in Moscow to his wife, intercepted by British Intelligence, says: 'Rose and Max are removing to their new flat today.' (*PRO KV2/1397*) That year one of her jobs was to find ways to send money to the newly launched *Daily Worker* in London, edited by Bill Rust.

Rose seems to have deceived herself into believing that the average Muscovite benefited as much as she and Max did from the revolution. She did not see the germs of the great terror that was to come, though they lived in Moscow at the time when Stalin was tightening his grip. In retrospect it all seems obvious, but many things look obvious with hindsight. We now know that in March 1923 Lenin, during his last illness, intended to denounce Stalin over his actions in Georgia. Stalin, who came from Georgia, wanted to create a great and indivisible Russia rather than a union of republics, and this involved more brutal repression of the Georgians than Lenin was willing to tolerate. Before Lenin died on 21 January 1924 Stalin created a triumvirate in the Politburo of himself, Kamenev and Zinoviev in order to block Trotsky.

Once Stalin was securely in charge, at the end of 1927, Trotsky was expelled from the Communist Party along with Zinoviev and Kamenev who then recanted, confessed their errors, and sided with Stalin. The next two years saw forced collectivisation in the country-side, the terrible famine in which millions died of starvation, and the exile of Trotsky.

Yet none of this seems to have touched Rose. No doubt like most convinced communists at the time, she easily transferred to Stalin the loyalty she had felt towards Lenin. In 1931 we find her studying in the evenings and working as a journalist during the day, and this is when she wrote to her old friend and London flatmate Eva Reckitt, the sister of Maurice Reckitt. Ironically in the light of subsequent events, one of the things she had written up was the trial of British Metro Vickers engineers on trumped-up charges of espionage, and no doubt this involved trying to justify their unjustifiable arrest.

In 1932 she did take Alyosha to London. Her demanding job meant that she was seeing too little of her son, and her efforts to teach him some English were having little effect, so perhaps she hoped a visit to Britain would achieve it. It was also a chance for her to see her sister Nellie and old friends like Eva Reckitt and Sidney and Beatrice Webb. Her visit to London was closely monitored by British Intelligence: a report of June 1932 says: 'As she is definitely interested in Intelligence matters her return to England may not be without interest.' Her movements, and even her rather innocent telephone calls, were carefully monitored and noted in Intelligence files which were only released seventy-one years later, in 2003. It looks as though the British thought she was a Russian spy, and the

Russians were beginning to wonder if she might be a British spy. But if British Intelligence was hoping for some killer facts from her visit, its officers were disappointed, judging by the innocent family conversations they solemnly recorded and guarded from prying eyes for seven decades: 'Later Rose rang up Eva RECKITT; she could probably manage to lunch with Monica Ewer and will ring her up about it'; that kind of material. (*PRO KV2/1397*)

It was also in 1932 that the *Workers' News* merged with another paper to become the English language paper *Moscow Daily News*, and Rose became foreign editor. With her heavy duties, and Petrovsky's senior job, they deposited Alyosha in their dacha outside Moscow in the care of a nurse, and stayed in their flat in Moscow, getting out as often as they could to see their son.

As late as 1934 Rose was still writing transparently happy letters to her sister Nellie Rathbone in London. In October, during what seems to have been a wonderful holiday in Georgia, she wrote:

I've been so 'busy' sun-bathing, sea-bathing, tennis, walking – and eating, that I have had no time to write letters. . . . So far the trip has been marvellous. . . . We stayed three days in Tiflis and nearly died of Georgian hospitality. We met the loveliest people there, who vied with each other to entertain us. You would probably hate the Georgian food, except that they put nuts in everything – but also a special kind of vinegar which they call wine vinegar. For instance, in chicken broth they add this vinegar and the beaten yolk of egg! And it's delicious. And as for their shashlik, there is nothing like it. A real Georgian dinner begins at 5 and goes on till about midnight. We had two such dinners in Tiflis and one in Batoum. And this is accompanied by steady wine drinking. Fortunately, they don't drink vodka, but delicious light Georgian wines, which leave no ill effect or make you drunk. You have to finish the glass at one go and, at special toasts, they drink out of tumblers. I kept my end up with the rest and was accepted as a 'sister'. A great figure on these occasions is the 'termada' or toaster. He is usually chosen as the wittiest person present and his toasts keep things going should they begin to flag. At one dinner we had the most famous termada in Tiflis. He was simply brilliant, and very witty in many languages, including pidgin English. After these 'orgies' we went for long drives along the Georgian Military Road. (*Rathbone collection*)

They must have travelled through the famine, the rural areas where people were literally starving to death, the areas that mocked the gargantuan meals they were enjoying, but Rose clearly did not understand what she saw (though it seems probable that Max did). There was only one drawback to the holiday: they had had to leave Alyosha, then nearly five, in Moscow, with a friend who had a son of the same age. 'I miss Alyosha terribly, and I'm wondering whether I will last out to the end of the month without him.' She didn't; she cut the holiday short to go back to him. (*Rathbone collection*)

Her very success, and perhaps her attitude towards those who did not share it, was making her some enemies in the Moscow expatriate community. 'Rose Cohen', wrote someone called Janet to Sally Freedman in London, in another letter intercepted by British Intelligence, 'is editor of the foreign department and is *very* unpopular. She's incredibly snobby, and earns a vast salary, and altogether is *not* a good advertisement for P (Petrovsky?) . . . Rose by the way was quite nice to me – but her general attitude is that she's no time for small fry. . . .' (*PRO KV2/1397*)

Another Englishwoman married to a Russian, Freda Utley, had already taken against Rose, for rather similar reasons. They had been close friends in London, but in Moscow Freda thought that Rose was living a privileged life among the elite which discriminated against Freda's Russian husband Arcadi Berdichevsky because he was not a party member. She wrote to Allen Hutt in 1928: 'Rose Cohen I have taken rather an objection to – she is so very smooth and insincere and also so terribly conceited. She really implies herself to be the power in the English section of the Comintern.' (*Morgan, Rose Cohen*) Freda Utley was to see Rose's pride take a fall, but, as we shall see, Freda by then had her own troubles to contend with.

Ivy Litvinov, the English wife of Maxim Litvinov, Stalin's Foreign Commissar, knew Rose well and liked her very much, but perhaps secretly saw a little more clearly than Rose the way things were going. Ivy had never been a political animal, which perhaps helped her both to see what was going on and, eventually, to survive it. She described Rose years later as 'a London Jewish girl, very beautiful, a sort of jüdische rose. I think she was a member of the party in the days of long, long ago.' Max was 'the ugliest man you ever saw, but very charming. He had one of those great drooping noses and he was a great hulking man, very much older than she was. . . . She was quite a little celebrity in Moscow. . . . They had a lovely apartment and they had a little boy and we all became great friends. I was great friends with Rose. And whenever I was alone with Petrovsky he used to make a pass at me. . . . Like some people did in Moscow, they dressed (Alyosha) terribly, in plus fours and cloth caps.'

Ivy Litvinov was born Ivy Low in 1889. Her father was a Jewish academic who died when Ivy was five, and whom she worshipped all her life. Her mother was the daughter of a colonel in the army, and mother and daughter never hit it off, especially after her mother remarried a man whom Ivy disliked. Ivy wanted to be a writer, and was busy introducing herself, brashly but effectively, into London literary life, when, in 1914, she met Maxim Litvinov, one of the penurious but ferociously committed Russian political exiles in London at the time. She was twenty-five, he was thirty-nine. She had no political ideas but a great love of literature. He rather disliked literature and was, like Max Petrovsky, a grimly committed Jewish Bolshevik and an intimate of Lenin. They were married two years later.

By the time the event Maxim had lived for, the Bolshevik revolution, happened in Russia in 1917, they had one baby and another was on the way. He wanted to go home to Moscow at once, but Lenin sent word that Litvinov was to represent the Soviet government in London. At once the British Foreign Office was bombarded with Maxim's demands, badly typed by Ivy: possession of the Russian embassy, a formal call on the Foreign Secretary, the right to use cipher. 'It will be a little difficult', recorded a languid

Foreign Office official in January 1918, 'for us to boycott Mr Litvinoff.' But in September, the British arrested him in a tit for tat action – the Soviet government had arrested a British official – and lodged him in Brixton prison until an exchange could be made. Then they deported him.

He and Ivy were reunited two years later, when Maxim became Soviet ambassador to the newly independent states of Latvia, Lithuania and Finland. In 1922 they went to Moscow, where Litvinov became Deputy Foreign Commissar and was later appointed Foreign Commissar. Ivy Litvinov, aged thirty-three, had arrived in the city where she was to spend most of the rest of her life. They got to know Max Petrovsky and Rose Cohen well. Ivy worked for a while under Rose at the *Moscow Daily News*. Ironically, it may well be that Max used his influence, while he had it, to protect Ivy; for when Litvinov was in disgrace, partly because the upper echelons of the Communist Party of the Soviet Union never quite approved of his unpolitical wife, and Ivy thought she needed to get out of Moscow for a while, she went to Max Petrovsky, whose brief included all the institutes of higher learning for industry. He sent her to Sverdlovsk to teach English, where she was out of sight and, she must have hoped, out of mind.

When the terror started, wrote Ivy many years later, Rose 'was always rather smug – "Well, I suppose they know what they're doing, don't you?" – "They don't take me" sort of attitude. And if we talked about overcrowding she would say: "Well, I think everybody has got a flat now, don't you?" I said: "Well, I don't, Rose, I don't think so just because you and I have." She had that sort of smugness and complacency, the cowardice that comes from shutting your eyes. She lived among Americans and had to keep the flag flying, and she didn't want to know, I think.' (*Carswell*)

There is probably a little retrospective embellishment in this. When Ivy wrote it, Rose and Max had been dead for many years. But it must be true that Rose was determined to hang on to her belief in the Soviet revolution. It had been good to her; surely it would be good to everyone. Ivy had never had that belief. Ivy was an intelligent but unpolitical woman drawn into the Soviet Union by a revolution which she would otherwise hardly have noticed.

* * *

In 1928 another clever young Englishwoman married to a Russian arrived in Moscow. Freda Utley was well thought of in academic circles – a research fellow at the London School of Economics, a writer, a teacher for the Workers' Educational Association. She was the upper-middle-class product of an expensive boarding-school education, first in Switzerland and then, from thirteen to seventeen, in England. English boarding schools for girls were pale imitations of those for boys, and Freda hated every minute of it, especially as her cosmopolitan background meant she spoke with a slightly foreign-sounding accent. She remembered all her life the humiliation of being forced to stand up in class to say 'stirrup' over and over again, because she could not say the R sound in the correct English way.

The school brought out the rebel in her, and her father, a leading left-wing journalist and Labour Party activist, gave her rebellion its socialist direction. 'Dimly I began to feel that the social hierarchy and the social code which governed our school were precisely that "capitalist system" which, as the daughter of a socialist, I had learned to think was the cause of all social injustice', she wrote later. Most of her fellow-pupils symbolised the English imperialist to her: 'class-conscious, sublimely self-confident and scornful of learning'. (*Utley, Lost Illusion*)

Born in 1899, short-sighted and hard of hearing, Freda had a formidable intellect, at least as good as Rose Cohen's, but not Rose's physical beauty. A rationalist and humanist by education and temperament, she was brought up by her socialist and atheist father to see religion as the shield of tyranny, intolerance and cruelty, and she had a passion for freedom and justice, which, as we shall see, was battered in every direction by the storms of her life. (*Farnie*) Freda (short for Winifred) passed the Cambridge University entrance examinations in 1914, but that year her father was ruined and later fell seriously ill. It was clear that she would have to start earning

28

money as soon as she left school, and Cambridge was out of the question. The headmistress, who had been rather proud of her clever pupil, at once lost interest in her, telling everyone that her family was destitute and her fees were no longer being paid. Her father died in poverty in 1918, and Freda kept her mother and herself by working as a clerk in the War Office. In 1920 she won a scholarship to London University, and paid her way through the course by giving English lessons to foreigners. (*Utley, Lost Illusion*) In 1923 Freda graduated from King's College, London, with first class honours in history, and took an MA two years later for a thesis called 'The Social and Economic Status of the Collegia from Constantine to Theodosius', then researched at the London School of Economics on eastern competition with the Lancashire cotton industry. (*Farnie*)

Through the Independent Labour Party she got to know many of the leading left-wing thinkers of the time, and Bertrand Russell became a close friend. She was invited to visit the Soviet Union as a representative of the University Labour Federation. There she came to know Rose Cohen and Rose's charmed circle, including Max Petrovsky, and, despite Russell's warnings, she joined the British Communist Party after the 1926 general strike, and became an admirer of its impeccably proletarian leader, about whom she wrote, years later: 'The fact that Harry Pollitt led the British Communist Party deluded me into thinking that it was still a revolutionary working-class party seeking to establish liberty and social justice.' In 1928 she travelled through Siberia to China and Japan, studying commercial competition between the Far East and Lancashire.

Back in London later that year, she took the decision which was to change her life. She married Arcadi Berdichevsky, a Russian Jew who had studied at Zurich University and then, in 1914, went to the USA, where he acquired a well-paid job. In 1920, in the wake of the Russian revolution, the Soviet government asked him to go to London, because they needed his commercial expertise in Arcos, the Soviet trade mission. It meant earning a fraction of his New York salary – £36 instead of £120 a month – but he thought he owed it to the first non-Tsarist government Russia had ever had to give it what support he could, and he brought his wife and son to London. There he met and fell in love with Freda Utley. (*Utley, Lost Illusion*)

Arcadi was about a decade older than Freda and had had one short-lived marriage in Switzerland during the First World War from which he had a son. He had then married again, and taken his wife to the USA. He left his second wife to live with Freda Utley, and sometimes called Freda his 'swan song'. He was by all accounts a gently humorous man of the world who, as a professional working for humourless Soviet bureaucrats at Arcos, used to say: 'I have to get my boss to order me to do so-and-so.' Nonetheless, with Freda's intellectual friends in London, he was sometimes slow – she told her son he always laughed at jokes a little later than everyone else. (*Utley interview*)

In May 1927 the Arcos office was raided by the British police, who found some evidence of spying activities. The office was closed and Arcadi, along with others of its staff, was expelled from Britain. He returned to Moscow, and Freda joined him there the next year. As Arcadi had done seven years earlier, she gave up well-paid work and a bright future to live in relative poverty in Moscow as a translator. The two of them were sent around the world on what seems, on her account, to have been secret missions on behalf of the Comintern, rather as Rose Cohen had done, though she was never trusted as much as Rose. When they travelled to China and Japan, Freda had secret Comintern documents for the Chinese communists hidden in her corset. In Japan they had what was to turn out to be the happiest year of their lives together. Then she returned to England, aiming to work for a while before going back to Moscow and joining Arcadi there on his return from Japan.

In London, by now a well-regarded academic writer, she threw herself into the work of the Communist Party, though she was starting to find its rigid sectarianism irksome. But she suppressed her doubts – she wanted to go on believing, and perhaps she also had in mind the fact that Arcadi's future, which she wished to share, was in Moscow. (*Utley, Lost Illusion*) Her year in Japan eventually resulted in a book, *Japan's Feet of Clay*, which established both her reputation and her communist credentials. She showed that labour costs of production in Japan were about half of those in Lancashire, and the disparity in labour costs was so enormous that no reduction in labour costs in Lancashire could ever restore its competitive capacity in the markets of the Far East. She condemned British employers for never having paid a living wage to the majority of their workers. (*Farnie*)

Back in Moscow in 1928, she heard that Arcadi had been unexpectedly ordered to go to China before returning to Moscow, and she was alone for three months. She did not live in the comparative luxury of the Hotel Lux, much less a splendid apartment of the sort that Rose Cohen had. Lacking Rose's communist credentials, and lacking Rose's advantage of having an old Bolshevik for a husband, Freda came far, far further down the food chain than Rose, and while Arcadi was abroad, she lodged with Arcadi's sister Vera and her two sons, and saw, as Rose did not, the hardship of the life of an ordinary Muscovite. 'With her Jewish sense of family solidarity and her Siberian tradition of hospitality, Vera unquestioningly gave me shelter and shared her food with me', she wrote afterwards. 'Having no job, I had no bread card and nowhere to get a meal. I got translating and editing work to do and wrote some articles, but this did not produce a food card.' Food was scarce, and the flat was very overcrowded. She worked for the Comintern, then as a textile expert at Arcadi's firm, Promexport, and at the Commissariat of Light Industry. Later she worked at the Institute of World Economy and Politics of the Academy of Sciences.

But Freda was beginning to feel a sense of rottenness, of impending doom, about Moscow. She met people at the Comintern who could boast of having spent time in prison in their own countries for the cause, and wrote cynically afterwards: 'How proud Communist Party members were if, when they went to Moscow, they could boast that they had been in jail in the class struggle. Such an accomplishment might be held to wipe out the stigma of their non-proletarian origin.'

Like Rosa Rust, she saw at first hand the care provided in Soviet hospitals. She had a miscarriage, and a day later was in extreme pain. At the hospital, 'I was strapped down upon an operating table and scraped by a "surgeon" who did not even wash her hands before operating, and whose whole painted appearance suggested a prostitute rather than a doctor. I was given no chloroform and the pain was excruciating. Then I was taken upstairs to a small room about 12 feet by 12 feet, with five beds in it. I was given an ice pack and then they left me. No one came near me, no one washed me. There was no nurse or attendant of any kind. The other patients begged me for the piece of soap I had brought with me.' She was unnecessarily scraped again the next day. It turned out that they had failed to make a note of the fact that it had already been done. When she asked for something to wipe away the blood, someone picked up a dirty piece of cotton wool from the floor and gave it to her.

Where Rose and Max were aristocrats of the revolution, Freda and Arcadi were not quite trusted. This was partly because Arcadi had never been a member of the Communist Party, and perhaps also because Freda had not been regarded as entirely reliable by the British communists. *Japan's Feet of Clay*, though academically respectable, seems to have contained what top British communist theoreticians considered to be ideological errors. Freda and Arcadi struggled to find anywhere to live, as many ordinary Muscovites did, lodging in the already overcrowded flats of Arcadi's friends and relations. 'For years every letter I wrote to my mother referred to our housing problem', wrote Freda later. 'The hope for an apartment in the spring, then in the autumn, then for the following year. At first I believed the promises; but after two years I was writing that I had given up having any confidence in Russian promises.'

And she added: 'The first lesson the Soviet citizen has to learn is that promises and contracts mean nothing at all. The government cheats its citizens all the time in big things and little, and every official behaves in the same way.' (*Utley, Lost Illusion*)

This sort of disaffection did not go unnoticed in Moscow in Stalin's time. However discreet you were – and Freda was probably not a naturally discreet woman – if you gave the slightest hint of your discontent, it was liable to get back to the authorities. We now know, from recently released Russian documents, something she never knew – that the Comintern was harbouring dark suspicions about Freda as early as January 1929, when she was in Japan. A Comintern representative in Tokyo wrote to Moscow: 'Recently the English communist, Freda Utley, left Moscow for Tokyo together with her husband Berdichevsky. Supposedly, Freda Utley had been sent on a special assignment to Shanghai. Many Soviet citizens in Tokyo have become aware of this. Freda Utley's Soviet links and her past have been uncovered. She has settled down, together with her husband and they are both behaving in a very suspicious way, leading outsiders to believe that she has links with our secret organisation. In Tokyo the British embassy has been trying to get in touch with Utley.'

The next month the same official was writing: 'Through recently received information we can report that Freda Utley is at the moment completely exposed. It has become known in Tokyo that she is a member of the party, that she came to Tokyo from Moscow via Irkutsk, where she was met, and then went on an assignment to Shanghai, having visited the Comintern in Moscow. She openly talks about the strong Communist Party in England, and also about the good party organisation in Shanghai.' (*RC*)

These suspicions probably had a bearing on what happened later.

In retrospect we can see the terror clearly as we look at the beginning of the 1930s. Between 1931 and 1934, seven million people died in the great famine. In 1932 Zinoviev and Kamenev, two men whom communists all over the world trusted, were expelled for a second time from the Communist Party, and sent to Siberia. They recanted and were allowed to come back in 1933. In 1932 Stalin's own wife committed suicide after being publicly rebuked by Stalin at a small dinner party. Yet still British idealists came to Russia to help build a brave new world.

* * *

Pearl Rimel was the second youngest of the eleven children of a middle-class London orthodox Jewish family of Austrian origin. Her father had come to London in the 1880s to represent a Hamburg firm of food merchants, which he did until the First World War when he set up his own business in London's East End selling eggs, butter and cheese.

Born in March 1912, Pearl went to school in Hackney in London's East End, and left school at sixteen to work as secretary to the managing director of the Black Cat cigarette company, whose splendid Camden Town office, still with the black cat proudly over its entrance, is now the headquarters of the magazine publishers East Midlands Allied Press. She is said to have been very witty, with quick repartee.

Some of her older sisters were by then convinced socialists and, influenced by them, Pearl joined the Labour League of Youth. Her life was mapped out in ways she could never have predicted at one of its social events, where she met and fell in love with a fellow-member, a young Dutchman called George Fles, in 1931. Pearl's orthodox Jewish parents were pleased to know that George was a Jew.

It was young love at its best and purest. Years later, one of the very few things Pearl told one of her grandchildren about his long dead grandfather was their first kiss. They were swimming with some friends in a lake and the two of them separated from the rest of the group, perhaps by accident, and then again perhaps not. They found a field where they kissed, and George started to kiss her body, and the 22-year-old girl, ignorant and naïve in a way that is hard to imagine today, feared that a kiss on her navel might make her pregnant. George laughed and laughed. A young man of twenty-four, he had had an affair in Paris, and was able to lead her and play the man of the world. (*Bower interview*)

George was travelling and acquiring confidence by leaps and bounds. In Amsterdam, where he was brought up, George, the youngest in a big family, with four older sisters and one older brother, had been thought a shy and sensitive young man. His middle-class, left-wing Jewish family called him by the pet name of Sjoppie.

His father, Louis Fles, had set up a thriving business dealing in typewriters, and both his parents, though without formal education, became fluent in several languages and voracious readers. It was a Jewish family, but not a religious one – Louis was a radical atheist and active in Dutch politics. Nonetheless, the family honoured several Jewish customs, including the Friday night family dinner, held every week in the big, comfortable house in the Baerlestraat in

Amsterdam where George grew up. George, perhaps tired of being the baby of the family, petted and protected by his brother and older sisters, left Holland in 1926, aged eighteen.

George's first stop was a long stay in Paris with one of his sisters, where he earned a living selling ties and braces from door to door. Then he went to Berlin, joined the Social Democratic Party, and got a job as a translator in a chemical factory. But the obviously growing strength of the Nazis and their clear and virulent anti-Semitism sent him back to Paris in 1929, where he became secretary to a salesman of American packing machines. There he again joined the social democrats, which in France were called the SFIO (Section Française de l'Internationale Ouvrière), but soon switched to the French Communist Party, the PCF (Parti Communiste Français). (*Berman*)

In 1931 he moved to London and lived by freelance translating. The shy young man his family knew seemed to have disappeared. Perhaps his travels had given him confidence, for the young man those who knew him in London remember is completely different from the shy teenager his family remembers. Sixty years later Pearl's sister Hetty laughed as she remembered the first time George and Pearl went into London with her. 'He had just arrived in England. We left the underground station, I think it was Piccadilly, and there was such a thick fog you couldn't see anything. And George spread his arms at the top of the stairs and shouted: "What a bloody country! What bloody weather!" Everybody in Charing Cross Road could hear. We had to laugh terribly but we were a bit embarrassed too because everybody turned around and looked at us.'

Hetty thought he was 'an enthusiastic, cheerful young man. He laughed a lot, he sang a lot and he had a strong voice, no matter if he sang or spoke. You would never hear him whisper. He had a great sense of humour and he could really laugh about his own jokes as well. Very ebullient, a bit eccentric. He was very popular in our group of left-wing youngsters.' George and Pearl and their friends went for country walks accompanied by a guitar and a revolutionary songbook, and organised parties and danced. George wanted to be a journalist, and told Hetty that he went from one country to another to broaden his mind and to increase his knowledge of languages.

35

But it was the start of the great depression, and work in Britain was hard to find. The second Labour government fell in 1931, the year of George's arrival, after an undistinguished two years in government, to be replaced by a National government (in reality a Conservative government) which immediately called a general election, and Labour went down to a crushing election defeat, the National government winning a majority of 500 over all the opposition parties. Communists were making little headway – the Communists still had the albatross of the Comintern-inspired Class against Class policy (of which more later) around their necks – and the Independent Labour Party, Labour's left wing, was in terminal decline. There was little in Britain to encourage an enthusiastic young Dutch idealist. In any case, the next year George was refused a residence permit – partly, he believed, because of his politics.

Where was he to go next? By then, he was not going anywhere without the girl he had kissed in the meadow by the lake, and Pearl was going to go wherever he went. According to Hetty, 'Pearl wanted to be independent, leave her constricting family, just like him. And she loved adventure: she was the first one in our family who travelled to the mainland, to Paris. None of us had ever got permission for that from our parents.' (*Bower interview*)

And it must have seemed clear to both of them, young socialists who believed that a better, fairer, freer world was their generation's for the taking, that they must go somewhere where they could help bring that world about. That meant one of two places. They could go to Spain and help the Spanish Republicans fight against Franco's fascists, or they could go to the Soviet Union and help build socialism. They tossed a coin. Russia won. George set sail, arranging for Pearl to follow when he had found work and a home. 'I came here to help build socialism' George later told his interrogators, truthfully.

George Fles's great-nephew, the Dutch journalist Thijs Berman, who has researched George's short life and to whom I owe much of what I know about him, has found photographs of the two of them: George laughing proudly with one arm round Pearl, who is wearing a summer dress; George in a London street, in a photograph on the

36

back of which he has written: 'Summer 1932. En route.' Thijs
Berman says: 'If you look at the photograph now, you are caught in
melancholy because of the energy and vitality which radiate from
him.' George was sure his linguistic skills – he had translated
German, English and French in all three of those countries – would
enable him to serve the revolution.

Pearl joined him in Moscow the next year. He was doing
translating work for the trade union international organisation, and
she worked as a secretary. They did not live in style like Rose Cohen
and her husband, but they lived well by Moscow standards – better
than Freda Utley – in a room in a small apartment, ideally situated
in the centre of the city between the Kremlin and Arbat Street.
Unlike many others in Moscow, they did not have to share a room
with other couples, which entailed using the cupboards, curtains and
sheets to put up partitions and provide some sort of privacy. But
their house was overcrowded nonetheless: the landlady and her
lover slept in the living room, the son slept in the hallway, there was
an aunt in the bathroom and a grandmother in the kitchen. During
the winter they used the space between the double walls as a freezer.
The house smelled of garlic, cabbage and drying laundry.

But they were happy. She was twenty-two and he was twenty-five.
They were in love, and filled with optimism for themselves and for
the world.

After two years they moved to Tbilisi. George was still working
freelance, and wanted to be a journalist; he was told he would stand
a better chance of a permanent job if he had experience of the rest of
the USSR. Tbilisi had a pleasant, mild climate, without Moscow's
harsh winters.

They had no jobs to go to, but they did have a letter of recommendation from an influential source. The queen of Moscow's
expatriate community, the beautiful and talented Rose Cohen, whom
George must have met at the *Moscow Daily News*, gave them a letter
of recommendation to give to a well-known young poet, Lydia
Gasviani, a great figure in fashionable Georgian society, whom Rose
had presumably met on her wonderful Georgian holiday. Lydia
helped George and Pearl to find students for private lessons in

English and French, and introduced them to her wide circle of Georgian intellectuals and artists. Their new life must have seemed a great blessing at the time. It was to be George's death sentence.

Thijs Berman found another picture of George and Pearl in Tbilisi, taken on 12 April 1936, with a deliriously happy Pearl and a protective George with his arm round her. On the back of it Pearl wrote: 'The happiest couple in the world, and they have just heard the most exciting news in the world: we celebrated baby's birthday today, two months old!' She was two months pregnant.

George found work at the observatory in Tbilisi as an interpreter. He had steady work in a healthy mountain climate. He wanted to stay there and be accepted as the observatory's permanent translator.

They decided that the baby should not be born in the Soviet Union, where even the most convinced communist had to admit that health care was rudimentary, and in the summer of 1936 Pearl set off by boat from Leningrad to London. In July she arrived in Rotterdam and met George's family. She told them happily that everything was going well, and George was to come and join her before the baby was born. Then they would return to live in Tbilisi. (*Berman*)

* * *

None of these people had any idea of the storm that was to overtake them. At least Rose Cohen and Max and George Fles still believed with all their hearts in the Soviet Union as the land of socialism, the place where all the injustices and suffering of capitalism was to be put right. Perhaps only Freda Utley and Pearl Rimel were starting to have doubts, but even they had no idea of the storm that was to overwhelm all of them.

Yet Rose and Max had a ringside seat for the moment when Stalin asserted his personal control over the Communist Party of Great Britain. Between 1927 and 1929, the British communists were required to change their policy dramatically. In 1927 they were still talking of uniting with other parties of the left, and trying to gain affiliation to the Labour Party, all of which is what Lenin had persuaded its leaders to do.

Lenin had not found this an easy task – many of Britain's Communist leaders believed there was no future in associating with the Labour Party, which they considered to have sold out years earlier. But he put hours of persuasion into it, taking time from all the pressing work of governing his huge country and consolidating his revolution, to showing leading British communists why he was right and they were wrong. He even wrote a special pamphlet designed to change their minds, and had it sent to Britain at the crucial moment in 1920. It was called *Left-wing Communism: an Infantile Disorder*.

By 1929, Stalin had forced British communists to adopt the policy which Lenin had talked them out of. This is how it happened. In October 1927 Harry Pollitt attended a meeting in Moscow where his party was roundly attacked for not being sufficiently scathing about the British trade union and Labour Party leaders who had so mishandled the general strike of the previous year. This, Soviet communists said, should have been British communism's moment, with the working class disillusioned by the nine day strike which their leaders had settled on humiliating terms. How had they let the chance slip through their fingers?

Stalin and Bukharin saw Pollitt privately and told him they wanted a sharp break from the united front line. Pollitt disagreed strongly. But he could not stop the Comintern instructing him to put forward candidates at the next general election wherever possible, even in marginal seats where communist intervention might simply ensure that the Conservatives won.

Lenin's arguments no longer applied, said a Comintern commission. First, Labour had now been in government in Britain (the short-lived 1924 government) and had demonstrated its failure to do anything for the working class. Second, there was now the prospect of a Labour-Liberal alliance. Third, Labour and trade union leaders had become more right wing. The Communist Party, said the Comintern, must now 'come forward . . . as the only party of the working class and more boldly criticise reformism'.

The next month Rose's husband Max Petrovsky, the Soviet mentor whom all British communists trusted, weighed in with support for the

Comintern view. There was, he said at another Comintern meeting in Moscow to discuss British affairs, 'a new situation' in Britain. Labour was now clearly seeking class collaboration, and was also gearing itself up for a further assault on communists. So communists must 'fight the consolidated bureaucracy by new means and new ways'. They had to criticise Labour 'in the sharpest way'.

One of the British communist leaders, Willie Gallacher, later to be a Communist Member of Parliament, was especially furious. As historian Andrew Thorpe puts it, 'Petrovsky seemed to be espousing just the kind of ultra-leftism out of which Lenin had talked Gallacher in 1920.' Gallacher said the situation had not changed, and anyway most British workers still backed the Labour Party. But he found that not only were the Russians and other foreign communists against him, but many of his own British colleagues had already been persuaded of the Comintern view. He reserved his fiercest scorn for the British supporters of the Comintern line, saying of Jack Murphy: 'Comrade Murphy has clearly not made up his mind fully whether he is with the party in Britain, or whether he represents the Political Secretariat here [in Moscow].' Petrovsky, clearly briefed to use his influence with the British communists, called Gallacher's speech 'a full capitulation in the fight against reformism'. He said the British Communist Party was in decline, and something had to be done to stop the rot.

Gallacher had not yet understood (he came to understand later) the realities of Moscow politics. He might not like the Comintern line, but it came right from the top, it applied everywhere and not just in Britain, and there was to be no avoiding it. In December, at the fifteenth Congress of the Communist Party of the Soviet Union, Stalin himself called social democrats 'capitalist lackeys' and said that the British Labour Party was moving to the right. Bukharin weighed in: never had there been such a gulf between communists and social democrats, he said. Forthcoming elections in Britain, France, Germany and Poland must be used 'to prove to the workers that the Communist Party is the only revolutionary party of the working class'. British communists must accept that things had moved on since Lenin spoke to them in 1920.

British communists left Moscow after that meeting committed to a 'merciless' campaign to expose Labour and the trade unions. Early in 1928 the Comintern spelled out the line which became known as Class against Class, which was to apply throughout the world, not just in Britain. Once he was back in Britain, Gallacher tried to tone it down, but most of his colleagues were quicker to understand that the die had been cast. (*Thorpe*)

Rosa Rust's father, Bill Rust, rather younger than Gallacher, understood more clearly where power lay, and by the end of 1929 he was seeking a purge of the 'leadership of the party from top to bottom'. Though the party went along with it, Rust was not forgiven at the time, and some of his colleagues privately never forgave him. They excluded him that year from the Central Committee – but Rust, back in Moscow, portrayed his exclusion as a deliberate snub to the Comintern, and demanded that continued deviation from the Comintern line should be 'mercilessly opposed'. He talked of 'veiled resistance' in the British Communist Party to the new line. He joined forces with Max Petrovsky to demand that Britain's communists should fall into line, accusing four other party leaders of sabotaging Comintern policy. (*Flinn*)

British communists were kicked into line after an attack by Comintern functionary Dimitri Manuilsky, which should have showed them the way the wind from Moscow was going to blow. 'How does it happen', asked Manuilsky 'that all the fundamental problems of the Communist International fail to stir our fraternal British Party? . . . All these problems have the appearance of being forcibly injected into the activities of the British Communist Party. . . . The German comrades carefully weigh every word spoken by anybody. They allow no deviation from the line, they attack the least deviation, respecting no persons.' But the British party, he said contemptuously, is 'a society of great friends'. The Comintern was determined to put right this sad state of affairs. In its place he wanted 'courageous, frank Bolshevist self-criticism'. (*Beckett, Enemy Within*)

It may have been the last time any substantial section of the British Communist Party leadership tried to defy Moscow, at least until the Second World War. It required them to end any attempt at collaboration with social democrats. The further to the left they were, the greater the danger, because they could mislead the workers away from the true socialist faith, which lay only in the Communist Party. The bitterest abuse therefore had to be reserved for Labour's left-wing faction, the Independent Labour Party, who must be denounced – Moscow even laid down the exact phrase to be used – as 'social fascists'.

Those with their ears most closely attuned to the mood music from Moscow, like the party theoretician Rajani Palme Dutt, saw it coming first. Dutt was impatient for his colleagues to adopt the new line. In February 1928, while his colleagues were in Moscow meeting the Comintern, Dutt wrote in his theoretical Marxist magazine *Labour Monthly* an article critical of the party leadership for their tardiness in adopting the new line. John Campbell, he noted, was still on friendly terms with Independent Labour Party leader James Maxton and miners' leader Arthur Cook, who had led the general strike.

The British Party Politburo voted for a 'severe censure' on Dutt for his 'thinly disguised attack on the party'. At once Dutt's friends in London and Moscow were besieged with long, detailed missives from Dutt's Brussels home, demanding (in one three-page closely typed letter) 'a specific charge to which I may reply' because of 'the damage that may already have been caused in the party'. Another letter soon afterwards noted that Andrew Rothstein, one of the British leaders with the strongest doubts about the new line, had criticised it in a private conversation with Dutt's brother. Rothstein must 'take steps to correct this so as to remove any injury he may have done to the *Labour Monthly* by the spreading of such statements'.

Dutt's letters at this time, which six years ago were to be found in the Comintern archives in Moscow but which I could not find there in 2003, are clearly those of a man under great strain and heading for a nervous breakdown, which he suffered in April. However, his view was that of the Comintern, and his neurotic monitoring of the smallest private conversation eerily foreshadows the dreadful Comintern investigations of the 1930s. And he won. After taking advice from the Comintern, the party's man in Moscow, Robin Page Arnot, wrote to London: 'In my opinion Comrade Dutt has shown great self-control in his notes. It is quite obvious to me that your "severe censure" will be treated . . . as a political act. This . . . may give the impression of a campaign against the Comintern resolution.'

The British party knew the game was up, and abased itself at once. A telegram went to Moscow: 'Central Committee unanimously accepts plenum resolution as meaning complete change policy stop withdraws own thesis grounds inadequacy mistakes. . . .' It was the humiliating climbdown Dutt had demanded, but it was still not good enough for the chief theoretician. He demanded more 'self-criticism' from his opponents for having been in the wrong. It was not until June that the censure was withdrawn in sufficiently grovelling terms to satisfy him, or to satisfy the Comintern. (*Beckett, Enemy Within*)

British communists were now embarked on the course which forced them to denounce non-communists in Labour's left wing as 'social fascists' – a policy which destroyed their chances of being effective, and ensured that they also destroyed the chance that Labour's left might be effective. They had also had a foretaste of the way in which total obedience was going to be demanded in the future, and the smallest deviation, even in private, could be held against you. It was another eight years before they were to find out what this spirit meant if you were not safely in London, but in the middle of the cauldron that Moscow was to become.

It's much easier to see in hindsight than it was for Rose Cohen, Harry Pollitt or even Max Petrovsky at the time, that this was the moment when it became clear that Stalin was not concerned with the realities of life in the small British outpost of the Comintern. Poor Rose went on believing she mattered in Moscow until the storm, with terrifying suddenness, overwhelmed her.

THREE

The Knock on the Door

Before Stalin's purges got properly under way, it was already clear that foreigners could spark suspicious paranoia as well as Soviet citizens. Even in the 1920s, Britons in Moscow were not always as safe as most of them liked to think. Abraham Landau, a 22-year-old London communist, was sent by Britain's Communist Party to work in the headquarters of the Communist Youth International, where Bill Rust was a senior official. He was arrested in his room in the Hotel Lux in January 1923 and executed two weeks later on a charge of espionage. (*McLoughlin*)

Jack Murphy, when he was the representative of the British Communist Party at the Comintern, was arrested in Moscow in the 1920s, on the flimsiest circumstantial evidence that he might be a British spy, and was greatly relieved when he was cleared, for he knew what happened to spies. The Russians, he wrote later, have a way of dealing with spies that ensures their offence can never be repeated. (*Murphy*) Harry Pollitt believed to the end of his life, wrongly, that Murphy was a British Intelligence spy who, on his return to Britain, spied on British communists. (*Foot*)

Murphy saw the Comintern warfare at first hand, writing that the 'great polemical battle' between Stalin and Trotsky 'went on from 1925 until it ended with the crack of the rifles of the firing squads of revolution in 1937'. He saw how polemical battles were waged in the Comintern: 'Everyone knew what was coming when the speaker

45

got to the point of saying: "And it is by no means an accident that Comrade So-and-so says this." Always it meant that we had now to listen to the political history of that particular person, how he had written an article 20 years ago, and on the speaker would go to prove that his opponent never was a Marxist. He was a Menshevik, or a Social Revolutionary, or some other term equally opprobrious.' (*Murphy*) Yet Jack Murphy did not at that time see what was brewing, remaining loyally on Stalin's side, even proposing the motion in the Comintern that expelled Trotsky from the Communist Party. It was not until the early 1930s that he left the Communist Party and joined Stafford Cripps's Socialist League.

The British communist leader's closest family were not exempt. The first leader of the British Communist Party, the fiery Scottish orator Arthur McManus, was a well-known figure in Comintern circles. After a hard day arguing with the leaders of communist parties in France, Germany, Bulgaria and the rest, he would lead them on drinking sessions described by one of his British colleagues as 'gargantuan'. Even the hard-drinking Russians struggled to keep up with him.

His brother-in-law, William Wheeldon, a communist school-teacher from Derby, emigrated to the Soviet Union in 1921 to work as a teacher. In Britain, Wheeldon's family – all socialists, all opposed to the First World War – had been accused of plotting to assassinate Prime Minister David Lloyd George, and he and his mother and sister were all sentenced to long periods of imprison-ment. A recent investigation by historian Dr Nick Riley has shown that they were framed by the British security services, and Lloyd George, who probably knew that, managed to arrange for them to be released after serving two years. But Wheeldon could not get his teaching job back because he had been in prison.

His sister Hetty married Arthur McManus when she was released from prison, and died soon after while giving birth to a stillborn baby. William went to the Soviet Union to start a new life, and took Soviet citizenship. He was arrested in 1927, and is thought to have been executed in the same year, though no one knows where or when. (*IoS 6/9/1992*) The next year McManus himself, who was probably an alcoholic, died, aged only thirty-eight, and his ashes were embedded in the walls of the Kremlin. There is no evidence that he made any effort to save his brother-in-law.

In 1933, forty-two engineers employed by Metro Vickers Electrical Company Ltd on the construction and maintenance of electrical power stations were arrested. Seventeen of them were brought to trial on unsubstantiated charges of espionage, wrecking and bribery. The Russians among them got long prison sentences. Two of the Britons received prison sentences of two and three years, but were released three months later, after the British government had threatened sanctions in the form of a ban on Soviet imports. (*McLoughlin*)

But the purges, as we know them, really began in 1 December 1934, when Sergei Kirov, Stalin's friend and associate and the governor of Leningrad, was assassinated. Stalin probably ordered the assassination, but at the time no loyal communist anywhere was in any doubt that Kirov had been killed by Trotskyists. That very day Stalin drafted a law which gave him power to have people executed, and Kirov's assassin and all his closest family were rounded up and shot. Two senior Bolsheviks, L.B. Kamenev and Grigori Zinoviev, were also arrested in Moscow, but were eventually released after confessing their 'errors'.

The big show trials were in August 1936, January 1937 and March 1938. The first famous and powerful Bolsheviks to go to the firing squad were the same two men whom foreign communists had been taught to regard as heroes of the revolution: Kamenev and Zinoviev. The Comintern laid down the correct line for the British Communist Party to take: that the two men were 'mean degenerates' and 'abominable traitors' who were in league with Trotsky and Hitler's Gestapo and had plotted 'huge crimes'. British communists were instructed to unite all socialist and anti-fascist bodies in Britain 'against this fascist gang'. (*Thorpe*) The Comintern might as well have instructed Harry Pollitt to fly to the moon.

This time recantation would not save Kamenev and Zinoviev, as it had before; they were shot. All the most distinguished of the old Bolsheviks followed them to execution: Krestinsky, Rykov, Piatakov,

47

Radek, Bukharin. All were first tortured into making extravagant confessions. Ordered by Stalin, the purges were organised by his secret police chief, N.I. Yezhov.

In Moscow the purges decimated the Comintern staff and paralysed decision making. Because it was apparently random, there was nothing you could do to ensure you would be safe. Loyalty could not be guaranteed to make you safe. So everyone lived in fear. Those who were not shot entered the camps – the gulag – which was scarcely a preferable fate, and the end result was generally the same: death.

But it was not confined to Moscow. The purges penetrated every corner of the vast Soviet Union. A decree of 2 July 1937 ordered all local authorities to set up troikas to try those suspected of crimes against the Soviet Union, and these troikas were given quotas and needed to keep the numbers up, otherwise awkward and dangerous questions would be asked.

No one knows exactly how many people were murdered over the next three years as the Communist Party and the Soviet Union were 'purged', but it runs into millions. Robert Conquest says there were six million arrests, three million executions and two million deaths in the camps. Subsequent writers have put the figures rather lower, but the numbers are still huge.

The terror extended to the families of those accused. In 1935 Stalin toasted the anniversary of the 1917 Revolution with these words: 'We will destroy any such enemy, be he Old Bolshevik or not, we will destroy his kin, his family. Anyone who by his thoughts and actions – yes, his thoughts – encroaches on the unity of the socialist state, we will destroy.' Typically, the wife of one executed minor bureaucrat, Alexander Tivel, was fired from her job and prevented from finding other work, her son was taken away from her and placed in an orphanage, and she spent nine years in prison camps and eight in exile in Siberia.

The army was decimated. Seven generals and a thousand officers followed the distinguished Marshal Tukachevsky to the firing squad. Historians, teachers, astronomers, philosophers, biologists, writers, theatre directors, musicians – all saw their professions 'purged' and unreliable practitioners executed.

The terror extended from the highest to the lowest in the land: from the minor functionary Tivel to the man who had ruled with Stalin, Nicolai Bukharin. After months of torture, Bukharin appeared before the Central Committee and was cross-examined by Stalin himself. And there, contributing briefly to the proceedings, was Max Petrovsky, the husband of Rose Cohen. Petrovsky, in fact, seems at that meeting to have had the temerity to question something Stalin himself said. Perhaps this was remembered against him later.

Afterwards, Bukharin wrote to Stalin from his prison cell. He was a broken man. Gone was the bravery and defiance he had shown when being cross-examined. Now he simply begged that if he was to die, he should not be shot:

I've come to the last page of my drama and perhaps of my very life. I agonised over whether I should pick up pen and paper – as I write this I am shuddering all over from disquiet and from a thousand emotions stirring within me, and I can hardly control myself. But precisely because I have so little time left, I want to take my leave of you in advance, before my hand ceases to write, before my eyes close, while my brain somehow still functions. . . . If I'm to receive the death sentence, then I implore you beforehand, I entreat you, by all that you hold dear, not to have me shot. Let me drink poison in my cell instead. Let me have morphine so that I can fall asleep and never wake up. For me this point is extremely important. I don't know what words I should summon up in order to entreat you to grant me this as an act of charity. After all, politically, it won't really matter, and besides, no one will know a thing about it. But let me spend my last moments as I wish. Have pity on me! Surely you'll understand, knowing me as you do . . . I implore you. Sometimes I look death openly in the face, just as I know very well that I am capable of brave deeds. At other times, I, ever the same person, find myself in such disarray that I am drained of all strength. So if the verdict is death, let me have a cup of morphine. I implore you . . . I am preparing myself mentally to depart from this vale of tears, and there is nothing in me towards all of you, towards the party and the cause, but a great and boundless love. (*Harvey*)

Stalin, pitiless, had his old friend shot.

Foreign communists were not safe – in fact, your record of communist activism in your own country could well be used against you, for at some time you might well have said or done something to bring suspicion upon yourself. In 1937, all twelve members of the Polish Communist Party resident in Moscow were executed, and the Polish party was wound up, on the grounds, apparently, that all its key positions had been taken by fascist agents. Foreign communists found that permission to enter and leave the country was constantly delayed, presumably while someone checked that the applicant was not currently regarded as an 'enemy of the people'.

* * *

In 1936, the year Bukharin was denounced, George Fles was living near Tbilisi, the Georgian capital, in a small mountain village called Abastumani. Originally he had been told that his chances of a job in Moscow would be much greater if he could show that he had worked in a faraway district, but with Pearl pregnant, they had both decided that Tbilisi's mild climate would be better for their baby, and George should try to settle down in an effort to make his job permanent. George worked at the observatory, translating scientific articles. Pearl listened to her mother's pleadings that the Soviet Union was no place to give birth, and went back to England to have her baby, stopping in Holland on the way to meet George's family. (*Berman*)

They had had coded, imprecise warnings from friends, but neither of them had worried too much about them. 'Evidently there were warnings among the English and American communities that Stalin was becoming slightly paranoid about the number of foreigners in the Soviet Union', says Pearl's sister Hetty, a former communist who is still, even today, picking with care the words she uses about Stalin.

In London, Pearl's family was having its own problems. Hetty had upset her orthodox Jewish parents terribly by 'marrying out' –

marrying a non-Jew, Reg Bower – and Hetty's marriage had also upset her sister Anita, who was a communist and opposed marriage as an institution. Anita had a very intimate and detailed correspondence with George and Pearl, in which, among other things, they discussed and analysed their shared faith in communism. Anita lived to regret this correspondence. (*Bower interview*)

The secret police came for George on 26 August 1936. An American friend of George and Pearl from their Moscow days, Ed Falkowski, who worked for the *Moscow Daily News*, was visiting at the time, and staying with George. That morning, George left the house to buy some bread. Ed waited for George the whole morning, on the veranda of the house – but in vain. Around noon a militiaman from the village came by, checked Falkowski's papers, and told him he must leave the village and the district at once. A couple of hours later, the militiaman was back, angry at finding Falkowski still on the veranda.

Falkowski left, and at once the militiaman sealed the door with a strip of paper. Back in Moscow, Falkowski told his friends that George had probably been arrested. Many found it hard to credit, because George was known for his strong communist beliefs. Over the next few months, the expatriate community in Moscow started to wonder whether the young, passionate Dutchman might really have been a spy all along, for why else would he disappear into prison and never come out? It would, they thought, explain his mysterious taciturnity, his departure from Holland, and his attempts to penetrate the socialist movement of every country in which he had lived, joining the Socialist Party in Germany, the SFIO and the French Communist Party in France, and the Independent Labour Party in Britain. It was, of course, rubbish. George's communist beliefs had never been anything other than simple, straightforward and sincere. But that was what people started to say when their friends disappeared, for the alternative – that the terror was random – was unbearable.

One of George and Pearl's Moscow friends was Bob Miller, Moscow correspondent for the US *Daily Herald*, and his wife Jenny. In truth they had been more Pearl's friends than George's, for

George was a little intolerant of non-communists in Moscow, and his socialism was more rigid than hers. He had by then dedicated himself to building socialism and the Soviet Union. When George and Pearl left for Tbilisi in 1935, Bob and Jenny were permitted to take over their room in Moscow. It was the bedroom of a small apartment, in a conveniently central location.

After George's arrest, Bob Miller found a pile of hand-written pages in the toilet, torn up to be used as lavatory paper and placed there by the landlady. He could see by the quality of the paper that it was western. They were Pearl's love letters. What had happened was that, after George was arrested, their belongings were sent to Pearl in London, but a box of George's with the bundle of letters had been left behind. Because paper was scarce in the Soviet Union, the landlady, who of course could not read them, had torn each sheet into four and put them in the toilet. Years later Bob Miller shamefacedly confessed to George's great-nephew Thijs Berman that he had reconstructed a few and read them. 'If I don't tell you, who will be able to tell you?' he said. 'There is nobody left. From those letters it was clear that those two really loved each other.'

They never saw each other again. Pearl heard from him once, and never knew what had happened to him. But now, thanks to a huge labour of love from a great-nephew he never knew, we know. (*Berman*)

* * *

They came for Freda Utley's husband, Arcadi Berdichevsky, four months earlier.

Freda, Arcadi and their two-year-old son Jon had just been allocated a flat, after six years of camping out in the already overcrowded little flats occupied by several homeless families. Now, for the first time, they had some sort of privacy as a family, and they loved it. But Freda's private disillusionment with the Soviet Union must have been showing. I suspect she was the sort of person who does not find it easy to avoid speaking her mind, and was still too trusting for the snakepit that was Moscow in the time of the purges. At all events, she wrote later that at her house-warming party on 10

March 1936 'I opened my heart freely' to an old Russian communist friend called Mentich, whom she knew shared her disillusion. He probably did not betray her, unless it was under torture, for he was arrested soon afterwards.

Exactly a month later, during the night of 10 April, Arcadi woke Freda and said: 'We have visitors.' There was a soldier in the hall and two uniformed police officers in the sitting room, together with the janitor of the block of flats in which they lived. The police warned them not to speak to each other, and started to search the flat, shaking out every one of their hundreds of books and going through all their papers. It took many hours.

'We sat silent and tense', wrote Freda. 'The slight up-and-down movement of Arcadi's right foot crossed over his left was all that betrayed his feelings. . . . When Arcadi's eyes and mine met, we gave each other a smile and a look of confidence and calm. . . . Will this nightmare pass, or is this the end of our life and our love?' The dawn came, but the search went on. The police were 'polite, silent, methodical'. They selected a few books to take away, including volumes of Marx and Keynes. They took all Freda's letters from Arcadi, her address book, some office papers he had been working on at home. At 7 a.m. their little boy, Jon, woke up and Freda gave him breakfast. At 8 they told Arcadi they were taking him away to be examined, but that the search had not yet been completed. Freda made him coffee. 'My mind now was filled with only one purpose: to strengthen him for the ordeal before him.' She knew how long and exhausting the examinations were, but did not yet know that innocence could not save you.

The police allowed the lovers to talk for a few minutes. 'I asked him no questions. I let him rest, half sitting, half lying on the couch with his head sunk down and his face very pale. I packed a small suitcase with brush and comb, soap, toothpaste, and a change of linen.' She asked him to whom she should go for help. He understood better than she did what was happening. 'No one can help', he said.

At 9 they took him away. She wrote later: 'No words of love passed between us. They were not needed. Reserved and calm to the last, he gave me a gentle smile and was gone. I never saw him again.

He passed out of my life on that lovely April morning, in his English flannel jacket, his head hatless, a slight figure between two khaki-clad Soviet secret police officers.'

Why did they take Arcadi? We don't know: the purges were utterly, terrifyingly random. Perhaps they were taking revenge on Freda for her increasingly unreliable beliefs. Perhaps it was all to do with a problem at Arcadi's office. He was working as finance manager for a sales organisation which had continued to sell goods abroad, although, according to a new policy, they should have been retained for use in Soviet industry. His boss had found out belatedly about the new policy, and had placed the blame for not following it earlier on those below him, one of whom had already been arrested. We do not know for certain why they took Arcadi, and we probably never will. (*Utley, Lost Illusion*)

* * *

'One of us has to break this long silence', wrote Rose Cohen from Moscow to her sister Nellie in London in April 1937, exactly a year after the secret police had taken Arcadi Berdichevsky. 'I seem to have stopped writing letters altogether. And yet I'm longing to hear from you. How are you all, and what are you all doing? I suppose the same as usual, but I would like to know the details. Hugo [Nellie's husband] is still of course at *Labour Monthly*. Tell him that the March number was really brilliant. I read every word with absorbing interest.' The letter ended: 'Do please write soon. M is away and I'm feeling very lonely.' (*Rathbone collection*)

'M is away.' In a letter that she knew would be opened by the authorities, Rose Cohen could not tell her sister the appalling truth. A few days earlier, on 11 March, the secret police had come for Max. A month later the British Communist Party's political bureau was told that he had been arrested as a 'wrecker' and all British communists who had had any contact with him were to make statements giving full details of what they knew about him.

Until that day, Rose was happy and seems to have felt safe and secure. A success in Moscow, trusted and prominent, content with her husband and child and doing important and interesting work, she did not share any of Freda Utley's doubts. It seems likely she convinced herself that the people who had been arrested – even those she knew well, like Berdichevsky, and George Fles, and Lydia Gasviani – must really have been living double lives, openly supporting the party while secretly plotting to overthrow it. She had applied to be transferred from the Communist Party of Great Britain to the Communist Party of the Soviet Union, stating that her father. was 'of proletarian origin'. (*RC*)

She went to London to visit her sister Nellie in 1936, and then, of her own volition, returned to Moscow. She could have stayed in London and been safe. This suggests she believed she was safe in Moscow, though Nellie thought she was distracted and a little unhappy, and had it not been for Alyosha might not have returned. Nellie put her sister's tension down to her being unhappy with Petrovsky, whom Nellie seems to have thought was something of a sexual philanderer. (*Rathbone*) But perhaps Rose was at last beginning to wonder about the Soviet system and her safety in it.

Nellie must have noticed that the April 1937 letter lacked the sparkle of previous letters from her clever, happy, exciting and hauntingly beautiful sister. But she did not know the dreadful truth. Harry Pollitt, who did, wrote a matter-of-fact seven-point letter to the party's man in Moscow, Robin Page Arnot, and point five was: 'Will you please give the attached letter to Rose Cohen from me?' Page Arnot delayed passing on the letter until it was too late, and Rose never saw it. It was an attempt to interest her and cheer her up: 'My visit to Spain [to the International Brigades fighting in the Spanish Civil War] gave me great satisfaction. There is quite a story about how I got there, which will make you laugh. . . .' And then, at the end, he wrote as much as he dared about her troubles: 'We all send our love. Don't lose heart.' She never saw Harry's letter. I found it, more than half a century later, in a dusty Comintern archive, where it was originally deposited so that it could be used, if need be, to help show that Pollitt, too, was a traitor. (*RC*)

When they took Max, Rose suddenly felt utterly alone and vulnerable. Until that day the most popular and admired member of the expatriate community, she suddenly found that old friends avoided her – even old British communist comrades based in Moscow, whom she and Max had always invited to their annual parties in their dacha outside Moscow.

She went to see her friend Ivy Litvinov, British-born wife of the Foreign Commissar Maxim Litvinov. The visit could have endangered Ivy. Her frightened husband had said to her: 'I hope you're not going to rush off and see Rose. It would be a terrible thing for you to do.' But Ivy's daughter Tanya went to Rose and brought her to Ivy. 'Not a single one of my friends has been to see me', said Rose to Ivy, who recalled later: 'She was utterly lonely and trembling.' Her greatest fear was that she would be arrested, and then what would happen to eight-year-old Alyosha? (*Carswell*) Twice in the previous two years Rose had cut short holidays she was enjoying because she could not bear to be parted from him. She knew something of the dreadful orphanages to which the children of 'enemies of the people' were sent, where they were treated harshly and forbidden ever to mention the names of their parents.

It was not quite true that none of her old friends came to see her. One, an Englishman called Tom J. Bell, who worked with her on the *Moscow Daily News*, spent a lot of time with her, and perhaps she realised he had been sent to spy on her, for she seems to have been very careful what she said to him. According to a British Intelligence report, 'Bell was instructed by his chief in the office to be very friendly with her and not to tell her that she was being watched, also to discuss her husband's arrest as often as possible and . . . to elicit her views on the matter. He [reported] that she never spoke of her husband as being guilty, and although he put it to her that he must be guilty, or implicated in some way, otherwise the OGPU would not arrest him, she always replied "An error has been made somewhere".' According to British Intelligence, 'it was decided to send him over for the trial if he would declare that Cohen had told him in confidence that she was implicated and her husband guilty. Bell said that she was watched night and day before her arrest, for over six months, and this had a very harmful effect on her health.' The oddest thing about this report, though, is that British Intelligence seems to think Bell was reporting to the KGB via Harry Pollitt. This, unless I and everyone else have completely misunderstood Pollitt, is not credible. (*PRO KV2/1397*)

Nellie must have caught the mood and replied at once, for on 4 July Rose wrote again: 'I was ever so glad to hear from you at last, and please thank Joyce [Nellie's daughter Joyce Rathbone] for her letter. Alyosha was particularly excited about the notepaper and showed it to all his friends. The snapshot is excellent of both of you. Joyce looks enormous. I'm glad she's as full of life as ever. Tell her it's difficult to send badges in a letter because of the sharp points. But I will try and send her some through someone.'

And then Rose came as close as she could to naming the fear that gnawed at her. 'Alyosha is very well and staying in a summer camp with his kindergarten. I paid him an "unofficial" visit yesterday. Visiting day is only once a month. I find this very difficult, altho' it's really best for the children, especially the little ones, as mothers tend to be a disturbing influence and upset the discipline of the camp.' Then much more about Alyosha – how sensible he was, how sensitive. Then how Alyosha had had measles in May: 'Two days he had a very high temperature and I was terribly scared. And just like my luck, I was all alone in the house during these days, as the nanya had to dash down to the village to fix up her pension.' Still she could not tell her sister just why she was all alone in the house, with no Max Petrovsky to share the burden. As for the nanya, in one paragraph she had just gone down to the village to fix her pension, but in the next it turns out that, after seven years with Rose, she 'has gone back to her native village as she has become too old and ill to work . . . I was upset at her leaving me, particularly at this time.' It's safe to surmise that the nanya knew, or was told, that Rose was no longer a safe person to be seen to be working for.

Then: 'Thanks for remembering my birthday and your greetings. They were more than welcome, for no one else remembered except my friend Masha in New York, who never forgets. I also feel very much ashamed that I forgot to send Joyce a card on her birthday. I remembered it for some time before and then forgot at the time.' Then she recites the names of old friends who have not written

57

recently, and ought to have done so. Then: 'I'm sorry this is such a dull letter but I'm feeling in a dull mood. So I had better stop. . . . Do please write oftener.' (*Rathbone collection*) Reading the letter now, knowing what was happening, you can feel the loneliness and terror. Rose, alone and far from home, obviously wanted more than anything to pour her heart out to her older sister.

Nellie could not know what was wrong, but she caught the mood and replied at once. Her letter was returned. The knock on the door at Rose's Moscow flat came at 3 a.m. on 13 August 1937. Freda Utley and Pearl Rimmel remained at liberty to ask, unavailingly, to be allowed to hear from their husbands again, but Rose was to share Max's fate.

Rose, it's said, broke down completely in prison, and cried constantly for Alyosha, right up to the moment, on 28 November 1937, when they took her out and shot her. Petrovsky was already dead: he had been shot in September. And Alyosha – but we will come back to Alyosha.

In Britain, no one knew for certain what had happened to her. The official Soviet line was that she had been sentenced to ten years in a Siberian labour camp. Few people returned from these places, and rumours circulated for years after her disappearance. In October 1939 there was a rumour that she had been released and sent to Britain. No one knew for certain until nearly twenty years later.

What had Rose done? At the time one of her many friends and admirers in England, Maurice Reckitt, wrote: 'The only evidence against her of which I ever heard was the report of a British comrade that she had declared that she would never let her child ride in a public vehicle, which was a counter-revolutionary sentiment! To anyone who knew Rose in London, and had ridden with her in the many public vehicles which were her only means of transport, the story is as incredible as it is trivial.' (*Reckitt*)

So what did they really have against Rose and Max? Max had been a friend of Trotsky. They were both Jewish, which was not necessarily fatal under Stalin, but did not help. The evident affection of the British Communist Party for Petrovsky would have been a mark against him in Stalin's book, for to suspicious Soviet

Communists this rather suggested that Petrovsky had gone native. (*Thorpe*) Stalin would not have appreciated the British party's protest, nine years earlier, when Petrovsky was taken away from day-to-day involvement with British affairs. The British Communist Party asked the reasons why Comrade Bennett [one of Petrovsky's aliases, the one he used in Britain] was withdrawn from the Anglo-American secretariat, 'and at the same time expresses the great appreciation of the British Party for the good work Comrade Bennett has done for the party. . . . The changes made, which were rather unexpected, will not alter the good relations that have always existed between Comrade Bennett and the Communist Party of Great Britain.' (*RC*) Stalin considered only one person to be indispensable, and it wasn't Petrovsky.

Perhaps Rose and Max suffered from being closely identified with the British party, which was regarded in some Comintern circles as unreliable. The secret police were not only out to build a case against the Petrovskys, but, more importantly, one against Harry Pollitt himself. There were plans, of which he knew nothing, for Pollitt to figure in a great show trial of Comintern leaders. Pollitt had been known to express doubts about the personality cult of Stalin, and Soviet officials were irritated at his reluctance to print long, boring speeches by Soviet leaders in full in the *Daily Worker*. Kevin Morgan suggests that they thought arresting Rose and Max would assist the preparation for this trial, for then Pollitt could be shown to have supported people now revealed as traitors. It is certainly the case that when some Comintern people were arrested, one of them, Hungarian Communist Bela Kun, implicated Pollitt as a 'collaborator' in his 'conspiracy' against the Comintern. Kun, in desperation, may have simply given the first name that came into his head to get them to stop torturing him, or let him have some sleep.

Rose was arrested on 31 August, the day that Pollitt arrived in Moscow to discuss the political situation in Britain. This would have been his first meeting with Rose after Petrovsky's arrest. Presumably the secret police did not want this meeting to take place. They may also have hoped that they could squeeze out of Rose something they could use against Pollitt. At all events they kept Pollitt kicking his heels for days in the Hotel Lux while they questioned Rose Cohen, Bela Kun, and the Russian Comintern official Osip Piatnitsky. (*Morgan, Rose Cohen*)

The case against Rose, Max and Harry Pollitt was being built up in the usual manner. An unsigned memorandum I found in a Comintern archive gives the flavour of this sort of exercise, with its half-truths and slavering innuendo; but what makes this one different is that it is in English and clearly comes from a British source – perhaps the Tom J. Bell who went to such lengths to seem to be her friend: 'Officially Rose Cohen was not Pollitt's wife but it was more or less well known that they lived together in Moscow and here. They might still be on intimate terms. Pollitt's wife and child lived with Cohen. Between Petrovsky, Cohen and Pollitt there was a close friendship. Pollitt often visits them when he is in Moscow, always brings her presents from her brother etc.' Claiming that many women are 'around Pollitt' when he comes to Moscow, the memorandum adds that 'Petrovsky was also at the party at Kerrigan's [Peter Kerrigan was another British communist leader] at the Hotel Lux. He came without Cohen. He was very friendly . . . Pollitt took Kerrigan's wife to the party at Petrovsky's . . . Petrovsky was there about two hours . . .' (*RC*)

The bohemian atmosphere this is supposed to conjure up corresponded with the image the Soviet hierarchy seem to have formed of the *Moscow Daily News* staff. Freda Utley, ironically, shared this attitude to those who worked at the paper, referring caustically to their attempts 'to recreate the London and New York radical Bohemian atmosphere of hard drinking and easy loving'. (*Morgan, Rose Cohen*)

For Max and Rose, the leadership of the British Communist Party was prepared to stir itself, just a little. They would lift not a finger for Freda Utley's husband, or for Pearl Rimmel's, but after Max's arrest, and before Rose's, they made an effort for Max. Pollitt, in London, received official notification from Moscow that Petrovsky had been arrested as a 'wrecker', and he reported to the Political Bureau that all British communists who had had any contact with him were required to make statements giving full details of what they knew about him. (*Thorpe*)

Just what was going on in the minds of Pollitt and his colleagues, who had regarded Max and Rose as close friends, who had stayed in their flat when they were in Moscow, who had gone to their regular parties for all English communists based in Moscow?

They wrote the statements. Several, including Pollitt and Page Arnot, wrote statements in Petrovsky's defence, praising him warmly. He and Rose were, after all, close personal friends of most of them. Page Arnot wrote: 'He was the one comrade to whom I felt the closest. This personal friendship existed also because his wife, Rose Cohen, a member of the Communist Party of Great Britain since 1920, was a close friend of most leading comrades. He has never uttered anything that is the slightest suspicious.' Pollitt wrote to the general secretary of the Comintern, Georgi Dimitrov, of his 'very warm personal friendship' with Petrovsky and his confidence in his unwavering loyalty to Stalin and the international communist movement. He had, said Pollitt, always emphasised that Stalin was 'the only man that could have carried [the Soviet Union] through to its present triumphant position.' Petrovsky, he said, had wanted him, Pollitt, to become the party's leader. The news of the arrest, he wrote, came as 'one of the greatest shocks of my life'. (*Morgan, Rose Cohen*)

But in public, Britain's communist leaders threw their old friends to the wolves. When the arrest of Rose became known in England, which was not until months after it happened, and other newspapers demanded that the Soviets at least charge her publicly and say where she was, the *Daily Worker* snarled at their anti-Soviet stance, and furiously insisted that the British government had no right to intervene. 'The individual concerned', said its editorial written, almost certainly, by someone who also knew Rose well, 'is married to a Soviet citizen and thereby assumed Soviet citizenship alike in the eyes of Soviet law as of international law. Any charge that may be brought against her will be tried according to the forms of Soviet justice. The British Government has no right whatever to interfere in the internal affairs of another country and its citizens. It is not surprising that the reactionary press is in full cry in support of the British Government protest. . . .' The editorial naturally found its way into the British security services filing system, where it will have done little to increase the desire of the government to try to help Rose.

It was a weaselly and discreditable way to abandon a woman whom every leading communist in Britain had counted as a friend. It is somehow even more distasteful because the editorial fastidiously declines to name her. William Gallacher, Britain's only Communist Member of Parliament, went to see Georgi Dimitrov about Rose.

Dimitrov was an international left-wing hero, and not just because of his brave showing in the Nazi court which had set out to frame him for the burning down of the Reichstag. Born in 1882, he left school at twelve. He had led strikes against the regime and been a socialist member of the Bulgarian Parliament from 1913 to 1923, and had split the Social Democrats, leading its left wing into the newly formed Communist Party after the 1917 Russian revolution. Dimitrov had come to prominence in Germany when he was put on trial by the Nazis on a charge of burning down the Reichstag. Twelve years later, in 1945, he was to rule his native Bulgaria.

Naturally, when the fascist coup came in Bulgaria in 1923, the Comintern blamed the Bulgarian communists for 'a crass opportunist mistake' in not opposing it effectively, and Dimitrov said later, in one of those gruesome 'self-criticisms' that were demanded on these occasions, that he regretted he had not been 'genuinely Bolshevik' and therefore could not 'successfully organise and carry through this historic popular uprising with the proletariat at its head'. (*Blagoyeva*)

After the coup, Dimitrov led an uprising, which was suppressed, and he was forced into exile and sentenced to death in his absence. By the time he arrived in Berlin in 1929, his three brothers had already met violent deaths: one in war, one in a Siberian prison camp in 1905, and one tortured to death by the Bulgarian secret police in 1925.

In 1933 the Reichstag burned down. The new Nazi government which had come into power that year was probably responsible, but it was determined that the communists should be seen to have been behind it. So, together with two other Bulgarian communists and a

Dutchman, Dimitrov was arrested and set up for a show trial, so that the Nazis could show the world that the fire was a communist plot. He was handcuffed day and night in prison, and told the penalty would be death. Meanwhile his wife died after a long illness. Nonetheless, he dispensed with the services of the German lawyer assigned to him, and, despite working in a foreign language, cross-examined the prosecution witnesses so effectively that they admitted they had been forced to sign false statements against him. When the top Nazi Hermann Goering came to give evidence, Dimitrov cross-examined him about the secret passage that led from his home to the Reichstag. The Nazis, having courted international publicity for what was intended to be a show trial, were forced to acquit him, and the next year, no doubt with a sigh of relief, they put him on a plane to Moscow.

This, then, was not a man you might expect to give way out of fear or cowardice. Yet, when Gallacher raised with him the question of Rose Cohen, Dimitrov looked at Gallacher gravely for a few moments and then said: 'Comrade Gallacher, it is best that you do not pursue these matters.' And Gallacher did not pursue them. He seems to have been cheered by the fact that he thought he had been better treated than Pollitt. (*Beckett, Enemy Within*)

Pollitt, after arriving in Moscow the very day of Rose's arrest, pressed his protests about Rose Cohen further than his colleagues thought wise. He had a long interview with Dimitrov, and according to Ivy Litvinov, he even saw Stalin himself, and asked him to send Rose back to England. (*Carswell*) Comintern officials started to suggest to other leading British communists that Pollitt was not as reliable as he ought to be, and they should think about replacing him. Things were worse for Pollitt than either he or they knew. Rose Cohen was one of several foreign communists and Comintern leaders who were arrested in the spring and summer of 1937. People will say anything under torture. We know that Bela Kun named Pollitt as one of his 'collaborators' in his Trotskyist 'conspiracy' and he may not have been the only one.

But Pollitt was capable of inspiring great personal loyalty, and his colleagues made it clear they stood by him. When he arrived in

Moscow on 31 August, Osip Piatnitsky, a former leader of the Comintern, was also in prison and undergoing torture, but he refused to 'confess'. If he could have been persuaded to name Pollitt as one of his 'co-conspirators' that would probably have sealed Harry's fate, for he could easily have been arrested while in Moscow.

It was during that visit that Pollitt went to see Dimitrov and raised the question of Rose Cohen and Max Petrovsky. After the meeting, he wrote thanking the Comintern boss for a conversation which was 'one of the most helpful things that I remember'. (*Thorpe*) We do not know what was said. Whatever it was, it may have been helpful to Harry Pollitt, but it was no help at all to Rose Cohen. Perhaps he was told that the more fuss he made about Rose and Max, the greater the chance that he would share their fate. Perhaps Dimitrov simply appealed to his loyalty and discipline.

Whatever was said, Pollitt and his colleagues not only ensured that the British Communist Party failed to protest, but also prevented effective public protests from anyone else on the left. Maurice Reckitt, who tried to drum up protest letters, found people telling him that Soviet justice could be relied on, that the future of the Soviet state was more important than an individual, even that it would be better for Rose if everyone stayed silent. Approaching public figures on the left, Reckitt found it hard to get significant left wingers to sign a very moderate letter to the *New Statesman* protesting at Rose's disappearance.

'When we turned to the left wing for help we were met with a blank refusal to give or suggest any assistance whatever', wrote Reckitt later. 'A few offered the lame pretext that it would be better for Rose if everyone kept silence; others added the barefaced assertion that Soviet justice could be relied on. . . . Others, again, still more scandalously asserted that no individual's fate was of consequence if they came into conflict with the interests of the Soviet Union.' These people, wrote Reckitt furiously, 'had been for years the very closest friends and admirers of the woman in this appalling predicament'. This illustrated 'the corrosive influence of Communist ideology upon rudimentary morals and natural affection'. (*Reckitt*)

The resulting lame letter in the *New Statesman*, far too little and far too late, is chiefly interesting not for those who signed, but for those who did not. Of course communist leaders did not sign, but where were the rest of the British left? Rose's old Fabian friends Sidney and Beatrice Webb, now converted to being admirers of the Soviet Union, seem to have confined themselves to making private (and, presumably, fruitless) enquiries.

And where were the old LRD luminaries Margaret and Douglas Cole? In later years, Rose Cohen's name was silently removed from their accounts of guild socialism and the Labour Research Department, as though its authors felt they had something to be ashamed of. It is not clear quite why they behaved in this way. Perhaps they still resented Rose for her part in moving the Labour Research Department away from Fabian socialism and towards communism. Perhaps it was simply because, by then, they were avoiding making any criticisms of the Soviet Union, for as the war approached, several people were starting to see the Soviet Union as an essential bulwark against the Nazis.

The month they shot Rose (though, to be fair, he did not know about that until many years later) we find Douglas Cole writing in the Communist theoretical journal *Labour Monthly*: 'Nor am I one of those who, when everything in the new and struggling Socialist community does not go just as they would like, turn their backs on the struggle and proclaim that the Revolution is being betrayed. Alas, men cannot make a new civilisation without growing pains, or liquidate a ancient tyranny without suffering.' (*Morgan, Rose Cohen*)

Privately Pollitt was distraught, and did not know what to do. An intercepted letter from a communist to her husband in April 1938, when the Soviets were saying Rose would go on trial, reports a meeting with him in London. 'The first thing he said to me, with a face as long as a yardstick, poor man, was "Have you seen today's papers?" He also said that since the day before yesterday his phone had not stopped ringing and that every newspaper in the country had been on to him. He seems to know where it is all coming from. Obviously he is terribly oppressed by the latest developments. . . . During the evening this was the only thing he mentioned.' (*PRO*)

Even the limited amount of help and loyalty which the British Communist Party gave to Max and Rose was denied to other victims of the murderous madness in Moscow. Pollitt, as we shall see, did not lift a finger for George Fles and his wife, for Arcadi Berdichevsky and his wife, nor for any of his other innocent British comrades and their partners who, as he must have known, were being flung into prison and shot, or tortured, or sent to the gulag.

The reasons for Stalin murdering his most loyal supporters are, as we have seen, obscure and confused, but the murders of Rose and Max were consistent with the foetid atmosphere of the purges.

You can get a feel of what killed Rose and Max from a document prepared by the Cadres Department of the Comintern in January 1939 about the British Communist Party and its leaders. It begins: 'The leadership of the Communist Party of Great Britain contains a number of people who were formerly connected with enemies of the people, and in some cases are currently connected with politically dubious people.'

The Department, it says, has 'materials on the connections between the leading communists in the CPGB with Petrovsky and his wife Rose Cohen, who turned out to be enemies of the people'. These 'materials' were the letters from Harry Pollitt and Robin Page Arnot in defence of Max Petrovsky, and Pollitt's last letter to Rose, which they did not let her see. 'It is clear from the materials that some of the leading comrades in the CPGB, particularly Comrade Pollitt, did not just have a business connection with Petrovsky and Cohen, but also a personal friendship with them.' This disturbing state of affairs persisted when Max and Rose went to Moscow, it says.

Pollitt's last letter to Rose was the clincher, though. 'It is clear from this that Pollitt was not only prepared to tell Cohen how he got into Spain, but also informed her of Gallacher's impending visit to Spain. From this one may conclude, among other things, that the position of conspiratorial work in the CPGB is far from satisfactory.' And then it quotes the deadly words from Pollitt's letter: 'We all send our love. Don't lose heart.'

The political history of CPGB leaders, says the document, betrays a woeful state of affairs. 'Many comrades in the leadership of the

CPGB have made serious political mistakes in the past.' In 1928 John Campbell 'adhered to a so-called majority of the Central Committee which underestimated the revolutionary strength of the working class and overestimated capitalist stabilisation'. This means that he had at first opposed Class against Class. Willie Gallacher had 'displayed left-sectarian tendencies' and got the line wrong more than once. And so on – few of the leaders escaped criticism for following an incorrect line at some time in their lives.

The document demanded, among other things, a 'purge' of Trotskyists in the Young Communist League, more discipline in the trade union communist groups, and constant vigilance against Trotskyist infiltration: 'Corrupting and demoralising Trotskyist ideas enjoy fairly wide credit among the British bourgeois intelligentsia.' There is, it explains, a woman in Macclesfield who used to belong to a Trotskyist front organisation in Germany. (How did they find that out?) She has in her home some German literature 'presumably produced by a Trotskyist publishing house'. Her husband, a Communist Party member, 'has declared that on all the main political questions he is in agreement with his wife'. Yet the party has let this go on! Bill Rust 'was compelled to warn the comrades concerned that such quietism and political indifference borders on rendering assistance to the most malicious enemies of the party, the Trotskyists . . .'

There is 'an unacceptable situation' in the *Daily Worker*, where 'the paper is making the most serious political mistakes' and its staff need to be 'purged'. The Left Book Club needs to be brought into line: it has published books by Trotskyists. (*RC*) And so on, and so on, pages and pages of it. That was the atmosphere of the purges, and the sickness entrapped anyone who came near it. It came, of course, right from the top. It was Stalin who had told the Soviet Communist Party's Central Committee in 1936 that Trotskyism was now 'a frenzied and unprincipled band of wreckers, diversionists, spies and murderers acting on instructions from intelligence service organs of foreign states', and that Trotskyists were now 'mostly Party people, with Party membership cards in their pockets', which opened the way for a worldwide purge. (*Thorpe*)

If British communist leaders behaved discreditably in abandoning Rose, so too did the British government. The Foreign Office seems to have been eager to seize on the excuse that Rose had given up her British citizenship and become a Soviet citizen, to wash its hands of her. Those who have written about Rose Cohen subsequently have accepted this version of events – that Britain could do nothing because she had voluntarily become a Soviet citizen. In fact, my reading of British Foreign Office documents now available suggests that it is most unlikely she did anything of the kind. She was a British citizen who had never given up her citizenship. The Soviet Union persecuted her falsely for being a British spy. The British government failed her because she was a communist.

News of her arrest in August 1937 took more than three months to reach the embassy, and when they did get it, though they did not know it at the time or for a long time afterwards, they had a matter of days to save her. Pollitt, who knew about it much earlier, did not alert anyone. The embassy heard only in December, and then indirectly, perhaps from a British communist source. Lord Chilston, the British ambassador, wrote to Foreign Secretary Lord Halifax, relying on some wildly inaccurate information from somewhere: 'Her illegitimate child, by a man who deserted her, has apparently been sent to a children's home. It is possible, indeed, that she no longer possesses British nationality, for she is certainly a Communist and was not registered at His Majesty's consulate.'

So the first whisper that she might not be a British citizen, entitled to such protection as Britain can give (and it could give some protection) came not from the Soviets, as has always been supposed, but from the British. In March the next year, the British embassy asked the Soviet Foreign Commissariat whether she had become a Soviet citizen. There is no evidence that the Soviets had even thought of the idea until the British put it into their heads.

In April 1938 the British embassy told the press about Rose, in the hope that this would increase pressure on the Soviets to release her. But by that time the Foreign Office was wondering whether it ought to be supporting her at all. A high-ranking official, R.H. Hadow, wrote a memorandum: 'The publicity likely to be given to

Miss Cohen's antecedents . . . may result in Questions in Parliament as to our support of a notorious Communist agitator, from right wing Conservatives.' Anyway, thought Mr Hadow, 'she may not still be a British subject'. At the end of April he was telling Chilston: 'The antecedents of Miss Cohen and doubts as to her nationality, which have now become known in England, make it inadvisable to continue to press the case pending its discussion in London next week. If approached therefore you should discreetly discourage further press publicity so long as the case is sub judice.'

Hadow did not have it all his own way. At the Foreign Office in London, Laurence Collier wrote: 'It seems to me wrong in principle to make distinctions between British subjects in these cases according to their political antecedents. . . . As regards Miss Cohen's nationality, I am at a loss to understand why, in the first place, the embassy went out of their way to suggest in their letter of March 1 that she might have become a Soviet citizen. . . . The fact that the Soviet government have never maintained that she is one is strong proof to the contrary. . . .'

Gordon Vereker, one of Chilston's aides in Moscow, agreed: 'The People's Commissariat for Foreign Affairs have in fact never questioned Miss Cohen's British nationality, and had they had the slightest doubt on the subject, they would certainly have made it a pretext for refusing to furnish us with any information about her.' He was right; but he was too late. The British had given the Soviets an idea to get them off the hook. Four days after Laurence's and Vereker's memoranda, on 9 May 1938, the People's Commissariat for Foreign Affairs did indeed claim she had given up her British citizenship. This was almost a year after Rose's arrest, when (though no one in Britain knew it at the time) she had already been dead for five months.

Presumably, because the Soviets could not produce her they wished urgently to show that she was no concern of Britain's. They told Chilston that she had applied for Soviet citizenship in December 1936 and it was granted in March 1937. This seems surprising, if she was as worried when she visited London in mid-1936 as her sister seems to have thought.

British records show that as late as 1935 she applied for, and was given, a new British passport. (*PRO: FO 371 File 714*) Soviet records show that as late as December 1935 she was writing 'British' in the nationality section of Soviet forms. (*RC 495/198/733*) So the change of heart, if she really applied to be a Soviet citizen in December 1936, must have been swift.

Collier was sure the Soviets were lying. The embassy picked up a rumour from Moscow's British community that Rose had become a Soviet citizen, but had regretted it and tried to revoke it after her husband had been arrested, and was told that it was too late; and that on her husband's arrest, she was expelled from the Communist Party of the Soviet Union. 'This story', wrote Vereker, 'is attributed to such of Miss Cohen's friends as still survive.' But surely, if she was trying to hang on to British citizenship and the Soviets would not let her have it back, she would have talked to the embassy, who could have given it to her.

Vereker argued that because Britain tended to take a firm line, its citizens were better treated in the Soviet Union than Germans, Turks, Persians and Greeks, whose governments were less concerned, and whose citizens in the Soviet Union were disappearing by the truckload. But the Foreign Office had had enough. 'In the case of Rose Cohen, you are authorised at your discretion to request the return of her passport', it wired Vereker. It had washed its hands of her.

Briefing the Foreign Secretary to deal with a question in the House of Commons from Josiah Wedgwood MP about Rose, officials said that according to the Soviet government, she was a Soviet citizen, so nothing could be done. They told him to say: 'In view of the above, it is not much use me urging the exercise of mercy in her case.' The briefing pointed out that one of her left-wing defenders had said she would not tolerate 'a word of criticism for Stalin and his government'. The official who briefed the Foreign Secretary commented smugly that now 'Miss Cohen would probably be only too ready to "tolerate a word of criticism for Stalin and his government"'. The British Communist Party, he said, seemed to carry little weight in Moscow, adding: 'The history of the Russian revolution shows that the "Bloomsbury Bolshevik" or "parlour pink" is the first to go to the wall.' Mr Hadow added a note in the margin. 'I wonder whether Miss Cohen is now solid or liquid?' – a reference to Stalin's opponents being 'liquidated'. Presumably Mr Hadow thought that was witty. He wrote to Josiah Wedgwood: 'We would do no good by continuing to make representations on behalf of someone whom we have no claim to protect as she is a Soviet citizen.'

The British embassy asked Foreign Commissar Litvinov for Rose's passport. Eventually, in October, it was returned. This of course does not prove that she gave it up to the Soviet authorities and became a Soviet citizen; they could just as easily have found it when they searched her flat. In fact, if, as they claimed, she had given it up voluntarily, it should, under international law, have been returned to the British straight away.

In London an excited official, Lascelles, minuted: 'The embassy does not seem to have realised what an interesting document this [passport] is.' Issued in 1935, it contained no Soviet entry and exit stamps, even though she had certainly travelled abroad. This proved she was also using Soviet identity papers, and was therefore suppressing the truth when applying for a passport, said Mr Lascelles: 'We always knew of course that she was a thoroughly undesirable person, and her case was only taken up with the Soviet government on general principles and despite her undesirability. I submit however that this revelation of the fact that at the time of her arrest she had no moral right to a British passport absolves us from any further obligation to interest ourselves in her case.' Interestingly, Mr Lascelles did not argue that she gave up British citizenship, only that she failed to reveal her Soviet identity papers when she renewed her British passport. Collier pointed out in reply: 'There are many persons who are quite validly in possession of more than one passport.' (*PRO: FO 371 File 714*)

British officialdom had, in fact, already devoted a good deal of time to analysing Rose Cohen's British passport. When she renewed it, in September 1935, the Passport Office sent the old passport to Scotland Yard with a letter saying: 'She asked for the return of her old passport. We thought it better, however, to keep it.' Scotland Yard returned it to the Passport Office later the same month: 'We have taken full particulars of journeys on the old passport which are of very great interest.' They had provided a new passport, as they were obliged to do – she had done nothing which gave them any excuse not to do so. (*PRO: KV2/1397*) But there seems to have been resentment that a notorious communist could travel the world on a British passport, and officials were glad of the excuse to abandon her provided by what seems to have been the fiction that she had become a Soviet citizen. They had plenty of time to spy on her, but none to try and save her.

The *Daily Sketch* gloated: 'A woman who was an apostle of this anti-democratic creed must rely now upon the protests of a "capitalist" state.' It was not much to rely on. The British government abandoned Rose Cohen to her dreadful fate with an audible and discreditable sigh of relief. But it was the Soviet government that murdered her.

FOUR

From Which No Traveller Returns

Sweetheart,
I am so big and fat and ugly that I am almost glad you are not here to laugh at me. I know you wouldn't but . . . I understand what my doctor means now. The chicken is really heavy now, there is a constant pressure on all my inner parts. Particularly since the little sweet is your son, hardly a moment's peace does he give me, wriggling, here, there, curling around . . .

The Herald Tribune and the rest of the newspapers are really simply scandalous in their anti-Soviet attacks, using the widespread rounding-up of Trotskyite terrorists as a ruse, alleging all sorts of startling lies about Soviet colonies in the capitals of the world . . .

Write soon precious. Your people have bought and forwarded an oil-stove, which they knew we wanted. . . . Write, write! Did you prefer the daily postcard? Come quickly. Your very very very own,

Pearl.

She was at home in England with her sister, waiting for her baby to come, in love, optimistic for herself and for George, for the baby, for socialism and humanity and the noble Soviet Union, and indignant about the Soviet Union's detractors.

They took the letter to George's cell and told him that he could read it, so long as he translated it into Russian for his interrogator to read, but that he would not be permitted to answer it. I know this from the research done by his great-nephew, the Dutch journalist Thijs Berman, who also, partly because he is a close relative, was eventually, after persistent badgering, permitted to see the record of George's interrogation.

George was isolated in a cell by himself, not allowed to talk to other prisoners, and interrogated for hours running into days and weeks by Vasiliev of the Georgian NKVD. George's poet friend Lydia Gasviani, to whom Rose Cohen had given him a letter of introduction, had been arrested a few days earlier on suspicion of being a Trotskyist. To the Georgian NKVD, Gasviani was just the sort of person who would be suspect: she had friends all over Europe, travelled a lot, and led an unconventional life. Her arrest had signalled the discovery of an 'international Trotskyite conspiracy' in Tbilisi, and Vasiliev's task was to convict George Fles of being a part of it.

The Georgian NKVD was run by the immensely cruel Lavrenti Beria. At that time it was his task to implement Stalin's instructions and find people to torture and kill so that the party and the people might be purged. Between 1936 and 1939 over 80,000 Georgians disappeared in camps, especially senior party members, intellectuals and artists. He did it so well that later he took over from Yezhov, and ran all of Stalin's secret police.

The first interrogation is dated 19 and 20 August, indicating that George had to answer questions the whole night through. This sort of interrogation normally started at 10 p.m. and continued until 6 a.m. The suspect had to stand up straight the whole time. Many gave false statements sooner or later just to be allowed some sleep. These statements provided evidence for the show trials.

So George stood all night long in the bare interrogation room of the NKVD regional office in Adigen. His interrogator took his time. The more tired George became, the easier Vasiliev's task would be. First, for hours, George had to tell the story of his life, his jobs, the names of the people he knew. He had to rehearse the tedious details which he had already written on a dozen forms of one sort or another in that bureaucratic country. And then, suddenly, and probably in the same toneless voice, Vasiliev asked him whether he had ever received Trotskyist literature in the Soviet Union. George said, truthfully:

In Moscow I had an intensive correspondence with my wife's sister, Anita Rimel. Back then Anita was still a member of the Independent Labour Party of England. [She later joined the Communist Party.] Sometimes she sent me texts from various political streams, including Trotskyist, to hear my opinion on them. She suddenly started with this in 1934. I received the texts by mail, together with her letters. All that material, including the Trotskyist texts, I gave to the Union, to comrade Norman, head of the Secret Department. When I visited a Dutch ship for my work in Arkhangelsk I received a pamphlet by Trotsky written in Dutch from a sailor. . . . I gave it to the head of the international club in Arkhangelsk. In September or October 1934 I received a couple of copies of the Trotskyist magazine *Red Flag* from Anita Rimel, by mail. I handed them over to Fierlov, the accountant of the Interclub, who conducted a secret correspondence and therefore could send them directly to the Secret Department of the International Union. The papers were in a sealed parcel and I did not tell Fierlov what it contained. Later on, after my return to Moscow, I asked Comrade Norman where the material was that I had sent him. Norman answered he had never received any magazines.

Those letters, as we shall see, preyed on the mind of Pearl's sister Anita for the rest of her life, after she learned what had happened to George. But was that all? Yes. In that case – and Vasiliev's triumph almost leaps off the page – what about this? 'Here I show you a German magazine with the title *Die Sammlung*. It was published in the Netherlands in June 1935 and contains an article by Leon Trotsky, *Soviets in America*. What do you have to say about this magazine?' George replied: 'I received this magazine by mail from my father who lives in Holland. I don't recall exactly when, maybe at the end of 1935.'

'To whom and under which circumstances have you shown Trotsky's article, published in this magazine?'

'I don't remember whom I lent it to. I think to Popov, a former employee of the State Movie Studios and a former employee of the Department of Culture. But I am not sure.'

'Do you have any other publications of Trotsky's articles in your possession?'

'I have another copy of *Die Sammlung* but there is nothing in it by Trotsky. I don't possess anything else of Trotsky's.'

'You confirm that you received the magazine *Die Sammlung* containing Trotsky's article *Soviets in America* by mail from your father in Holland?'

'Yes. And once, when I was in Tbilisi, I got a few books by mail from Moscow, which my father had given to someone who travelled from the Netherlands to Moscow.'

'You declared that you previously handed over Trotskyite literature which you received from abroad to the responsible Soviet authorities. Why didn't you give this magazine to the responsible Soviet organisation here in Tbilisi?'

'I didn't think Trotsky's article in this magazine was that important, though I believe now I have acted irresponsibly.'

'As a foreigner who has lived in the Soviet Union for a long time you probably knew that all the works of Trotsky were declared anti-Soviet and anti-revolutionary a long time ago?'

'Yes, I knew.'

'Have any magazines which your father sent you from Holland ever disappeared?' 'That has happened. It became clear through the correspondence with my father.'

'Did you give the magazine to Lydia Gasviani for her to read?'

'No, I did not. That I recall quite clearly.'

George told Vasiliev that his baby was due in the second week of November. And as soon as November came, Vasiliev suddenly stopped allowing him to see Pearl's letters, and refused to answer George's questions about her.

His son Michael John was born on 11 November 1936 in the Royal Free Hospital in Hampstead, north London. George, who had now been in prison for three months, was not told. They saw that he was frantic for news, and kept it from him. But the day after his son's birth, George's resistance broke, almost as though he knew what was happening that day in faraway London. He gave a statement which he must have hoped contained enough by way of confession to get him out of prison. It was very long. Vasiliev's summary of it for his superiors began:

(1) I believe I am prosecuted rightfully according to article 58–10.
(2) Although I have shown an apparent loyalty towards the Soviet Union since my arrival and although I have even tried to convince others, these activities don't show my real nature. I tried in vain to become a Soviet but I didn't succeed all the time.
(3) Prior to my arrival in the Soviet Union, during my stays in Germany, France and England, I found myself in a Trotskyite environment. I came to the Soviet Union with a Trotskyite conviction and kept that conviction even after my arrest.

Vasiliev tried to get George to implicate others. George named a couple of Soviet citizens he had met who, he said, expressed mild criticism of the Stakhanovite movement, a government initiative designed to get workers to work harder. Later on, probably when he had despaired of ever being allowed to know any news about his wife, he tried hard (and of course unsuccessfully) to withdraw the names from his statement. Vasiliev also got a clearer self-incrimination from his prisoner. George said, or at least signed a statement to say that he had said: 'I arrived in 1932 to live here and to help build socialism. After having arrived in the Soviet Union I was immediately disappointed. Ever since I arrived in the Soviet Union I have tried to fight Trotskyist tendencies, in me as well as in others. But I must confess I didn't have much success.'

George Fles had been 'exposed', as Vasiliev put it. Vasiliev asked: 'From all your former statements and from material evidence, the conclusion was drawn from the preliminary inquest that not only did you fail to fight Trotskyist tendencies, but that you went as far as to support and distribute these tendencies. The evidence for this fact is formed by Trotskyist literature which you received from abroad, which you read yourself and handed to others for them to read. And finally you protected persons whom you knew were Trotskyists. Do you confess?'

The answer, far too pat and formal to be George's own, reads as follows: 'I confess that my activities in the USSR had an outspoken Trotskyist character through which I damaged the Soviet Union.'

Vasiliev wrote an indictment against him. It said that George had systematically received counter-revolutionary Trotskyist literature since 1933, which he had lent to others; that he was in touch with Trotskyists; and that he was a Trotskyist himself. He was taken to the city prison of Tbilisi, where, for a change, he shared his cell with other prisoners. From there, in March 1937, he wrote a request to the public prosecutor:

> During the investigation, letters from my wife, who is currently in London (England) were regularly shown to me. Yet, after her letter of November 6 . . . they refused to hand over her letters which they undoubtedly received afterwards. And they refused to give me any recent information about the state of her health. The interrogator replied to all my questions saying that there are signs that she is still alive. . . . She was due to have a baby in the first part of November. So far I don't know anything about the outcome of her pregnancy . . . I wasn't given an opportunity to send her the most superficial information: that I am alive and healthy, which is nothing more than basic justice. Considering the current residence of my wife, she cannot visit me personally, a right that is granted to everyone whose preliminary inquest has been concluded. All my requests to my investigator, the Public Prosecutor and to the People's Commissar of Internal Affairs of the Republic of Georgia have been in vain.
>
> I admitted all my mistakes and blunders, but I don't have any chance to show their real extent and with that to prove my loyalty to the state of the Soviet Union.
>
> I realise that it is inevitable in this situation to exert a little pressure, but as far as I understand Soviet justice, its aim is not to

submit someone to unnecessary, avoidable suffering. Anyway, I refuse to believe that it is acceptable according to Soviet law to torment a woman without any reason, not to mention the possible negative consequences for her child.

He also asked for 'inaccuracies' in his written statements to be corrected – Vasiliev had said these were unimportant. He wanted to sweep out of the record the names he had given, for he must have known by now the sort of fate to which he might have helped to condemn them. Then he added: 'I have been detained in the isolation-ward of the NKVD in Tbilisi for three months, dressed in summer clothes, while I didn't receive any necessities like a sheet, underwear etc. And currently I am detained in an unheated building of the prison in Tbilisi, without a winter coat, a hat or other necessities, despite all the promises which have been made to me in this respect . . .'

They sent him to Moscow, where he was imprisoned first in the Lubyanka, headquarters of the NKVD, then in the Butirskaya prison. Some political prisoners were executed in the cellars of the Lubyanka after they had been forced to undress themselves. The corpses were piled up and taken in lorries to the mass graves in the woods outside the city. In Butirskaya, seventy or even more prisoners could sometimes be locked up in one room. The floors were covered with planks to sleep on. Narrow fold-away beds were connected to the walls. There were no mattresses. Instead of a toilet, every cell had two buckets, and the smell was appalling.

He was there from April to June 1937. Usually, when a foreigner was led into the cell, the other prisoners turned away in disgust, believing he was probably a spy. In every cell there were informers, which ruined all attempts to make friends. There are more letters from George to the prosecutor, on the files from Butirskaya, in an increasingly small and unsteady hand: please may I have a bath, please may I have clean underwear, please may I clear up 'inaccuracies' in my statement, please, please may I have news of my wife.

On 26 April 1937 George Fles was sentenced to five years imprisonment for counter-revolutionary activities. He was put in

Smolensk prison, where we now know that he died on 31 May 1939. He never knew that his son had been born safe and healthy. Pearl never knew what happened to him, or when he died. For many years she believed that she would see him again one day. Today, we have the date of his death, but we do not know how he died, though Thijs Berman has established that he was not shot.

He knew, even if Pearl did not, that he would never come out of his prison alive. We can be sure of that because one day, on a Moscow street, a man came up to one of Pearl's English Moscow friends, Jack Miller (not to be confused with George's American journalist friend Bob Miller). The man handed him a tiny, grubby piece of thin paper, and rushed away before Miller could ask him anything about it. 'It was dirty, it smelled as if it had been in the mud and it was the size of a coin', Miller told Thijs Berman. It was the last letter from George to Pearl, written in Russian, presumably so that the man who smuggled it out for him could check the contents. Every millimetre of the sheet was covered with tiny handwriting. In it, George said that he would not survive the *dolgonochnaya mrachnost*, the darkness of the long night. Pearl, he said, should marry again while she was still young. She carried the letter everywhere with her in her purse until, forty years later, when she was in her sixties, she was mugged on the streets of Los Angeles and her purse was stolen.

George's prediction was hardly surprising. His friend Lydia Gasviani spent two years in the prison in Tbilisi, two years of night-time interrogations and torture. Thijs Berman has seen a police photograph taken prior to her execution: it shows her as a shrunken, destroyed woman, he says. She had just turned thirty. Most of her friends and acquaintances were shot. (*Berman*)

While George was dying by degrees in squalid Russian prisons, his family did everything they could to find him or get news of him.

It took time for Pearl to realise that something dreadful had happened. She and George wrote to each other at least once a week, and then, suddenly, George's letters stopped. Pearl was staying in London with her sister Hetty, but she instinctively did not confide the fear she felt in Hetty or Anita, then or later: they had by now left the Independent Labour Party and joined the Communist Party, and Pearl, says Hetty, was very cagey with them.

Soon after her baby was born, she accepted the Fles family's invitation to spend Christmas and the new year with them. By the time she got to Amsterdam, she was seriously alarmed, and she found that George's family had not heard anything either. Back in London, she went to the Foreign Office. It was a depressing interview. The official she saw started by asking her why she had married a foreigner. Then he told her abruptly that she should realise that she and her husband had caused their own problems, by emigrating to the Soviet Union. All the Foreign Office would do was to send a telegram to the British embassy in Moscow asking for information. (*Bower interview*)

The Ambassador, Lord Chilston, wrote to the Commissariat for Foreign Affairs asking to be informed of George's whereabouts, and if he was in custody, of his state of health, whether he could write to Pearl, and whether a foreign consul might be permitted to see him. It fell to Laurence Collier – whom we last met as the lone London FO voice advocating energetic support for Rose Cohen – to write to Pearl on 2 February 1937 with Lord Chilston's answer. He had been told 'that Fles was arrested last August for counter-revolutionary activities'. A further embassy telegram added: 'It is most improbable that they will be able to tell me anything further for some time.' The embassy would keep a watching brief on it 'so far as this can be done despite the fact that we have no *locus standi*' – because, of course, George was Dutch, not British. Collier added: 'I am sorry that I have not anything more definite to tell you at the moment; but I hope we shall soon hear something further.' (*Berman*) They never did. Today all the Foreign Office files on George Fles have gone into the FO shredder.

Pearl went to London to see Harry Pollitt. Pearl and her sisters were all socialists, and some of her sisters were still reliable communists, so she must have felt she had a legitimate claim on Pollitt. 'What can I do?' said Pollitt helplessly. 'They won't listen to me. They've arrested Rose Cohen. I know she's innocent. I've known her from a child.' He also said: 'I know your sisters, but I don't know you and I don't know your husband. I cannot get information about Rose Cohen. What chance is there for me to get information about a Dutchman about whom I know nothing?'

Hetty says this made Pearl very bitter. Hetty herself had, and still has, some sympathy for Pollitt's position. 'Whether she realised that Harry really could not find out anything, or whether she thought he was stalling for fear of opening a Pandora's box, I've no means of knowing.' (*Bower interview*)

By now the relationship between the sisters was strained, and the reason is clear enough from what Hetty wrote many years later about her feelings at the time: 'As we were aware of George's irrepressible extrovert behaviour, we assumed he had either been seriously or foolishly engaged in some stupid activity which had aroused suspicions. We did not think him guilty of any 'crime', but equally could not be absolutely sure.' Pearl, she felt, had switched suddenly and fervently from the ILP to the Communist Party, and was now making another sudden and strident switch towards anti-communism. 'Reg maintains that Pearl's political understanding was extremely limited, her knowledge of Marxism non-existent (with which I agree.) Her and George's flippant decision to go to work in the USSR was purely adventurous with a certain emotional attachment to the idea of socialism without any real knowledge of that either.' (*Bower autobiography*) It is not hard to see why Pearl did not feel she could talk openly to her sister.

It was not a lot of use going to the Dutch government: they still refused to recognise the Soviet Union (and continued to refuse until they found themselves enmeshed in Hitler's tentacles in 1943). Dutch interests in Moscow were looked after by the German Embassy. Desperate though she was, the Jewish socialist Pearl Rimel refused to ask the assistance of Nazi Germany for her Jewish socialist husband.

She left London, where she had been living uneasily with Hetty, and went with her son to live in Amsterdam, to be near George's family. She found a job as a secretary at the American Consulate in Amsterdam, and was able to use this contact to ask the American Embassy in Moscow to do something for George as well, but with no result.

Pearl's sisters clung to their belief in the Soviet Union. The last survivor of the family, Hetty Bower, née Rimel, explained to Thijs Berman how they rationalised it to themselves: 'We never believed he was a spy. We thought they had arrested him because he had been tactless to a party boss, that he had called some bigwig "incompetent" or "mad". We knew he was capable of that, because tact wasn't his strongest feature and he wouldn't ask himself if he could say something like that. He was too honest for that – he was a very open and honest man. So we assumed that he had unwittingly offended someone.'

Her husband, communist loyalist Reg Bower, could not feel quite sure George might not have been a Trotskyist. 'Perhaps he had listened to their arguments. I would have done that, without agreeing with them at once. You want to know what they have to say. In my opinion the revolution was a continuing process and there were external attempts to interrupt that process. That is why I was prepared to accept much of what was happening or at least to understand a number of the reasons. Besides that the only information that we got was what they were willing to give us – I believed that they might have had something against George of which I was not aware. But I did not have any certainty.'

Hetty reminded her husband: 'You actually said in those days: why did George leave the Netherlands, go to Germany; why did he join in with the Young Communists over there and later again in France and England? At first sight it was exactly what someone who wanted to spy would do.' That was the same reasoning that George's Moscow friends applied. Thijs Berman says that poor George was condemned unjustly twice: once by the Soviet Union, and again by his friends.

But, at last, the Rimels heard that the Fles family had been told by the Soviet authorities to stop sending money or parcels. Then, says Hetty, 'the main question was what had happened to him, if he had been shot, or if he had joined the army. Pearl did not confide in us. We felt guilty, we were still members of the party, we were still supporting the Soviet Union and we did not want to condemn completely what was happening there. We felt guilty towards Pearl and her ruined life, because of what had happened, as if it was our fault.'

As for Pearl, she talked very little about George, and what her son John Michael Fles knows about his father was only told to him long after her death, after Thijs Berman went to Russia.

In 1937, in Holland, George's father, 65-year-old Louis Fles, wrote letters to the Soviet government, asking about his son's state of health, and received no reply. He asked if his son could receive visits, or foreign mail. Poor Louis Fles never knew that it was his own innocent decision to send reading matter to George, along with the reading matter sent by his sister-in-law Anita Rimel, which had helped to seal his son's fate. He wanted to travel to Tbilisi himself. Lord Chilston advised that this would be pointless, but when his letters went unanswered Louis Fles travelled anyway to look for the youngest of his six children. In Moscow, Pearl and George's friend Jack Miller acted as his interpreter.

Miller was the first person, apart from Ed Falkowski, who knew that George had been arrested, and he had alerted Pearl. Miller found out because he had received another bundle of magazines from George's father, and had forwarded the parcel to Tbilisi. The parcel was returned to Moscow, and the post clerk who gave it to Miller said he could tell by the way it was returned that George had been arrested.

Lord Chilston was able to tell Louis that George had been transferred to Smolensk prison. Louis hoped to visit him there, to take him food parcels and put courage into him. But his visa was only valid for Moscow. He knocked at the doors of several government offices, asking for a visa that would take him to Smolensk. Every day for two weeks, he went to the office in the morning for a visa, and they told him to return the next day. Then there was a knock on his hotel room door one night. Two KGB men told him to pack his bags and go with them to the station. Their orders were to put him directly on the train to the Netherlands, and to arrest him if he refused to go. The only thing that Louis achieved in the bureaucratic maze was a monthly allowance through the State bank for his imprisoned son. According to Jack Miller, 'only

Rosa Rust (circled) aged twelve, with other pupils at the school for the children of important foreign communists at Ivanovo-Vosnesensk. (*Rust family*)

Above, left: Six-year-old Rosa Rust in Moscow, with some of the street children she befriended while her parents were working. *Above, right*: Rosa aged nineteen in London. (*Both Rust family*)

Rosa and her mother Kay cut the cake at Rosa's twenty-first birthday party. (*Rust family*)

The wedding of Rosa Rust and George Thornton. Seated is Rosa's mother's old friend Paul Robeson, whose Communist sympathies were to get him into deep trouble in the USA. (*Rust family*)

Rosa aged forty-two. (*Rust family*)

Rosa in 1995, while being interviewed by the author. (*Joe Cornish, Independent*)

British communist leader Harry Pollitt (standing, left) and Rose Cohen (standing, right) with another senior British communist, Bob Stewart (standing, centre) and Stewart's wife and daughter (seated) in Moscow in the 1920s. The inscription on the back of the photograph (inset), in Pollitt's handwriting, reads in part: 'Rose Cohen, who I am in love with and who has rejected me 14 times.' A few years later Pollitt was pleading unsuccessfully with Stalin to spare Rose's life. (*Both People's History Museum*)

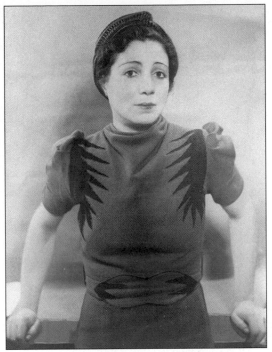

Harry Pollitt on his return from visiting the British Brigade which fought along-side the Republicans during the Spanish Civil War. (*Marx Memorial Library*)

Bill Rust's second wife, Tamara Kravets, whom he met in Moscow and for whom he left Rosa's mother Kay. (*Marx Memorial Library*)

Bill rust in the editor's chair at the *Daily Worker*, 1939. (*Marx Memorial Library*)

Above, left: Freda Utley in her twenties, sailing. *Above, right*: Freda's husband, Arcadi Berdichevsky in Moscow before his arrest. (*Both Jon Utley*)

Freda in the United States in 1943. (*Jon Utley*)

Above: Freda with her son Jon Basil Utley in Washington. (*Jon Utley*)

Freda Utley with William F. Buckley at a party he gave to celebrate the publication of her autobiography, *Odyssey of a Liberal.* (*Jon Utley*)

Pearl Rimel and George Fles, Tbilisi, 6 April 1936. (*Thijs Berman*)

Pearl in later life, at work in Los Angeles. (*Rimel family*)

crumpled-up receipts returned from the prison and a little later nothing at all'.

The last person to try to find George was his 33-year-old brother Barthold, known in the family as Bap, a literary agent living and working in New York. Bap flew to Berlin and drove through a city covered in swastikas, which terrified him because he was strongly aware of having a very Jewish nose. The next day he left early for the Soviet Union.

Jack Miller was no longer in Moscow, and Bap had to try to find his way about without an interpreter. The Ministry of Foreign Affairs had him come back in vain a few times and he must have spent hours in the queues of the NKVD. In the end they suggested he take a train to Kiev, but George was not in the Ukraine and there was no file on him in Kiev. And in Kiev, Bap was even further away from Smolensk, which may have been the ministry's intention when they sent him there. Threatened with arrest if he stayed, Bap went back to New York. From that time on this scion of a socialist family always referred to communists as 'red fascists'. For the rest of his life he felt guilty about not being able to do anything for his brother.

A greater sense of guilt was to overwhelm Bap. He tried and failed to persuade his parents and brothers and sisters to come to the USA before the Second World War started. When Germany invaded the Netherlands, his father Louis Fles committed suicide by poison. Louis assumed he was on a blacklist for his series of anti-fascist speeches on the Secularist Broadcasting Company, and anyway he was a Jew. He decided not to wait for his arrest. His wife Céline followed him in 1942 when Dutch police officers came to get her. She too took poison.

Two of George's sisters, Mina and Harry (Henriette), were deported to Germany and died in Auschwitz in 1942. Harry, remembered as the beautiful, dark sister, was living in Paris in 1940 with her husband and two children, but she rushed back to Amsterdam with her family directly after the German invasion of France. She and her two children, Rudolph, aged fourteen, and Nicole, six, were killed in Auschwitz on 12 August 1942, and her husband Meijer followed them into the gas chamber on 30 September. A third sister, Rosina, had moved with her husband to San Francisco, and she died there of natural causes in 1939.

Of the two parents and their six children, only Bap and Clara survived the war. Bap was in the USA, and Clara was spared because she was married to a non-Jew. She is the grandmother of Thijs Berman, the journalist who uncovered most of this information.

Pearl and her son escaped from Holland to the USA just in time to avoid being rounded up by the Nazis, thanks to the American embassy contacts she had made while working there. Her fare was paid by Lockheed, an American company for which she had also worked in Amsterdam, and which was later to employ her in California. (*Berman*)

* * *

The morning after they took Arcadi Berdichevsky, his wife Freda Utley went to the secret police office where the arresting officers had said she would be told the reasons for his arrest. It was closed. She went the day after and joined the queue for hours, only to be told that there was no information for her yet, and she should call again tomorrow. She called tomorrow, and the next day and the day after, for weeks. She tried the Commissariat for Foreign Trade, which governed Promexport, the organisation for which Arcadi worked, but they had no information to give her either. She went to the chairman of Promexport, Kalmanovsky. He met her in a dark room lit by a small lamp on the writing table. He was nervous, and there was panic in his eyes. There was no help to be had from him, and she wondered if he had denounced Arcadi to save himself. She went to a friend who had once worked for the secret police. He made some enquiries and told her Arcadi was being held in connection with the case of another Promexport man, and that everything would be all right in the end: her husband would not be held responsible for the problem simply because, as finance manager, he had signed the fatal contract.

Like Rose Cohen, Freda found that old friends feared to speak to her. At the Academy of Sciences where she worked, several colleagues avoided her. She wrote afterwards: 'When someone is arrested in the USSR it is as if a plague had struck his family. All are afraid of any contact, afraid to be seen talking to the stricken relations. I was comparatively lucky. Several friends stuck by me.'

She had a contract in England to finish her book about Japan, and was grimly aware that her son Jon did not have the protection of a British passport, having been born in Moscow: he must be spirited out of the country while it was still possible. Freda was luckier than most: she already had a visa to go to England. She persuaded herself that she would be able to return to Moscow later to collect Arcadi, and Jon could be left safely in England. She left a letter at the Lubyanka prison for Arcadi, saying she was going but would return. She never knew whether he was allowed to see it.

Jon, now two, searched for his father in cupboards and under chairs in the Moscow flat for ten days before she took him by train for the three-day journey to Berlin, and thence to London. 'Jon is safe, Jon is safe', she said to herself in time to the noise of the train. But Freda left 'with my political beliefs and my personal happiness alike shattered'.

Almost as soon as she got to London, Arcadi's sister Vera telegraphed that the police were taking away Freda and Arcadi's flat, and she should come at once to reclaim it. She did, leaving Jon at a nursery in England; and the news on her arrival was grim. Vera had discovered that Arcadi was accused of a political offence, which was much more serious than the administrative one she had previously been told about.

Every day Freda went to the public prosecutor's office and stood in line for hours waiting her turn to talk to an official there. Every time they said the same thing: come back tomorrow, come back in four days, come back in a week. Every time she was told that the case was now in the hands of a new official, and the person to whom she was speaking had no information to give her. After five weeks of this she met an official who told her that it was all due to some remark Arcadi had made in Japan six or seven years earlier.

She wrote letters: to the prosecutor, to the secret police chief Yezhov, to Stalin. She never had an acknowledgement. She went twice a week to the NKVD headquarters to fill in a form (she always had to fill in a new form) asking to be allowed to visit her husband in prison.

Arcadi, she was told, had, like George Fles, been moved from the Lubyanka to the dreadful Butirskaya prison. This could mean that he had been condemned. The only way to find out was to go to the prison every three days to see if his name was on a list they posted at the gate of those being sent to a concentration camp. Through a friend of a friend of Vera's, whose husband was one of the few to be allowed the occasional visitor in the Butirskaya prison, they found out that Arcadi had not yet been condemned, so his examination must still be going on.

This meant that she was allowed to deliver food to him every eight days and clean linen every sixteen days. To do this, she had to go early in the morning with a sack or pillowcase, stand in line, and fill in a form describing its contents. Each time it took hours for it to be her turn to hand her sack to the NKVD official. But she saw suffering far greater than her own. She wrote afterwards of the 'poor, illiterate women in the queue who could not write and feared their pitiful supplies of black bread and onion might be rejected unless they could sign their names on the form. Many of the women, with their breadwinners arrested and children to support, were obviously half starved themselves, but they brought bread for their husbands. . . . I began to be ashamed of my grief. I had food and Jon had food.' And there was a great consolation: it meant she knew her husband was alive, because in the afternoon the women were given a receipt signed by the prisoner. And at least he knew that his son was safe, and his wife had an English passport and an academic reputation, and it would be an embarrassment to arrest her. Threats against his family would not work with Arcadi.

When she was first allowed to deliver clean linen and underwear, she was given in return what he had been using. 'The stuff we got back was filthy, sweat-stained, black with grime. Somehow this brought back to me more vividly than anything else what he must be suffering.' He was, she knew, a fastidious man. 'I heard of one arrest after another among our friends and acquaintances', she wrote. 'The scythe was sweeping higher. Everyone I knew looked afraid. Panic spread.'

Freda was tortured by the idea that she was in some way to blame for Arcadi's predicament. 'I had never done anything against the Soviet government, but I had thought a lot against it. I had not always been cautious enough when on trips to England. Occasionally I had revealed a little of the truth on conditions in the USSR to intimate friends.' She was probably right. What we know now suggests that it is quite likely his association with her was part of what they held against him.

In July, four months after Arcadi's arrest, Freda went back to England. Her publishers wanted her to correct the proofs of her Japan book, and Jon was restless without either of his parents. The Soviet officials gave her an exit visa, but would not give her a return visa. That must be obtained in London, they told her. She left everything she owned behind in Moscow, including her money, which she left with Vera, telling her to continue the payment of 800 roubles a month to Arcadi's former wife and her son, though she seems to have resented this last: 'Anna Abramovna had had a job for some years past, and Vitia was now in his teens.' And she wrote a long letter to Arcadi explaining what she was doing. She told him she loved him. Life without him was unbearable. If he were condemned, she would come back to be with him, but would leave Jon in England. She never knew whether Arcadi was allowed to see the letter.

She wrote later: 'Nine years before, almost to the day, I had stood in Red Square for the first time, my heart full of enthusiasm and faith. Now I was flying away to the west leaving the dearest person in my life inside the prison house which the Soviet Union had become.' (*Utley, Lost Illusion*)

Her book *Japan's Feet of Clay* was a huge success, cementing her reputation and rescuing her precarious finances. Banned in Japan, the book became a bestseller in England and in the USA and was translated into French, Swedish, Danish, Norwegian and Chinese. The Japanese government thought it largely responsible for the initiation of a boycott of Japanese goods in America. Two more books on Sino-Japanese relations followed in quick succession. (*Farnie*)

But Vera telephoned to say that Arcadi had been sentenced to five years' imprisonment in an Arctic concentration camp for 'having been friendly or acquainted with a Trotskyist'. From Archangel he sent a postcard, saying he loved her and she was to be cheerful. In January 1937 came another card, from Siberia, and another in May, saying he lived for the day when they would be together again. Then nothing, ever, again.

In one of these cards he said he had found an old friend among the prisoners. Freda hoped this might be Mentich, whom she had described affectionately as 'ponderous as a bear and with a laugh that warmed one's spirit', and to whom Freda had unburdened herself a month before Arcadi's arrest. Mentich was arrested a month after Arcadi. It might, she thought, be some comfort to both men if they were in the same camp.

She knew that her flat had been confiscated, and Vera evicted from it. Vera had been arrested, and Freda's money and possessions taken by the secret police. In the summer of 1938 foreign commissar Maxim Litvinov told British Ambassador Lord Chilston that Arcadi was still alive, but Freda doubted it. Litvinov offered no proof, and it was in the Soviet Union's interest for Freda to believe he was still alive and could be made to suffer if she stepped out of line. Freda was a distinguished writer and academic who could command a hearing in Britain. She suspected that the Soviet authorities wanted to use her fear for her husband as a means of making her keep silent. (*Utley, Lost Illusion*)

Like Pearl Rimel, like Rose Cohen's sister Nellie, Freda rested some hope in 16 King Street, the Covent Garden headquarters of the Communist Party of Great Britain. Probably realising that she was not trusted there, she asked Harold Laski, a much respected academic and a key figure in the Labour Party left, to make the approach to King Street for her. But he got an even poorer reception than the others. Freda was not an intimate of Britain's communist leaders like Rose, not even someone considered politically reliable like Pearl and her sisters. She was a freethinker, unreliable, and a nuisance. The party's senior theoretician, the grim and doggedly Stalinist Rajani Palme Dutt, wrote back a firm reproof to Laski:

'Least of all have we in other countries who have made a complete mess of our own labour movement . . . any right to pose as superior critics and censors of those who have shown in practice that they are able to judge correctly the necessary measures to defeat the capitalist enemy.' (*Manchester*)

Freda was careful what she said, but she made use of every possible public platform to draw attention to what was happening to her husband. The British Communist Party did its best to take these platforms away from her. There is an illuminating letter in the Comintern files from Harry Pollitt to Robin Page Arnot, who represented Britain's communists in Moscow at the time. Pollitt is a man I praised, in an earlier book, for his warm humanity, but reading this letter, I wonder whether I was wrong.

He is complaining that Harold Laski refuses to write for the Communist Party theoretical journal *Labour Monthly*, edited by Rajani Palme Dutt, while Arcadi was still in prison, and that Laski has made it a condition of appearing at a Left Book Club rally that Freda Utley also be among the speakers. This, Pollitt says, placed him in a difficult position. He ought not to be sharing a platform with Utley, but to refuse would deny Pollitt himself an important platform. He writes: 'I finally decided that in spite of Freda Utley's presence I should take part in this meeting. She is absolutely foul in the way she is getting propaganda against the Soviet Union across.' He notes that the left-wing Labour MP W.J. Brown is supporting her: 'This is probably due to the fact that Brown and Freda some years ago had one of those affairs which strong-minded men like you and I have never experienced, and she is using him in order to draw attention to Utley's position.'

It could, just, be argued in Pollitt's defence that he was trying to help Arcadi by making clear to the rulers of the Soviet Union the harm his detention was doing in Britain. But he must have known they were past caring about that. The harsh truth seems to be that, knowing innocent people were being sent to their deaths, Pollitt was devoting himself single-mindedly to justifying the terror. Page Arnot told him the approved line on 9 February 1937 in these words: 'This is the opportunity to give Trotskyism its death blow. . . . Those who were against the August trial must be got to eat their words, until the point is reached where no true leader or intellectual dares raise his voice on behalf of these murderers, or in any way dares to popularise Trotskyism.' Pollitt replied two days later that Stafford Cripps (later to be Chancellor of the Exchequer in the 1945 Labour government) had told him the members of the Inner Temple were confident of Soviet justice: 'In the *Daily Worker* we have done the best we could. We tried to answer the questions that were in the workers' minds. I find the two things on which there is the greatest difficulty in getting conviction is, first of all, the character and completeness of the confessions [of people like Kamenev and Zinoviev in the show trials], secondly why did they risk so much, and how could such old timers try to make an alliance with fascism. It is this last point that is still the hardest to get over.' (*RC*)

A private appeal to the Soviet government was signed by several distinguished left-wing people whose good opinion Soviet leaders might have valued, including Bertrand Russell, *New Statesman* editor Kingsley Martin, and Laski. The British embassy tried to find out for Freda what had happened to Arcadi, but they were in a weak position because he was undoubtedly a Soviet citizen, and the British government had even expelled him from Britain on a charge of espionage.

Meanwhile Freda was still working. *Japan's Feet of Clay* earned her a job as a war correspondent in China for the *News Chronicle*, which provided the material for her next book, *China at War*, published in 1939. She was careful what she wrote: with Arcadi perhaps still alive in a Soviet prison, she needed to appear to be a friend to world communism, though her beliefs, as we shall see, were changing fast. Her writing at this time always had one eye on the hoped-for release of Arcadi. Professor Douglas Farnie writes: 'First, she hoped to establish her reputation in England in order to enhance her bargaining power. Secondly, she wished to prove that she was a wholly reliable Stalinist line Communist and that Arcadi should therefore be freed to rejoin her.' It was, of course, too late for that: Pollitt, and the Soviet government, already had her marked down as an irredeemable anti-Soviet.

At the end of 1939 she emigrated with Jon to the USA, and there, in September 1940, all the anger she felt spilled into the pages of what her admirers consider was her best book: *The Dream We Lost: Soviet Russia Then and Now*. Freda called herself 'the only Western writer who had known Russia both from inside and from below, sharing some of the hardships and all the fears of the forcibly silenced Russian people.' The Soviet Union was 'a savage and barbarous Asiatic despotism'. She had seen for herself the 'comradeship of the damned' within a 'vast prison house'. She condemned the 'storm of terror, hate, regimented sadism, hunger, cold and wretchedness and . . . nauseating cant and hypocrisy'. She wanted to show 'the plan-mad liberals of the Western world that Russia's reputedly planned economy is a myth'. She compared Soviet Russia to Nazi Germany, and advocated a negotiated peace between Hitler and England, even at the price of recognising German hegemony over the continent. There was no going back now. (*Utley, The Dream*)

A few years later, she rewrote the book for publication in Britain, and gave it a new title: *Lost Illusion*. It was published in 1949, and Bertrand Russell wrote an introduction: 'I knew Freda Utley first when she was in process of becoming a Communist; I continued to know her through the stages of her disenchantment, the tragedy of her husband's arrest, and the despair induced by the failure of all her efforts to procure his liberation, or at least to discover his supposed crime. At all periods, her love of humanity and her indomitable courage commanded the highest admiration.'

Years later she learned that Arcadi died in Komi, two years after he had been arrested. She never knew how. Perhaps his heart gave out – she knew it was under strain even before he went to prison. Perhaps he was shot, or died of cold, ill-treatment or lack of food. She never knew. Nor did she ever know whether her letters reached him. (*Utley interview*) In fact, he had died in a prison camp on 30 March 1938. Litvinov had lied to her. He told her Arcadi was living in the summer of 1938, a matter of months after Arcadi's death.

* * *

If Freda Utley's political unreliability was held against her in King Street, Rose Cohen's absolute reliability and her closeness to the British Communist Party's top brass gained her nothing. Even for her, the loyalty due from her friends was not there when she needed it. It might well, of course, not have saved her, but it's hard to forgive men like Harry Pollitt for not even trying. No doubt Pollitt thought he was being loyal to the Soviet Union. This sort of loyalty is ultimately corrupting. In March 1938, when most of the Russian communists he had been taught to admire, and his dearest friends Rose Cohen and Max Petrovsky, had been shot, Harry Pollitt wrote an article for the *Daily Worker* which began:

> The trial of the 21 political and moral degenerates in Moscow is a mighty demonstration to the world of the power and strength of the Soviet Union. The fact that the Soviet Government has been able to bring to the dock the criminals who have been plotting for years against it is a proof of unity and stability. And it offers a tremendous contribution to the cause of world peace.

He closed with a quote from Comintern chief George Dimitrov:

> The touchstone in checking the sincerity and honesty of every individual active in the working class movement . . . and of every democrat in the capitalist countries, is their attitude towards the land of Socialism. . . . You cannot be a real friend to the USSR if you do not condemn its enemies – the Trotsky-Bukharin agents of Fascism.

How could he write such rubbish? Here is the best defence I can offer, and it comes from his own pen. Pollitt wrote the following words on the Russian revolution, and there is no doubt at all that they were utterly sincere:

> The thing that mattered to me was that lads like me had whacked the bosses and the landlords, had taken their factories, their lands and their banks. . . . These were the lads and lasses I must support

through thick and thin. . . . for me these same people could never do, nor can ever do, any wrong against the working class. I wasn't concerned as to whether or not the Russian revolution had caused bloodshed, been violent and all the rest of it.

Reviewing Stephen Spender's *Forward with Liberalism* in 1937, he wrote: 'When a people have finally conquered power as in the Soviet Union, they will never again take any risks that can lead to a restoration of capitalism, they will break with rotten liberalism in their politics, and when Trotskyite traitors are found, will deal with them as they deserve.' (*Morgan, Pollitt*)

When the Second World War began, Harry Pollitt, for the first and only time in his life, disobeyed a Comintern instruction, and for a time had to give up the leadership of the Communist Party. He had enthusiastically led his party in support for war with Nazi Germany until the signing of a non-aggression pact between Germany and the Soviet Union in August 1939. Then, the Comintern instructed communist parties everywhere to denounce the war as a capitalist plot. Pollitt was unable to swallow the about-turn on policy required of the party, which would require him to campaign against a war he had previously supported. Later, he wrote a private note for his family explaining his behaviour: 'I had impressed upon my comrades their duty was to vote for [the Comintern line] in order to preserve the unity of the party. This was advice I ought to have taken myself, whatever the character of my personal views and feelings. . . . I understood, but insufficiently as it seemed, the supreme necessity of discipline.' He never rebelled again.

Douglas Hyde, who later became news editor of the *Daily Worker*, recounted in his memoirs a sort of British show trial which he himself had conducted as a leading London communist in the late 1930s. Of course it mattered far less – the worst he could do was expel someone from the party. But the principle seemed remarkably similar to the ways these things were conducted in Moscow. He was trying a woman who was a foundation member of the party and had worked in Moscow for the Comintern. She was in trouble for her attitude towards the Soviet Union and Stalin. She had been overheard telling members of the local Cooperative Women's Guild that she had lived in Russia, that things were not perfect there, and that Stalin-worship had gone too far.

Hyde says he opened with the usual long 'political statement', an analysis of the political position throughout the world with particular reference to the role of the Soviet Union. 'The sabotage', wrote Hyde, 'had been purely on the ideological plane and so, if they and all present were to see the full seriousness of the charges, it was necessary to ensure that all felt that an attack on, or even lukewarm support for, Russia and its leaders amounted to an attack on peace-loving people everywhere, upon the cause of communism and upon the British communists themselves.'

When warned that she risked expulsion, the woman had stopped talking in public about her views of Stalin and the Soviet Union, but was known not to have changed her private views. For this, the branch secretary angrily denounced her for a Trotskyite, a petty-bourgeois deviationist, and a saboteur. She stood up firmly for herself, and 'angry recrimination and personal abuse would follow from both sides'. She stressed the years she had spent in the party, her Moscow experience, but confessed she had been indiscreet. 'She ended', says Hyde, 'with an impassioned plea that those present should understand that she had not intended to betray the cause to which she had given her life. She . . . wept as she pleaded against her expulsion.' Hyde's committee recommended a twelve month suspension, and Hyde was later told that he had been far too lenient.

Sadly Hyde gives no clue as to who this woman was. But whoever she was, she must have known at least some of the principal characters in this book. She certainly knew Rose Cohen, for all British communists based in Moscow knew Rose; and she must have known that Rose had been arrested. Yet, even after all that, keeping her party membership mattered desperately to her. She still believed. And she was still prepared to accept party discipline as a matter of course. It does not seem to have occurred to her that this must be the sort of trial to which Rose was also being subjected, but for Rose, there was much, much more at stake.

If Harry Pollitt was prepared to demand that sort of discipline and loyalty from his members, it is hard to see how he could fail to show it himself just because the arrested woman happened to be someone he loved. That's the most charitable explanation I can think of. Alison Macleod, author of *The Death of Uncle Joe*, has a more charitable one, which she offered in a letter to me in March 1995. A few months before the *Daily Worker* washed its hands of Rose Cohen, a communist called Percy Glading was imprisoned in Britain for spying for the Soviet Union. His spying activities had been reported to MI5 by Olga Gray, who was Pollitt's secretary and close confidante (there was a rumour that they were also lovers) – and who was also an MI5 agent infiltrated into the party to report on its activities. Alison Macleod writes: 'So the revelation that she had been spying on him must have been a great shock to Pollitt. Perhaps he thought that, having been wrong about Olga, he might have been wrong about Rose Cohen.'

She points out that the Comintern document intended to provide evidence for a possible show trial of Pollitt makes no mention of Olga Gray, yet this would have made a much stronger case against him than anything they did mention, so it must be assumed that Moscow did not know. 'My own theory', she writes, 'is that the very small group of people who were leading the Communist Party by the end of 1937 knew that Stalin was mad. . . . So they all rallied round Pollitt and helped him to cover up his connection with Olga.' Covering up for Pollitt over Olga Gray would have been much harder if the party had made a public fuss about Rose Cohen.

A third explanation comes from Jack Murphy: that Pollitt and his colleagues actually believed what they wrote. Incredible as it sounds, Murphy, writing in 1941, after he had left the party, still seemed able to convince himself that old, loyal Bolsheviks like Bukharin and Zinoviev were guilty of the crimes to which they confessed in the show trials. He rejected the obvious truth, that these confessions were extracted by torture, and offered the odd idea that they were in tune with the confessional Russian way of thinking. He recalled meeting these old Bolsheviks in the early days of their power, back in 1920: 'There was no shadow across the hall to warn us of their tragic exit from the scenes of their triumph . . . Zinoviev, Rykov, Kamenev and Bukharin lie buried somewhere after the firing squad of the revolution laid them low.' (*Murphy*)

Whatever the truth, Pollitt's obedience earned him no favours in Moscow, and failed to persuade Stalin to help him limit the damage the purges were doing in Britain. He asked Stalin to give an interview about the show trials to a British newspaper: Stalin refused. Comintern decision making was paralysed by fear, and the Comintern staff was decimated: a huge proportion of them were taken, and all the rest lived in daily terror of the midnight knock on the door.

Britain's communists seemed to get little in return for their loyalty except occasional dollops of money, and that was drying up in the 1930s. They had never been able to ensure that British communists in Moscow were treated properly. Some of their requests are almost laughable, mixing the stiffness of their politics with the most modest demands. In October 1937, while Rose Cohen was in prison and terrified of what was to happen to Alyosha, and a month before she was executed, the British Communist Party's man in Moscow, Ben Francis, was busying himself trying to get some help for a British party member in Moscow called Irene Anderson, who was working as a Comintern courier. He pointed out how well connected she was – she was the granddaughter of former Labour Party leader George Lansbury, and had been living with her aunt, communist loyalist Violet Lansbury, and Violet's ex-husband. But Violet had moved out. And Violet's ex-husband had been expelled from the Soviet Communist Party. So Comrade Anderson could hardly be expected to live with him, 'on moral and political grounds'. But even with this compelling reasoning, he could get nothing done for Comrade Anderson. Could she not have a room, permission to go home, maintenance while she waits for an exit visa, the month's wages she was promised? (*Manchester*)

Harry Pollitt's regular requests on behalf of his comrades in Moscow – a visa for this person, a flat for another, medical attention for a third – were routinely ignored. Seldom has a politician given so much and received so little in return.

FIVE

Rosa in Kazakhstan

It is time to return to Rosa Rust. Until 1940 she was safe in her boarding school in Ivanovo-Vosnesensk, and knew little or nothing of the purges. Her mother Kay knew all about them, though. In Moscow, after Bill Rust left her for his new Russian love Tamara Kravets, Kay struck up a relationship with a Russian called Misha. She seems to have married him, though we have no record of it, but sometimes in later years she would refer to Misha as her husband.

Her daughter Rosa liked Misha very much. He was not at all like her father's sour mistress Tamara. He was kind and bubbling, a bear of a man, she said. The secret police came for him at 3 a.m. one night early in 1937. He was shot soon afterwards. The charge is thought to have been Trotskyism.

We do not know exactly what happened after that, but Kay seems to have been somehow warned that if she did not leave the country, she would share her lover's fate. She would have known Rose Cohen well – she had worked for the *Moscow Daily News* under Rose – and she must have realised, as all the foreign community in Moscow did, that her arrest was a grim warning. If they were going to take someone like Rose, they might take anyone.

Kay was almost certainly told she could not take her daughter out of the country with her. The Soviet government liked to have under their control someone close to top foreign communists like Bill Rust.

It helped keep people in line, though all the evidence suggests that Rust did not need much keeping in line. Kay paid a hurried visit to twelve-year-old Rosa in Ivanovo-Vosnesensk in 1937. She promised to come back soon to collect her – but she never came. Rosa was on her own. A part of her knew at once that that was how things were going to be.

You had to leave the school at fifteen, so in 1940 Rosa was sent to Moscow, to a hostel for political immigrants in Gorky Street, now Tverskaia, the same street as the Hotel Lux. In Moscow she was to study for more examinations, together with fifty or so others of her age. She was very happy there, and always remembered it as a beautiful house, with a lovely dining room and a room in which to listen to the radio and to dance. It had belonged to the Russian royal family, and had chandeliers and parquet floors.

The part of the house not occupied by Rosa and her fellow pupils was filled with political refugees. They were all damaged men and women: one, she remembered, had been in prison so long that he would stand and talk to his own shadow.

But the main disadvantage of the house, from Rosa's point of view, was that it was run by a woman called Sophia Petrovna. 'She was awful. Like Mrs Thatcher, you know, that type', Rosa told me years later. Rosa's dislike was returned, in spades. A dry Comintern report I found in a Moscow archive about Rosa says: 'She lived in the house for political émigrés in Moscow. She was a bad student.' Sophia Petrovna took a terrible revenge on what I suspect was a clever but wilful teenage girl. Perhaps it was more terrible than Petrovna realised. (*RC*)

Despite Petrovna, Rosa loved her time in Moscow in 1940 and 1941. She went to school in the mornings, and in the evenings to the theatre or cinema, or a concert. While London was enduring the blitz, Moscow was at peace, because Stalin had signed a pact with Hitler. Bill and Kay in London must have been pleased that their daughter was somewhere safe.

But without warning, on 22 June 1941, Germany attacked the Soviet Union. Rosa remembers it vividly. 'Suddenly one morning in summer, it was a Sunday, I was listening to some beautiful music on the radio and they said there was going to be an announcement. Then Molotov [Soviet Foreign Minister] announced that Germany had attacked. I remember that Molotov had conquered his stammer but it came back that morning.' No wonder his stammer came back. The infallible Stalin had insisted, against all the evidence, that his pact with Hitler would protect the Soviet Union from invasion. For hours Stalin refused to believe the news, or to allow his generals to fire a shot at the Germans, and he went to his dacha in shock. When the Central Committee arrived, he thought they had come to arrest him, but they had come to beg him to take charge of the war that must now be fought.

Rosa, of course, knew nothing of the panic in the Soviet government. 'The next day I went out, and all the shops were empty. Everybody started buying everything they could lay their hands on and the shops were stripped of everything.' This behaviour offended against the Soviet patriotism Rosa had learned in Ivanovo-Vosnesensk. 'I was angry that they should react like that. Didn't they know the Red Army would drive the Germans away? I didn't realise that the Russians knew, from history, from experience, what was going to happen. I was naive, and oh so patriotic. I thought they were traitors to do that. A month later Moscow was bombed. I couldn't believe these things were coming. They were flying so low I could see the bombs, just coming down and destroying everything.' It had its upside, though. It meant she got to see the splendid bomb shelters, the wine cellars of the Tsars. 'Those wine cellars were built to last, German bombs could not destroy those.'

In Britain her father Bill Rust was required to do another quick ideological somersault. From denouncing the war against Hitler as an imperialist war, he had to switch quickly to becoming the most ardent advocate of total war against fascism. Bill was used to it; there is no evidence that it caused him any lost sleep. Quite soon, Harry Pollitt was reinstated as Britain's communist leader. In Moscow, ideas of a show trial in which Pollitt's 'treachery' would be 'exposed' were no longer mentioned.

The purges had placed the Soviet Union in a poor position to defend itself, for most of the army top brass had been killed or exiled, and the rest lived in daily fear. Even though Stalin had called a halt to the mass purges in 1938, the fear of the midnight knock on the door was still real. The sixteen-year-old Rosa had no idea of the sad state of the Red Army on which she pinned her hopes. She and the others were put to work emptying attics and putting sand in them, to protect houses from bombs. She thought this strange, for she was sure the Red Army would chase all the bombers away. But it soon became obvious to her that the Germans could bomb Moscow any time they liked.

Despite the bombing, Rosa was still having too much fun to do a lot of work, and when the examinations came she received a lower mark than her evident ability would have warranted. Sophia Petrovna punished her by keeping her in Moscow while the other fifty teenagers were sent on holiday to the countryside. If she had been able to go with her friends she would have been spared the horrors to come, because while the others were away, the Comintern gave instructions that the children should be returned to Ivanovo-Vosnesensk, and that was where all the others went. No doubt Comintern officials thought that foreign communists had important work to do in wartime, and they did not want them worrying about whether their children were safe. But anyone already in Moscow had to stay there. So while her friends went back to school, Rosa, once again, was on the loose on the streets there, just as she had been before she went to school. (*Rust*)

In London, Bill Rust was back at his old desk at the *Daily Worker*. He had given up the editorship in 1931 to return to Moscow, and had then worked for the British Communist Party in Lancashire, where he had a serious motorbike crash. Next stop for Bill was Spain. In December 1936 the Communist Party appealed for volunteers to travel from Britain to fight for the Republican cause and against General Franco's fascists in the Spanish Civil War. Within a month, nearly 500 men had gone to Spain, and the British Battalion was formed. By the time the war ended in 1939, well over 2,000 volunteers had gone to Spain, and between a third and a half of them were communists. More than 500 were killed.

But they did not confine themselves to fighting fascists. In May 1937 there was fighting behind the Spanish Republican lines.

Communists, reflecting Moscow paranoia about Trotskyists, were in conflict with the supporters of POUM – the Workers Party of Marxist Unity. The leadership of the British Battalion were recalled to London to explain the alleged lack of discipline in their ranks, and when they went back to Spain, they were accompanied by a political commissar, there to make sure British soldiers followed the party line. This was Bill Rust. In Spain he was said to carry a handgun everywhere, and to analyse people's politics with cold brutality. He certainly maintained records on the soldiers, in which he frequently denounced their political heresies.

After another visit to Moscow in November 1938, he was back in London in time for the declaration of war with Germany in 1939, and along with the rest of the party, he advocated a vigorous prosecution of the war right up to the moment when Stalin and Hitler signed a pact and the Comintern instructed communist parties everywhere to denounce the war. Then, when general secretary Harry Pollitt and *Daily Worker* editor John Campbell rebelled against a Moscow instruction for the first and only time in their lives, Rust became, alongside the grim party theoretician Rajani Palme Dutt, a principal advocate of the changed line.

Since Campbell could not bring himself to defend Stalin's pact with Hitler, or to obey the consequent order from Moscow to denounce Britain's war effort, he could no longer edit the paper, and Rust took back the editorship. Bill had no such problems. He firmly believed that Moscow knew best. He was now recognised as one of the most able people Britain's Communist Party possessed, and one of the two or three stoutest defenders the Soviet Union had in Britain. That is how, in June 1941 when Germany attacked the Soviet Union, Bill Rust came to be in the editor's chair at the paper. After the German attack, although Harry Pollitt took back the job as general secretary, John Campbell did not return as editor. Bill Rust stayed in the job.

The Red Army's contribution to the war effort, and the enormous casualties it suffered, helped make the British Communist Party popular and respectable, and gave it the greatest influence it ever had in the whole of its seventy-one-year history. Membership reached an all-time high of 56,000 in 1942. Bill shared platforms with leading

Conservatives. Harry Pollitt had frequent meetings with Lord Beaverbrook, the Minister for Aircraft Production, and travelled the country quelling strikes. (*Beckett, Enemy Within*)

* * *

At first Rust had no worries about his daughter. In 1941 he probably thought she was in Ivanovo-Vosnosensk. 'My father and mother thought I was somewhere safe, and I wasn't', Rosa said to me. She had been told to join a group who were to do something for the war effort, and to travel out of Moscow with a German group. She asked where and was told: 'You will find out.' She asked, 'Where are my friends?' and was told, 'They will follow.'

The group went to Stalingrad. It took several days to get there, but she remembered all her life how beautiful the city was, and afterwards she was pleased that she had seen it before it was destroyed in the war. Two days later they set out on a barge down the Volga river to a small village. There, she was near the front, in the Volga German Republic, with a group of German exiles from Moscow. The village beside the Volga seemed to be a desert. 'I couldn't see any trees or anything, it was all sand. There were fleas in the sand, they attacked your legs. It was windy, locals used to wear a chiffon scarf across their faces so the sand wouldn't go into their eyes.'

There she made one of the most important friendships of her life. She met a German woman, about the same age as her mother, called Hannah, and Hannah became a kind of surrogate mother to her. Hannah was alone too: she had come, only a few years before, from Berlin, to live in Moscow with her husband, and had then parted from him. Years later Rosa described Hannah for me: 'She was one of those miniature, lightweight, lovely Jewish women; she used to say' – and Rosa, who was a natural mimic, imitated the low, gentle, loving voice – 'Rosa, liebchen, liebchen'. Rosa looked after Hannah 'because I was strong, you know'. She said 'strong' loudly and firmly, flexing her arm. 'Hannah was very weak physically, she only weighed about seven stone, she smoked this very rough tobacco called Mahourka, they usually smoked it in newspaper.' The two women found a deserted house to shelter in, and the sixteen-year-old girl was put to work doing 12 hour shifts in a canning factory, while Hannah stayed in the house and looked after her, 'like my mother', said Rosa, who had never really known a mother.

'Camels would arrive with boxes of vegetables and the men would carry these into some kind of a tank. My job was to take these empty boxes back again and stack them. One night it was pouring with rain, and I had to walk about 50 yards in this downpour to stack them in a shed with the camels. I'd never been so close to a camel before, these huge animals with lovely eyes and eyelashes. They chew sideways, you know. I said to the camel, it's all right for you, you're just a camel and in the shelter, look at me, I'm wet. So the camel spat at me.' She doubled up with helpless laughter. 'This dollop of chewed-up grass and spit straight in my face! Ugh!'

After three months, Rosa came home one day exhausted after her shift and Hannah looked at her with frightened eyes. She had had a visit from the militia. All Germans must leave the area. These were orders from on high, because Stalin believed that the Volga Germans were preparing to welcome the advancing German army. They had forty-eight hours to pack.

Rosa was terrified of being left in that appalling place alone and went to the militia station. That was where she learned that she was in the Volga German Republic. She had not realised that. She just knew that there were a lot of funny people in the village, and that the older ones could speak a peculiar language called German. It was not the German you hear in Berlin, but an antiquated language which Rosa described as 'sort of Catherine the Great German. Germans do not understand them at all.'

Rosa had stumbled into one of Stalin's crimes – the forced migration of hundreds of thousands of Volga Germans, thrown out of their homes and sent to the far corners of the vast country. A decree of 18 August 1941 ordered the deportations of the Germans, who had lived by the Volga for nearly 200 years, accusing them of being traitors and preparing to sell out the Soviet Union to Hitler. The deportation began the next month. About 330,000 people lived there, descendants of settlers brought from Germany by Catherine the Great in 1763, mostly Lutherans escaping religious persecution. The community had survived the anti-German persecution brought on by the First World War, and the Bolshevik dislike of its religion, and under communism their land had become known as the Volga German Autonomous Soviet Socialist Republic. Its people – though not their priests – had even survived Stalin's purges.

But in 1941, Stalin's decree wiped that place from the map, for ever. When, years later, some of them tried to go home, they found their homes occupied by Russians, who drove them away again. A second, secret decree spelled out how it was to be done: 'The entire family will be transported to the entrainment station in one vehicle, but at the depot the family heads will be loaded into special, preselected railway cars . . . their families will be deported to special settlement locales in remote areas. . . . They must not be told of their impending separation from the family head.' (*Macleod*)

Most of the Volga Germans have never been heard of since. It was one of Rosa's most insistent questions: where are they now, the Volga Germans? It was not until 1955 that the Soviet Union admitted what had happened to them, and they were never able to return to the land they had been given by Catherine the Great.

Rosa was a girl with no roots. At that moment Hannah was the only person in the world who mattered much to her. Perhaps she could have escaped then – she might have been able to show she was not a German. And perhaps not: the Comintern archive entry suggests that her card was already marked. In any case, she did not try to escape. Where would she go? How could she leave the tired, terrified, fragile Hannah? She went along with her surrogate mother, and they spent two days on horse and cart to get to Astrakhan, which was to be the meeting point for all the Germans who were to be deported. She described the scene for me. 'Suddenly there were thousands of them. Thousands! You know the refugee syndrome, this sad group, carrying bundles of clothes, all their possessions on their backs, loaded down like animals, with that cowed look because the soldiers spoke roughly to them and called them bloody Germans. I started feeling nervous, hanging round my friend Hannah.'

At Astrakhan they were herded on to a ferry. When that was full, the rest were put in a big open barge which was towed by the ferry, and stayed there, in the open, for a three-day journey along the Caspian Sea. Rosa was lucky: she was on the ferry. Rosa said:

When you are young you are resilient, you can't dwell too long on what is happening. Children have to concentrate on something pleasant or they cannot survive. I found a lot of young boys and girls and we became friends. They said they lived in some village where they had a farm, and some men in uniform came and said: you have to leave. I said, did they tell you why? Are you Germans? Well, yes, I think so, we're called Volga Germans. Do you speak German? No, my grandfather does. How does your mother feel about it? She's crying her eyes out all the time. My father's in the army. We're not the only ones. It was the same for everyone in the village. The soldiers said, because we're Germans we must be preparing to meet the Germans when they invade.

They were taken to a big railway station at a town called Guryev.

It was a big junction, engines whistling, dirty and noisy, lots of cattle trucks. I thought, oh my God, where am I going? There were about fifteen cattle trucks and they told us to climb in. It was just an open truck, and a shelf, and a bit of straw on the floor. No one told us anything, the train just went.

We made friends with the driver and said, do you think you could stop every two hours or so somewhere in a field, so we can all go to the toilet – there were no lavatories on the train. Men went from that side and women went from that side. It was getting more and more disgusting, the conditions became filthier, we all got lice in our hair, lice in our clothes, we always itched. We couldn't wash anywhere. We had hardly any food. We travelled for six weeks like that.

A young German woman was nursing her four-month-old baby girl. Sometimes the train would stop at a station, and every time that happened, the mother rushed to search for hot water for the baby's feed, to dilute the little condensed milk she was carrying. One terrible day they said the train would stop for two hours, and it started as she went to get water. She missed the train. Sixteen-year-old Rosa was left holding the screaming baby. She and her new friends gave the baby some milk with cold water, which the baby did not appear to like very much. Someone had a water melon, and Rosa cut off a piece and the baby sucked it.

Rosa's friends asked the driver to try to stop the train where there was a lake or a bit of water, so that they could wash the rags they used as nappies. Once she washed the baby in a lake. It was dreadfully cold. In later years Rosa laughed happily at the memory. 'The driver stopped the train for us because he liked us, because we were cheerful. The conditions were so grim and depressing, to be young and alive was something important. The baby was all right, she didn't even get diarrhoea. I was very pleased with myself.' The baby's mother was frantically hopping from train to train trying to catch up with the refugee train. After a week she made it. 'She looked about ninety years old, she said' – Rosa comically mimicked the mother holding the baby and weeping – 'Oh Rosa, oh my little one. I said, I'm afraid she's a bit stinky. She said Oh-oh-oh she's alive.'

Food was very scarce. Years later Rosa met a survivor from Belsen who told her what real hunger was, and she understood exactly. 'It's not like you feel peckish. This occupies you twenty-four hours a day, you just think about food all day, you become dehumanised, you think and breathe food. We were reaching that state. We often went days without food.' One day she was called on to distribute bread:

I found a group, I said how many in the family, they said seven, I could only count six. I said, where is the seventh? They said, grandma died. Where's the body? We threw it out. What were we supposed to do with the body in the middle of nowhere? The train was going to travel maybe five hours, seven hours non-stop, we didn't want a dead body stinking it out. Someone said, you should have kept quiet, you could have claimed food for seven people. I remember the look of disbelief on their faces that this young person was asking stupid questions and wasting time when they could be eating.

I was very young to come across incidents like that. My childhood was disappearing fast. At sixteen you still try to remain cheerful. Every time the train stopped I tried to find out what was happening but the guards were so full of self-importance, they tell you nothing. You learn you can't be cheeky to anyone in uniform because they are very powerful people and wear guns. So you nod and obey. I used to get upset about it. But Hannah, she was a Jew from Berlin, she knew what brutality was.

But at last they did stop. Rosa opened a door and said to the others: 'I think we've arrived.' She saw perhaps 200 carts and horses and asked a militiaman where in Russia they were. The answer startled her. They were not in Russia at all; they were in Kazakhstan. She looked back to her travelling companions. Did any of them know where Kazakhstan was? No one did. They were herded into the carts and travelled along bumpy roads for hours on end, seated on a little wooden ledge. It was a very tight squeeze. Rosa was hanging on to Hannah, and Hannah said, in a tiny, comforting voice, 'Oh, liebchen, we are together.'

They came to a village at 3 a.m. and a militiaman took Rosa and Hannah to a small house. He banged imperiously on the door and said to the very old woman who answered it: 'Receive. There are two people who are going to live in your house.' And he left. The old woman said sleepily to them: 'Who are you? What do you want with me?' Rosa said she was sorry, and she was tired, and could they please sleep on the floor and talk about it in the morning. The militiaman returned in the morning and the old lady tried to explain that her house was full, but he told her: 'It's wartime, they're refugees, they've got to live somewhere. They will work, they will give you money, you feed them.'

Five of them slept in one small room: Rosa, Hannah, a teacher from a local school, the old woman's daughter and the old woman herself. The room also held a big stove where meals were cooked, and two or three times a day Rosa took buckets to fetch water, breaking the ice in winter. The village was full of lice. Hannah poured petrol on their clothes and burned them. They put paraffin

109

on their hair to get rid of the lice. But for the villagers, lice were part of daily life. Every Friday after they bathed, they would put their head on someone's lap, and their friend would look for lice, and squash them between a knife and a fingernail.

This was when Rosa really started to appreciate Hannah. 'Hannah was a very important person in my life. She taught me tolerance. I used to look at these peasants who were primitive, and she used to tell me, liebchen, they have lived here for hundreds and hundreds of years, we are guests in their village, don't you laugh at them, show a little respect, liebchen.' Hannah had been a dressmaker in Berlin, and she taught Rosa to sew and make dresses which they sold locally to buy food. Rosa remembered the lessons years later when she had children: all her life she sewed and made clothes in the way that Hannah had taught her.

She saw terrible things. A new group of refugees arrived even hungrier than Rosa and her companions. They had come from the siege of Leningrad, and Rosa could see that they were walking skeletons. She did not understand what they were telling her, for she had read no newspapers and knew nothing of the Leningrad siege. She always remembered a little boy who said nothing, just cried. Rosa gave him a tiny piece of bread and he put it in his pocket. He was only about four, and he already knew that he should hoard it, for there might be nothing at all to eat tomorrow.

After a few weeks, while Hannah stayed in the house and sewed garments, Rosa went to a nearby mining village called Belousovka and found a job in the factory. They worked three shifts so that the machines need never stop. Then they sent her down the mine. And there, while Bill Rust wrote pro-Soviet editorials in London, his young daughter was worked almost to death mining copper, 100 miles from the Chinese border. Her job was to push huge, heavy trucks full of copper along rough railway lines and turn them sideways to empty them.

The hooter would go at 5 a.m., waking the whole village, and she entered the mine every day at 6 a.m., before dawn, and came out after dark. She never saw the sun, nor had anything like enough to eat, nor had any protective clothing. Malnutrition caused near-blindness and she could see nothing in the dusk. Her body reacted to being deprived of sunlight. She felt her energy going. If she got even the smallest cut it went septic: the cut refused to heal and the skin went rapidly yellow. She became steadily more unwell. Everyone working in the mine became ill. Many of them died. The teenage girl saw death all around her.

One day a woman peddler knocked at the door of her cottage, took one look at her and said: 'You need onions.' Rosa had neither money to buy them, nor anything to exchange for them. 'I felt so ill, my legs were so swollen. She said, are you sure you haven't anything to sell? Two hours later she brought me a string of onions and she said' [Rosa assumes a sepulchral voice] '"Eat them raw or you'll die." And I did and I got better.'

Rosa, though strong and young, knew she could not survive long. Many others had died already. She thought a lot about her mother and father, and wondered what they were doing. She had no idea what had happened to her friends from school, but she wrote to one of them, asking that the letter be shown to someone in authority. The letter arrived in Ivanovo-Vosnesensk, the friend took it to the principal of the school, and in the spring of 1943 a letter arrived for Rosa containing a pass signed personally by Georgi Dimitrov, secretary of the Comintern. There was also 500 roubles to get her to Moscow. It seemed like a fortune: she had been earning 55 roubles a month. (*Rust*)

Rosa thought they had found out for the first time where she was, and taken instant action to ensure that the daughter of an important foreign communist was not to be left to rot as though she was just anyone. But it looks as though she was being kinder to the Comintern and the Soviet bureaucracy than they deserved. Comintern files suggest that, whatever they may have told Bill Rust, they knew where his daughter was. Kay and Bill were certainly concerned that they had heard nothing of her whereabouts. Even given the war, and the problems of communicating between London and Moscow, they would have expected a scrap of news from their daughter – especially since it was possible for the Comintern to communicate with British Communist Party

111

headquarters. They may have thought she was in Ivanovo-Vosnesensk, but they certainly could not be sure of this.

Kay was constantly demanding that Bill should find out what was happening to her, and pointing out that he was supposed to be an important Comintern figure so he ought to be able to sort it out. Bill told the *Daily Worker*'s man in Moscow, John Gibbons, to try and find out something. But if the Comintern told Gibbons they did not know where Rosa was, they were lying. The Comintern memorandum quoted above, which is dated February 1943, says: 'She was sent to Stalingrad, and then to Eastern Kazakhstan, where she is at the moment.' It describes rather euphemistically what work she had done ('working in a workshop' and 'training to be a plumber' are slightly inadequate descriptions really). Therefore, it says, 'the statement by J. Gibbons that Rosa Rust has been forgotten is not absolutely accurate'. They had not forgotten. They had simply omitted to tell her parents, and had left her there to rot.

It would be possible 'to call Rosa Rust back to Moscow in the future and arrange for her to work in one of the Moscow firms as she is indeed in a difficult economic position and is isolated from her English comrades'. A month later another Comintern memorandum reads: 'According to the directive of Comrade Dimitrov, the daughter of William Rust, one of the leaders of the Communist Party of Great Britain, should be recalled to Moscow.' (*RC*)

'Recalling her to Moscow' in practice meant sending her the pass: it did not mean actually getting her to Moscow. The pass got her past militiamen, but did not get her on to trains. At her nearest station she asked when was the next train and people laughed. They had been waiting three weeks. Trains did pass but they were so full of soldiers that it was impossible to get on them. It took weeks to get back to Moscow. At one station she waited for three weeks while people struggled to get on trains full of soldiers, until at last she managed to get on to a train unnoticed – 'and I sat still and did not breathe, and at last the train started, and I sighed, whoosh'. It took her to the Kazakh capital where she needed to make another change of trains.

The journey was full of adventures. She met gypsies and remembered their ways from her time on the streets of Moscow, so

that they took her in as one of their own. At one station she met a
man who she thought was going to try to steal a piece of bread the
gypsies had given her. But he said he was a deserter, so she gave him
a piece of her bread. When the evening came he hid in a toilet. At 3
a.m. there was a loud noise as dozens of jackbooted soldiers came
on to the platform. Rosa picked a row with them and shouted a lot
to wake the deserter and give him time to escape. An old lady
nearby whispered to her: you mustn't talk to them like that, they're
not very nice people.

Her food ran dangerously low, and she feared she would not get
to Moscow before her documents ran out – they were only valid for
two months. She got on her last train, to Moscow, by shouting at a
woman soldier with a rifle in an official-sounding voice, saying she
was an important Comintern official and the woman would get into
trouble for holding her up. The soldier lowered her rifle for a
moment, and Rosa rushed into an already crammed carriage where,
for the whole of the seventeen day journey, the passengers took it in
turns to lie on the floor and sleep for four hours.

In Moscow she went to the Hotel Lux and asked for her Japanese
friend Mishka from Ivanovo-Vosnesensk. Mishka came rushing
down and Rosa insisted that they must play a piano duet together, as
they used to do. After what she had been through, the Lux seemed
like unbelievable luxury. Five teenage girls shared a big room with a
shower and kitchen, and she had tickets to go downstairs for
breakfast. The Hotel Lux was where she met John Gibbons, a young
man with wavy hair. 'Your father's been looking for you for years',
he told her. Kay, he explained, had been pestering Bill for news of her.

Gibbons cabled Bill, and Bill cabled back: does she want to stay in
Moscow or come to England? Rosa, who could neither remember
England nor speak English, said that she wanted to go to England.
But she also said that she was not going anywhere until Hannah and
a few other German friends were brought out of Kazakhstan. She
badgered Comintern officials, and got them out. Hannah came to
Moscow and Rosa met her at the station, carrying a sandwich in
case her friend was hungry. Hannah was. She looked at the
sandwich: 'Rosa, liebchen . . .'. Hannah met her husband again after

that, and they decided to try living together again. They had a baby, a son. After that Rosa never saw her again and had no idea what happened to her, which was a great sadness to her: 'Hannah was a very important person in my life, she taught me many things.'

She was taken to see Dimitrov. She thought he looked sombre and ill, but he shook her hand with a strong grip. He was glad her ordeal was over, he said, and her parents had been told she was safe. This was a man with a lot on his mind. The Germans were at last in retreat from the Soviet Union. The Comintern was about to be wound up, and Dimitrov was increasingly preoccupied with the politics of his native Bulgaria, which was occupied by the Germans. That year the King of Bulgaria died under mysterious circumstances after returning from a meeting with Hitler. The next year the Soviet army was to invade the country, and Dimitrov was to return home for the first time since 1923, to become leader of a communist government in 1946, to execute the leader of the opposition Agrarian Party in 1947, and to die in a Moscow sanatorium in 1949.

But on that day in 1943 he took time off to work out what to do with Bill Rust's daughter. She wanted to go to England, and she wanted to go by the quickest possible route, whatever the dangers, so Dimitrov arranged with the British embassy for her to travel with a convoy of ships, leaving from Murmansk on 2 March 1944, which took her on a three-week sea journey to the Scottish port of Leith. It was a very dangerous way to travel – she had rejected a safer option because it would take longer. She saw one ship of her convoy being sunk, and German planes attacking the men in the lifeboats. She thought several of them must have been killed, but according to the ship's captain, they were all saved. Anyone else would have thought what a dangerous and uncomfortable journey it was, but after what Rosa had been through she hardly noticed.

At Leith she had been told to take a train to Edinburgh. 'I couldn't read English, and it was crowded and I was standing in the corridor. The station names had been obliterated and all I could see was an advertisement for Virol, which was some kind of drink. And I thought, this is the third station called Virol. Then suddenly the

114

train stopped, people started moving, I heard them all muttering this funny word "skoosme".'

The train was clearly going no further, so Rosa reasoned that this must be Edinburgh. It was. 'These two very English people from the Foreign Office, with bowler hats and striped trousers, came towards me and bowed. "Miss Rust?" I said: "Da." One of them spoke rather poor Russian. He said: "Only one box? We have two cars for your luggage." I said: "Don't you know there's a war on?"'

After a few nights in Edinburgh they put her on a train to London, and her parents met her at Euston station. It took a while before she and her parents recognised each other. 'I hadn't seen my father for so long. And they missed me! I was so big, they remembered a little girl. They looked so old suddenly!' Bill Rust was forty. 'I hadn't seen my father since he came to speak to the school. They had this bunch of flowers, I said what lovely flowers, what are they, my father said Dafferdiws.' Rosa's remarkable ear for accents got her father's cockney tone perfectly, even though when she heard it she still knew no English. Her mother corrected his pronunciation. 'Thass what I said din I, dafferdiws.' Rosa said: 'Whenever I look at daffodils I can hear my father say dafferdiws.' (*Rust*)

She started slowly to learn that nothing in politics is quite what it seems. With Britain now the ally of the Soviet Union, the Foreign Office and the British Communist Party were working secretly in close collaboration. Neither wanted the world to hear that in Stalin's Soviet Union, innocent people were herded about the country in cattle trucks and forced to work down copper mines in inhuman conditions. So his daughter's arrival, welcome though it presumably was, presented Bill Rust with a problem. Alison Macleod, then a *Daily Worker* journalist, who, like most of Bill's colleagues, did not know at the time that Rosa existed, puts it crisply: 'If anyone had described in our office one-tenth of what Rosa lived through, Bill would have denounced these anti-Soviet lies and slanders.' Macleod went to work for the *Daily Worker* in 1944, and it was not until nearly fifty years later that she even knew Bill Rust had a daughter. (*Macleod*) British communists always tried to keep Bill's first wife and his daughter in the background, as we shall see.

Partly, perhaps, for this reason: Rosa's relationship with her father never flowered. She said it was the same with many of the children who were brought up in the Soviet Union away from their parents. 'We went back to our various countries and were introduced to our parents, this is your father and your mother, love them. Like hell you do. You are such very different people. I did not know my father at all. He could not adjust to the idea I was grown up. He was probably suffering from the same thing, this is my daughter, love her. I used to think he looked like Mr Pickwick.'

Though he was undoubtedly fond of her, and he did not hide her away, Bill did not exactly spread around the news that he had a daughter. No one knew who did not have to know. Bill suggested she go and work in a factory, and she suspected this was because he thought it would be good Communist Party propaganda. Kay was furious, pointing out that Rosa had already done more than her fair share of factory work. But for Rosa, her experiences since 1941 were getting more unreal by the day. 'I feel as though all the things that happened to me did not really happen, because there's no record of them', she said.

She was obviously unwell, and the doctor who saw her was concerned that she had not had a period for three years. But otherwise, he said, she was in remarkably good shape, all things considered. She needed rest, quiet and proper food. She was sent for six weeks to an agricultural camp in Bedfordshire, where you could combine a cheap holiday with doing useful war work. She liked it there, and the muscles she had developed in the copper mine meant that she could carry two sacks of peas where the others could only carry one. Six weeks of open air and proper food turned her once again into the healthy and beautiful young woman she had been in Moscow. (*Macleod*)

Then she returned to live in London with Kay, and learned English at Regent Street Polytechnic (now part of the University of Westminster), where she made the welcome discovery that she loved English poetry as much as she loved Pushkin. She still remembers the whole of G.K. Chesterton's 'The Donkey', her first-ever English poem. The passion and intensity of her strong, deep voice and the rhythm of the words were given an extra dimension by her Russian accent:

> When fishes flew and forests walked
> And figs grew upon thorns,
> Some moment when the moon was blood,
> Then surely I was born.

All her life she was able to recite every one of those English poems she read in those first months, just as we can remember poems we read when we were small children. 'What is this life if, full of care . . .', 'When fishes flew and forests walked . . .' Just give her the name, and you could hear the whole poem, in her rich, multi-layered voice. (*Rust*)

SIX

Rosa in London

Rosa never joined the British Communist Party. 'I didn't like the people in it, they lacked humanity', she told me. She told her father that he was wrong to take Stalin's side against Tito, which must have irritated him greatly. Stalin and the Yugoslavian leader Tito had fallen out, and Bill naturally had swiftly turned his lively admiration for Tito into the hatred proper for a traitor. She also told him she thought the *Daily Worker* unreadable, which must have irritated him even more. But she never escaped her father's politics. In one way or another – because of the attentions of the party itself, or because of the attitude of the British government and establishment towards her – the party cast a shadow over her whole life.

Learning English was the first hurdle. At Ivanovo-Vosnesensk the second language pupils were taught was German, and she was reasonably proficient in that, but she knew literally not a word of her native language. However, she had an actor's or a musician's ear for cadences, and learned English fast, though she always spoke it with a Russian accent. She worked first for *Soviet Weekly*, a magazine subsidised by the Soviet embassy, and then as a translator for the Soviet news agency Tass.

She lived with her mother Kay in a flat in Bedford Square, in central London. Kay had lost her job at the Foreign Office after Rosa arrived in England. It is not at all clear how she came to be working there in the first place, or why she was forced to leave. It seems likely

119

that someone who knew Russian, had lived in Moscow, and had connections with Britain's top communists, might be regarded as useful in wartime when the Soviet Union was Britain's ally, and an embarrassment when the cold war loomed on the horizon.

So after the war ended the two women lived in genteel poverty, with only Rosa's very modest earnings to live on. They were frequently invited to receptions at Eastern European embassies, and they took big handbags and rifled the buffet, taking the food home for later. Kay had what her grandson, Rosa's son David, describes as a bohemian lifestyle. While Rosa probably preferred Kay to Bill, she was not that fond of Kay either, partly because Kay criticised her a lot.

Though she disliked the Communist Party's top brass, the party provided Rosa's social life. Where else was she to find the company of other young people, when she had not been in Britain since the age of three? It was at a Young Communist League social event that she met a clever young history student called George Thornton.

Bill Rust would have approved of George Thornton's credentials. He was impeccably working class, with a labour movement pedigree: his father had been a National Union of Railwaymen shop steward and a Labour councillor. He had fought in the Second World War and, after being demobbed, he managed to get into King's College London to study history – a remarkable achievement in those days for a working-class man without money. He joined the Young Communist League, which, back in the 1920s, Bill Rust had led.

His tutor at King's College was Andrew Rothstein, a Balliol College historian who had been one of the British Communist Party's most important leaders in the 1920s. Rothstein had fallen foul of the Comintern line in the 1930s by opposing Class against Class, and he had at one point even found himself in a Moscow prison, hours away from execution as a Menshevik. For this reason he fell from grace in the party, but he was still a loyal and convinced member. Rothstein considered George to be a considerable historian with an important future. He was particularly impressed when one day he told George that the best textbook on a particular subject was in Polish, and George learned enough Polish to be able to read it. George and Rosa shared a love of poetry and music. George was devoted to the works of Shelley, a poet Rosa had not yet come across. (*Thornton*)

One day in 1949, Rosa telephoned Bill Rust at the *Daily Worker* and said: 'I want to meet you tonight and introduce you to the man I'm going to marry.' Bill promised to meet her later at Tottenham Court Road in central London, and they could go to a pub for a meal.

It was a busy day for Bill. Furious at UK newspaper attacks on the Soviet Union, he had published an editorial in the *Daily Worker* headlined 'Fleet Street dungheap', a blistering attack on journalists. The Central London branch of the National Union of Journalists, of which, naturally, Bill was a member, was outraged, and demanded that he should come along and account for himself. He was due there that evening. He seems to have been looking forward to the NUJ meeting: Bill liked a good scrap. But first he had to attend a series of party meetings, and it was while he was at 16 King Street that he murmured that he felt ill, and then collapsed. It was a massive stroke, and he was dead by the time he reached hospital. He was forty-five.

Kay phoned Rosa at work and barked two words: 'Bill's dead'. George Thornton claimed in later years to have reflected that 'It was a drastic way of avoiding meeting me'. (*Rust*)

Bill Rust, in those last years of his short life, had flowered as a journalist. When he first edited the *Daily Worker*, back in 1930, he had done it like the Comintern functionary he was, printing great slabs of unmediated and unreadable Comintern statements. When he came back to edit the paper from 1939 until his death in 1949, he had a much better idea of what journalism was about – and no doubt the paper benefited from the fact that communications with Moscow were not so easy in wartime. Recognising that he had no journalistic experience, and that this mattered, he made full use of experienced and talented journalists like Claud Cockburn and Allen Hutt. The *Daily Worker* enjoyed its best years under his editorship.

'Rust', writes Andrew Flinn, 'was the prime example of a generation of revolutionary activists. They joined the party in their youth under the influence of Lenin and the Bolshevik revolution. Lacking experience, they knew little of political struggle outside the insular world of the party. Isolated from real life in Britain and inspired by what they saw as the triumphs of the USSR, they embraced the sectarian politics espoused by the Comintern. In this atmosphere, they learnt that ruthlessness and lack of sentiment were cherished revolutionary values. Many like Rust also received their political education in the International Lenin School or the Young Communist International, while in the party they owed their preferment to the patronage of the Comintern. This youthful enthusiasm for Moscow would lead to eventual complicity in the crimes of that regime.' (*Flinn*)

The Communist Party did funerals in style. It planned a procession through the streets for Bill's coffin, it planned who should be there – and it planned who should not. Kay and Rosa were asked to stay away. The reason for this extraordinary request was that Bill was now married to Tamara Kravets, and the party wanted to adopt an appearance of strict respectability. So it tried not to let it be too widely known that Bill had had a previous wife, by whom he had a grown-up daughter. Tamara too seems to have wanted Kay and Rose airbrushed out of Bill's history, which seems, on the face of it, to be an amazingly insensitive way to proceed; but we will never quite know the truth of it, because for the rest of her long life Tamara refused to talk about that or anything else to do with politics or her past.

As it happens, Bill also had an illegitimate daughter by a communist he had worked with before the war, though no one except perhaps one or two top communists knew it at the time, or for another fifty years. (*McConnell*)

The party was probably also not at all keen on Rosa having a high profile because of her Russian accent. It was by no means certain that, if someone asked her how she came by it, she might not tell them the whole story – a story that did not reflect credit on the Soviet Union, and would endanger the secrecy of a shameful episode in Soviet history which, at that time, no one in the west knew about: the expulsion of the Volga Germans.

Kay made it very clear to King Street what she thought of the instruction not to attend her husband's funeral, and the row reached

Harry Pollitt, who had brains and humanity enough to realise that the instruction was wrong in principle and dangerous in practice. Of course they must be there, he said, and Kay and Rosa walked in front of Bill's coffin past the 5,000 who lined the North London streets to pay their last respects.

Rosa's wedding was a much happier affair, though she might have preferred not to have Harry Pollitt giving her away, standing in for her dead father. Pollitt climbed into the car beside her to take them to the wedding, a little drunk she thought (Harry was drinking a lot of whisky by then), and said to the 23-year-old bride: 'By the way, do you know the facts of life?' No doubt he thought he was doing his duty as a kind of surrogate father. But the music-loving couple were terribly pleased to have the great Paul Robeson, the black American communist actor and singer, at their wedding. Kay had known Paul Robeson through the Anglo-Soviet Friendship Society, and had set up his tour of the USSR. (*Rust*)

Rosa and George were happy together for the next half century, but the shadow of the cold war and their own communist past hung over their lives and their marriage like a pall, and never left them alone.

When they were married, in 1949, Britain's Communist Party thought its best times were just starting, but the truth was that they were ending. It was another false dawn, just like the one it had known in the early 1930s, when Harry Pollitt first became its leader. In those far-off days, it seemed that it might be able to make a new beginning, having managed to jettison the Moscow policy of Class against Class, which demanded that it should try to brand others on the left as 'social fascists'. Pollitt was a fine speaker with an attractive personality and an instinctive ability to relate to people. The Labour Party in government had manifestly failed, the Independent Labour Party was disintegrating, and it looked briefly as though the Communist Party's time might have come.

Stalin's purges put an end to any such hopes. By the end of the 1930s, the purges had ruined the party's chances, and placed every-one's loyalty under strain. To make things worse, in 1939, when the war began, voters were treated to the ugly spectacle of the Communist Party first calling for unremitting warfare against Hitler;

then, when Hitler and Stalin did a deal, condemning the war and calling for peace talks; and then, when Germany attacked the Soviet Union, calling for unremitting war against fascism again. The Communist Party managed to make itself look as though it had no mind of its own, and simply parroted the latest line from Moscow, and that, indeed, was the sad situation Stalin had forced it into.

Once the war was well under way, the party looked briefly like a success story again. The Soviet Union was popular as never before, and it was temporarily convenient for government ministers to treat with Harry Pollitt. The Comintern was wound up during the war, and communications between London and Moscow were difficult, so British communist leaders for the first time had the luxury of formulating their reactions to events themselves. They managed rather well. At the 1945 general election two Communist MPs were elected, and the party attracted so many votes that, in a fairer electoral system, it would have had a powerful parliamentary party.

In 1945 the message the Communist Party had to offer was in tune with the spirit of the times. Winston Churchill, prime minister in the war years, was a national hero, but he was also the leader of the Conservative Party, which people blamed for the gross inequalities and hardships of the 1930s. The election of Clement Attlee's Labour Party was a clear signal that Britain wanted a government which would redistribute wealth and power, as communists advocated. Attlee and his ministers set about doing just that, in a more thorough and determined way than any government has ever done, before or since.

The Communist Party really needed Attlee to fail as the previous Labour prime minister Ramsay Macdonald had failed, in order to show that no one was prepared to tackle the injustices of capitalist society other than the communists. But if Labour was not to fail, then the next best thing was to be a part of Attlee's success. About a dozen of the 393 Labour MPs were either secret Communist Party members or close to the communists. The Soviet Union was popular in Britain, for people knew the war could not have been won without the massive sacrifices of the Red Army and of Soviet civilians. Communists were still seen as the only people who, before the war, had done anything effective to oppose anti-Semitism; that was what won the party its second parliamentary seat, in the strongly Jewish Mile End division of Stepney in London's East End.

The rise of communist parties was a Europe-wide phenomenon. In France, the Parti Communiste Français was a partner in government, having won more seats than the social democrats.

Bill Rust's *Daily Worker* was bigger, better and more influential than ever before, and Rust aimed to turn it into a popular mass paper. He was able to use Moscow's money to build a splendid new office close to Fleet Street, without having to take too many of Moscow's instructions to print every word of every long, boring speech given by every Moscow bigwig. He had to be careful to get the line right, of course, but the days when the theoretician Palme Dutt could step in and stop him running racing tips had gone.

Bill had working for him, in the Lenin School-trained Allen Hutt, probably the best newspaper designer in Britain, as well as some famous names in journalism, like Claud Cockburn and Llew Gardiner. In 1948, the year before Rust's death, circulation was higher than it had ever been, at 120,000. Rust died believing that this was just the start, and that the only way forward was upward. He was wrong. *Daily Worker* circulation had peaked, and eight years later it was down to 63,000.

The reason was that, all too soon, the old Stalinist spirit draped itself round the elegant headquarters which Lenin had bought for the party at 16 King Street in London's Covent Garden. The demise of the Comintern proved only a temporary halt to Soviet control. In 1947 Stalin set up the Communist Information Bureau, or Cominform, with headquarters in Bucharest, which quickly laid down how communist parties the world over were to behave. Harry Pollitt did not hear about it until after the communist parties of Eastern Europe, France and Italy had been fully briefed, but when he did, he rushed to welcome the new body, with the usual depressing self-abasement for not foreseeing it. 'We . . . clung to old formulas and agendas.'

While this was happening, the world was dividing into two armed camps. The previous year Winston Churchill, now leader of the opposition, had formally launched the cold war in a speech in Fulton, Missouri: 'From Stettin in the Baltic to Trieste in the Adriatic, an iron curtain has fallen across Europe. . . .'

The cold war smothered the hope and optimism of 1945 like a frozen shroud. The party was over. Communists went back to futile obedience to the edicts issuing from Moscow. As they became identified with the interests of a hostile foreign power, the British version of McCarthyism, less virulent than the American version but poisonous to those it touched, was soon to begin. The hysteria was triggered by spy scandals.

In 1950 the atomic scientist Klaus Fuchs confessed to supplying secrets to the Soviets, and the next year saw the defection of Guy Burgess and Donald Maclean. The Labour Party started expelling MPs who were close to the Communist Party, and there was a purge of communists in the civil service. But the real victims of the cold war were often people like George and Rosa. Young people with songs in their hearts and hope for the world are often those who suffer for the sins of elderly politicians. George was a communist (though not for long – he soon took his battered idealism elsewhere). Rosa had spent her formative years in Moscow, and her father had been one of the two or three best-known communists in Britain.

It was in that atmosphere that George and the three other members of Andrew Rothstein's tutor group all came up for their final examinations – and all of them failed. A year or so later, Rothstein was forced out of academia in the growing clamour against communists, and especially communist historians. Despite his well-attested ability as a historian and a teacher and a spirited legal defence mounted by the lawyer, politician and communist sympathiser D.N. Pritt QC, his career in the academic world was over.

The party rescued Rothstein, and he became director of the Society for Cultural Relations with the Soviet Union. But there was no such rescue for George Thornton. He and Rothstein both believed that the latter's students were being used as a weapon with which to attack Rothstein, and unjustly marked down. It is impossible to prove, but it is very likely, especially to those of us who had the pleasure of talking about history with George Thornton and admiring his insight and his well-stocked mind. George's son says the result had a 'crushing psychological effect on him throughout his life'.

Soon after that, in 1951, the British foreign office closed down the Soviet news agency Tass. The party protested, although privately, according to Alison Macleod, *Daily Worker* journalists celebrated: no more tedious statements which they were not allowed to ignore. But it meant something more serious for Rosa: it meant she no longer had a job. However, their oldest son was born that year, and George and Rosa nailed their left-wing colours to the mast by naming him David after David Guest, an International Brigader who was killed in the Spanish Civil War. (*Thornton*)

But Rosa's job had gone, and so had George's desperately hoped-for academic future. And while the British establishment had their suspicions about George and Rosa and were unlikely to give them any help, the same applied to the Communist Party; for Rosa had refused to join it and George was showing disturbing signs of thinking for himself. There was no future there.

SEVEN

1956: The Prisons Yield up their Secrets

Secret

To the International Department of the CPSU; Central Committee of the CPSU – Membership sector; for the file. Decision of the Committee of Party Control, Protocol No 1021/10 of 3 March 1958.

The case of COHEN, Rose Morisovna (member of the CPSU from 1927, Party card No. 1160681).

In view of the fact that the accusations against Cohen R.M. were without foundation – to rehabilitate her as a member of the party.

Supreme Court of the USSR. Decision No. 4N-012577/56

Military Collegium of the Supreme Court of the USSR.

Having examined at the session of 8 August 1956.

THE CONCLUSION OF THE CHIEF MILITARY PROSECUTOR

In the case of COHEN, Rose Morisovna, born in 1894, a native of England, sentenced by the Military Collegium of the Supreme Court of the USSR on 28 November 1937 on the basis of articles 58-6, 58-8, and 58-11 of the Criminal Code of the RSFSR to be shot, with confiscation of property.

Cohen was found guilty of having been a member of an anti-Soviet organisation existing in the ECCI (Comintern) and a resident agent of British Intelligence.

In the conclusion of the Chief Military Procurator it is incumbent to rescind the sentence in relation to Cohen and to quash the case against her in the absence of evidence against her on the basis of the fact that a new investigation has been carried out and it has been established that she was without foundation found guilty of anti-Soviet espionage activity . . .

To rescind the sentence of the Military Collegium of the Supreme Court . . . in relation to COHEN Rose Morisovna and to quash the case against her in the absence of evidence against her. . . . (*RC*)

After Stalin died in 1953, stories of the great terror started to leak out, and the leadership of the Soviet Union seemed to have lost its appetite for blood. By 1955 the battle for the succession had been won by Nikita Khrushchev, and on 25 February 1956 Khrushchev made a four-hour speech to the Twentieth Congress of the Communist Party of the Soviet Union, detailing many of the crimes of the Stalin era.

Stalin, using his unlimited power, allowed himself many abuses, acting in the name of the Central Committee, not asking for the opinion of Committee members, or even informing them. . . . Many Party activists who were branded in 1937–38 as 'enemies' were actually never enemies, spies, wreckers, etc. but were always honest communists, and often, no longer able to bear barbaric tortures, they charged themselves with all kinds of grave and unlikely crimes. . . . Of the 139 members and candidates of the party's Central Committee who were elected at the Seventeenth Congress, 98 persons, i.e. 70 per cent, were arrested and shot. . . .

The same fate met not only the Central Committee members but also the majority of the delegates to the Seventeenth Congress. Of 1,966 delegates, 1,108 persons were arrested. This very fact shows how absurd, wild and contrary to common sense were the charges of counter-revolutionary crimes. . . .

Mass repressions grew tremendously from 1936. The mass repressions at this time were made under the slogan of a fight against the Trotskyists, but Trotskyism was completely disarmed. . . . Confessions of guilt were gained with the use of cruel and inhuman tortures.

He quoted several examples of 'odious falsification and of criminal violation of revolutionary legality'. One was a former candidate for the Central Committee Politburo, 'one of the most eminent workers of the party and of the Soviet Government, comrade Robert Eikhe, a member of the Communist Party since 1905.' He went on:

Comrade Eikhe was arrested on April 29 1938. . . . Under torture, Eikhe was forced to sign a protocol of his confession prepared in advance by the investigative judges. In it, he and several other eminent Party workers were accused of anti-Soviet activity.

On October 1 1939 Eikhe sent his declaration to Stalin in which he categorically denied his guilt and asked for an examination of his case. In the declaration he wrote: 'There is no more bitter misery than to sit in the jail of a government for which I have always fought.' A second declaration of Eikhe has been preserved, which he sent to Stalin on October 27 1939. In it [Eikhe] cited facts very convincingly and countered the slanderous accusations made against him, arguing that this provocatory accusation was on one hand the work of real Trotskyites whose arrests he had sanctioned as First Secretary of the West Siberian Regional Party Committee and who conspired in order to take revenge on him, and, on the other hand, the result of the base falsification of materials by the investigative judges.

Eikhe wrote in his declaration: 'On October 25 of this year I was informed that the investigation in my case has been concluded and I was given access to the materials of this investigation. Had I been guilty of only one-hundredth of the crimes with which I am charged, I would not have dared to send you this pre-execution declaration. However I have not been guilty of even one of the things with which I am charged and my heart is clean of even the shadow of baseness. I have never in my life told you a word of falsehood, and now, finding both feet in the grave, I am still not lying. My whole case is a typical example of provocation, slander and violation of the elementary basis of revolutionary legality. . . .'

There was only one thing he was ashamed of, he said, and that was his confession of guilt:

'I am now alluding to the most disgraceful part of my life and to my really grave guilt against the party and against you. This is my confession of counterrevolutionary activity. . . . The case is as follows: Not being able to suffer the tortures to which I was submitted by Z. Ushakov and Nikolayev – especially by the former, who utilised the knowledge that my broken ribs have not properly mended and have caused me great pain – I have been forced to accuse myself and others. The majority of my confession has been suggested or dictated by Ushakov. The rest is my reconstruction of NKVD materials from Western Siberia for which I assumed all responsibility. If some part of the story which Ushakov fabricated and which I signed did not properly hang together, I was forced to sign another variation . . .

I am asking and begging you that you again examine my case, and this not for the purpose of sparing me but in order to unmask the vile provocation which, like a snake, wound itself around many persons in a great degree due to my meanness and criminal slander. I have never betrayed you or the party. I know that I perish because of vile and mean work of enemies of the party and of the people, who have fabricated the provocation against me.'

Khrushchev continued:

On February 2, 1940, Eikhe was brought before the court. Here he did not confess any guilt and said as follows: 'In all the so-called confessions of mine there is not one letter written by me with the exception of my signatures under the protocols, which were forced from me. I have made my confession under pressure from the investigative judge, who from the time of my arrest tormented me. After that I began to write all this nonsense. . . . The most important thing for me is to tell the court, the party and Stalin that I am not guilty. I have never been guilty of any

132

conspiracy. I will die believing in the truth of Party policy as I have believed in it during my whole life.'

On February 4, Eikhe was shot. It has been definitely established now that Eikhe's case was fabricated. He has been rehabilitated posthumously.

From 1954 to the present time the Military Collegium of the Supreme Court has rehabilitated 7,679 persons, many of whom have been rehabilitated posthumously.

Khrushchev blamed one individual, Stalin, for all of this:

Stalin was a very distrustful man, sickly suspicious. We know this from our work with him. He could look at a man and say: 'Why are your eyes so shifty today?' or 'Why are you turning so much today and avoiding looking me directly in the eyes?' The sickly suspicion created in him a general distrust even towards eminent Party workers whom he had known for years. Everywhere and in everything he saw 'enemies', 'two-facers' and 'spies'. Possessing unlimited power, he indulged in great wilfulness and stifled people morally as well as physically.

When Stalin said that one or another should be arrested, it was necessary to accept on faith that he was an 'enemy of the people'. Meanwhile, Beria's gang, which ran the organs of state security, outdid itself in proving the guilt of the arrested and the truth of materials which it falsified. And what proofs were offered? The confessions of the arrested, and the investigative judges accepted these 'confessions'. And how is it possible that a person confesses to crimes which he has not committed? Only in one way – because of the application of physical methods of pressuring him, tortures, bringing him to a state of unconsciousness, deprivation of his judgement, taking away his human dignity. In this manner were 'confessions' acquired.

The wave of mass arrests began to recede in 1939, Khrushchev said, and he proceeded to denounce Stalin's role in the war, his 1939 pact with Hitler which he ought to have known could never hold, his failure to direct the armies properly or to pay even one visit to the front. 'Documents that have been published show clearly that as early as April 3 1941, Churchill, through his ambassador to the USSR Sir Stafford Cripps, personally warned Stalin that the Germans had begun regrouping their armed units with the intent of attacking the Soviet Union. . . . Stalin took no heed of these warnings.'

Just before Stalin died came the affair of the doctor's plot. On 13 January *Pravda* 'uncovered' a vast conspiracy among Jewish doctors to murder Kremlin leaders, including Stalin. This would probably have signalled the start of another terrible round of purges had Stalin not died two months later. It was, said Khrushchev truthfully, 'fabricated from beginning to end', and confessions were extracted from the doctors by torture.

This speech marked the beginning of perhaps the strangest part of Harry Pollitt's strange life. Most of Pollitt never quite believed Khrushchev, whom he saw as a small man attacking his hero Stalin. The bust of Stalin in the living room of his small north London home stayed there, defiantly, until Pollitt died four years later. Yet, telling no one, five months after Khrushchev's speech, Harry Pollitt wrote to the Central Committee of the Communist Party of the Soviet Union a letter which he may have been secretly composing for twenty years.

Dear Comrades.
The relatives of Comrade Rose Cohen asked me to try to obtain some information about her. . . . In Moscow she married Comrade Petrovsky. She had a son called Alyosha, who must now be about 20 years old.

In the 1930s Petrovsky was arrested, as was his wife Rose Cohen subsequently. In 1937 or 1938 I personally requested news of Rose Cohen from Comrade Dimitrov and Comrade Manuilsky, but received no information. In 1938 the late Beatrice and Sidney Webb were very interested in Rose Cohen, because in 1919–21 she had worked in their office.

Rose Cohen's family has great influence in Jewish circles in Britain. Following the publication of reports of wrongful arrests, they are again raising that question and are bombarding me with requests.

I should be extremely obliged if you would let me have some information about Rose Cohen in order that an unpleasant fuss in the British press may be avoided. . . . (*Morgan, Rose Cohen*)

Pollitt was being economical with the truth. Rose's family was not particularly influential in Jewish circles. They had not suddenly renewed their requests for information, and they were not likely to create a particular fuss in the newspapers, which were, in any case, full of the crimes of Stalin throughout that year. And by then Stalin had anyway thrown away all the support and sympathy he had had in Britain's Jewish community by fitting up the Jewish doctors and torturing them into confessions of a plot to murder top Kremlin figures.

Now sixty-six, Pollitt, writes Kevin Morgan, 'unable to grasp the implications of Khrushchev's revelations, continued to deploy long-practised arguments about the dangers of adverse publicity, as if that could now matter to the Russians in the year of the secret speech.' (*Morgan, Rose Cohen*)

It looks as though Harry still clung to some sort of hope that Rose might one day walk out of one of those terrible labour camps, old, bent and ill, no doubt, but still Rose. It must have been a secret, despairing hope that he could never confess to anyone, and he knew Moscow well enough to know that such human considerations would cut no ice there. If so, the reply, extracts from which appear at the start of this chapter, told him the worst, that the love of his life had been dead for twenty years.

The Soviets told Pollitt nothing about Alyosha. They could have done, as we shall see. But they chose not to. The *Daily Worker* did not print so much as a sentence to say that Rose had been rehabilitated. Three years previously, the paper had printed Harry Pollitt's obituary of Stalin: 'Never . . . have I met anyone so kindly and considerate.'

Rose Cohen's older sister Nellie had never tried to trace Alyosha, because she had been warned, by someone with good Soviet contacts, that it might be held against Alyosha. She must have realised many years earlier that her sister was probably dead, though, strangely, it does not seem to have shaken her communist beliefs or those of her husband, Hugo Rathbone.

But after Khrushchev's 1956 speech Nellie had her first news of Alyosha, a letter from Ivy Litvinov telling her that Alyosha had become a fine young man, and had been to see Ivy in Moscow. But she did not say much about him, for she was writing from Moscow and had to be careful. (*Rathbone*) Ivy wrote a note for herself a few years later:

> And so this pathetic, extraordinary, wonderful young man came to see me, looking a terrible physical wreck; a great tall young man. . . . He was such an interesting, charming and pure person. . . . He had no telephone. I could never get in touch with him. He used to ring me up. . . . He has still got relations in England. I would love to get in touch with them and bring him news. But I don't know if I will ever be able to find him again. (*Carswell*)

Nellie had a daughter, Joyce, born in the same year as Alyosha, 1929. In 1936 Nellie married another English communist, Hugo Rathbone, who had spent time in the Labour Research Department and the International Lenin School in Moscow, and Rathbone adopted Joyce.

In the 1980s, after Nellie's death, Joyce Rathbone went to see Andrew Rothstein, whom we last met when he taught history at King's College to Rosa Rust's future husband George Thornton, and was hounded out of the university because of his communist views.

Rothstein, born in 1888, was the highly intellectual Balliol-educated son of Theodore (Fydor) Rothstein, a Lithuanian Jewish communist who had fled Tsarist persecution and settled in Britain in 1891. Theodore was a friend of Lenin's, and became a major figure in international communism and a key figure in the formation of the British Communist Party and in its relations with Moscow. After the 1917 revolution he returned to Moscow and became an important Soviet diplomat. Andrew Rothstein played a key part in British and international communist politics all his life and, like many others, spent time in a Moscow prison during the purges, and is thought to have narrowly escaped execution. In the 1980s he was the only person left alive who knew most of the secrets of the relationship between Moscow and the British Communist Party, but he chose never to discuss them, and they went with him to his grave at the age of ninety-six in September 1994.

Rothstein agreed to help Joyce to find her cousin. A month later he gave her, without explaining how he came by it, an address where Alyosha was living in Moscow. She wrote to the address, in English, and for months she heard nothing. Then one night her telephone rang. It was Alyosha's son Misha, now himself a young man. He told her that it might be difficult to meet his father, because he was a geologist and his work was considered secret. But he did agree that she should come to Moscow, and Misha would try to arrange a meeting.

Joyce flew to Moscow and Misha met her at the airport to tell her that Alyosha would not see her. Alyosha had said: 'How do I know this is really my cousin? Perhaps it is a trap.' After the fate of his parents, and the effect it had had on his own life, it's hardly surprising that Alyosha wanted to be quite sure nothing he did would attract the attention of the Soviet Union's authorities. But Misha said he still hoped to change his father's mind, and invited Joyce to his own flat for supper, hoping his father would come too.

Alyosha came. He wept over the book Joyce gave him with his mother's name in it, the photograph of his mother, the family tree she showed him. 'He could not stop looking at them', said Joyce. He told her about his life. He had been sent to a series of tough orphanages where he was forbidden to mention the names of his parents. (*Rathbone*) These orphanages were well known in the Soviet Union. They were cold, spartan, strict places to which the children of 'enemies of the people' were sent, designed for children who needed to be punished for the sins of their parents.

Eventually the parents of a school friend found him, got him out of the orphanage, adopted him, cared for him and loved him. 'I had a very tough time but I met some noble people who were kind to me', was how he had put it to Ivy Litvinov. (*Carswell*) He was now a geologist, and looked like his father.

But the strangest and saddest thing of all, Joyce says, was how anxious he was for her to understand that his parents were not really Trotskyists. It had all been a terrible mistake. Had they not, after all, been rehabilitated? (*Rathbone*)

* * *

Freda Utley and Pearl Rimel made the best of their new lives in America. I do not think they ever met there, or knew of each other's existence, but for both women, their experiences had turned them from idealistic communists into ardent anti-communists. After 1956, Freda was able to find out what had happened to Arcadi, but Pearl never knew for certain what had happened to George Fles.

Pearl had found a job working for an airline and used her free flights to visit her family in England and George's in Holland. But these visits were not always happy family occasions, because – so her sister Hetty told me, still, in 2003, with a sense of disapproval – Pearl had become bitterly anti-communist. 'She did not confide in me because I was still in the Communist Party at that time', says Hetty. 'Right at the beginning she wasn't as bitter as she became later.'

Pearl had kept George's last letter, the letter which he somehow smuggled out of prison and persuaded one of his guards to hand to Jack Miller for her: the letter written in Russian so that his guard could read it, on a tiny, dirty, crumpled piece of cheap paper, which said he would never escape the *dolgonochnaya mrachnost,* the darkness of the long night: the letter in which he told her to marry again while she was still young. But she disobeyed George's last instruction – she never remarried. For many years she refused to give up the idea that one day there would be a knock on the door, and he would be there, having served out his years in a Soviet prison. For her there was never even the certainty that he was dead. She did not have the contacts or the know-how to get definite information, as Harry Pollitt and even Freda Utley did.

Khrushchev's 1956 revelations destroyed Hetty Bower's peace of mind. To the distress felt by most British communists at the betrayal of their idealism was added a sense that she had somehow betrayed her sister. Yet even then, she and Reg were not quite sure about George Fles. 'We were completely bewildered,' she wrote later, 'and totally unable to judge whether in fact George had been guilty of any indiscretion or worse, or whether he had been a completely innocent victim of Stalin's madness. Reg and I only knew that somehow we felt guilty personally; that Pearl's tragic circumstances, bereft of her husband and father of her child, was something we had to atone for, and the many financial sacrifices we had made for Pearl seemed trivial, and in the years after 1956 we did even more to try to compensate.' (*Bower autobiography*)

Pearl worked in California for Lockheed, the company that had helped her escape from Holland before the Nazis arrived, for many years, and then for a time for California's public service broadcasting company, KCET. Younger relatives who visited her from Britain remember her as 'lovely, vivacious, beautiful blue eyes, a lovely smile, very good looking and sure of herself'. They recall her occasional visits to England, and one in particular, when she joined the family for Passover and made jokes all the way through the readings. (*Rimel*)

As a single mother keeping her son on what she could earn, life was not easy. At first her letters home to her sister Anita were full of worry about how she was to earn enough to keep a small child, and to look after him as well. Earning the money meant spending long hours away from him. Eventually she sent him to boarding school from 1943 to 1950, when he was aged seven to fourteen, so that she could work – a decision which she seems to have regretted, and which filled her with guilt.

In 1950, when John Michael Fles was fourteen, Pearl put him on a plane to London by himself to meet his family, and to stay with Pearl's sister Hetty. Pearl told him for the first time that he was Jewish, and that he would find in London a Jewish grandfather and several aunts and uncles. 'That was the first time he knew he had any connection with Jews', says Hetty, who was seven years older than

139

Pearl. Hetty, who had children of her own, found her nephew a strange, difficult teenager. Her husband Reg Bower, who had lost his own father when he was young, told her that such a loss was not an excuse for poor behaviour. (*Bower interview*)

Pearl was now, as her son put it recently, over-compensating for her sense of guilt for what seemed to her to have been a childhood deprived of parental love. She was alarmed at his use of drugs in the 1960s, when he became a beatnik, but accepted him as he was, though her family in England watched with disapproval. 'She let me be free', is how Michael Fles (as he is now known) puts it today.

Anti-communist she may have been, but she kept it in proportion. Unlike Freda Utley, who (as we shall see) joined eagerly in the witch-hunt for communists initiated by Senator Joseph McCarthy and his House Un-American Activities Committee, Pearl was horrified, seeing McCarthyism as something rather like Stalinism. She lived in California and had come to know as friends some of the theatre people targeted by McCarthy, and did what she could to help them.

Pearl Fles (as she was always known in the USA) died in Los Angeles in 1983, on the eve of her seventy-first birthday, of stomach cancer. Her friend and lover for the last few years of her life, Ray Goldstone, wrote to one of her relatives: 'At first I was just numb when she left us, and relieved that she would not have to suffer any more. Now the quieter pain has set in. That I won't be able to enjoy the warmth and love and wit that she had in such abundance.'

Hetty in faraway London (Pearl had not wanted her to come to California) was full of self-reproach and sadness, seeing, perhaps for the first time, George as a victim and Pearl's life as heroic. She decided to place an obituary notice in the British Communist Party newspaper, which had by then changed its name from the *Daily Worker* to the *Morning Star*. Hetty wrote that Pearl's husband was a 'victim of the Stalin terror'. (*Bower interview*) Those who have no knowledge of communists of that generation cannot understand the heart-searching that it cost her to write that.

Hetty telephoned her older sister Anita, still a convinced communist, to tell her what she planned to do. Anita said: 'You mustn't do that. It would be wrong for you to put that in the *Morning Star*.' She was 'vehement in her disapproval and dismay' wrote Hetty later. Anita also claimed that she had letters she could show Hetty which would put things in a completely different light. So Hetty's obituary notice in the *Morning Star* simply said that Pearl and George had 'lived and died with great courage'. Hetty always hoped that Anita would show her the letters she referred to, especially after Anita, too, left the Communist Party, but Anita never did. Anita may have died without knowing that her own presents of German socialist magazines had helped to seal George's fate. But Hetty has a suspicion – no more than that – that Anita did know a little of what happened, and kept it to herself. Hetty is not quite sure. (*Bower*)

Anita Rimel worked for a large part of her life as personal assistant to J.D. Bernal, the distinguished scientist and communist and author of several influential books on the relationship between Marxism and science. Some of her closest relatives say that in the later years of her life, they think that she slowly began to believe that the magazines and letters she sent to George may have been the cause of his death. She did not like to talk about him, but they believe she was tormented by guilt, and that this may even have hastened her own death in 1993 from cancer. Her own disillusion with communism came at the time of the brutal suppression of Chinese students at Tiananmen Square in 1989. (*Rimel*)

Freda Utley and her son Jon Basil Utley became US citizens in 1950. Freda never lost the fear that something she had said might have contributed to Arcadi's arrest, though she was sure they would have taken him for something, sooner or later. Freda's idealism mingled with her anger and bitterness, and went through the shredder of her fiercely powerful intellect, to turn her into one of the most effective right-wing communist-hunters of the McCarthyite era. She was not the first socialist to have reacted violently to what she saw of the methods of the Comintern and the Soviet Union. Back in the 1930s, Jack Murphy wrote after he left the Communist Party that communists themselves, by their methods, were recruiting sergeants for the fascists. To Freda, Britain's declaration of war in 1939 was a tragedy: Hitler and Stalin should have been left to fight it out between them.

The events of 1956 at last gave her a chance to find out what had happened to Arcadi Berdichevsky, and the high-level political contacts she had made in the USA enabled her to take it. She asked former US Ambassador Llewellyn Thompson to find out for her, and he agreed to ask Khrushchev's deputy Anastas Mikoyan at a state dinner. Months later, in a letter dated 27 December 1962, Thompson relayed Mikoyan's answer to her. 'The Soviet Ambassador has now confirmed that Berdichevsky, Arcadi Yakovlovich, died in Komi on March 30 1938', wrote Thompson.

She devoted herself to alerting her adopted country to what she saw as the communist menace. She knew Senator Joseph McCarthy well, and helped him compile his notorious lists of highly placed people suspected of communist sympathies, providing him with the material for his 1950 denunciation of Owen Lattimore, the journalist and academic who was accused (and acquitted) of spying for Chinese communists. She believed to her dying day that McCarthy's methods were essentially right, the only way to neutralise the evil that was communism. One of her contributions to McCarthy's work was to compile a list of the books in the American library in occupied Germany, in order to substantiate her claim that they were nearly all pro-communist, with hardly any anti-communist literature. McCarthyism's ultimate failure, she believed, was due to McCarthy's heavy drinking and his 'capture' by the far right. She grew to love the USA, believing it represented everything she had originally liked about communism, in particular the ideas of freedom and opportunity. (*Utley interview*)

Her polemical writing was widely admired. She is still today, years after her death, still often quoted by the American right, and denounced by the American left. She considered communism a greater evil than fascism, and is even denounced in Deborah Lipstadt's *Denying the Holocaust* as a Holocaust denier. Lipstadt writes: 'Eventually Utley would become one of the most vocal of Senator Joseph McCarthy's supporters, branding one of those he accused of being a Communist spy as a "Judas cow," an animal who led others to be slaughtered'.

142

Lipstadt adds that certain writers 'tried to neutralise German actions by directly comparing the Nazis' annihilation of the Jews and murder of millions of others with Allied actions. They contended that the United States had committed wrongdoings of the same magnitude. The ardent isolationist Freda Utley made the same point in *The High Cost of Vengeance*: "If imitation is the sincerest form of flattery no one ever paid a higher compliment to the Nazis than their conquerors. . . . We reaffirmed the Nazi doctrine that might makes right. Instead of showing the Germans that Hitler's racial theories were both wrong and ridiculous, we ourselves assumed the role of a master race." The argument that the United States committed atrocities as great, if not greater, than those committed by Germany has become a fulcrum of contemporary Holocaust denial and a theme repeated continually in their literature.'

The High Cost of Vengeance was Freda Utley's most controversial book, and one of the main reasons why she earned Lipstadt's attention. It was written after a long visit to occupied Germany, in which she argued that Allied policy towards Germany after 1945 was worse than what the Germans had done during the war: 'Compared with the rape and murder and looting engaged in by the Russian armies at the war's end, the terror and slavery and hunger and robbery in the Eastern zone today, and the genocide practised by the Poles and Czechs, the war crimes and crimes against humanity committee by the Germans condemned at Nuremberg to death or lifelong imprisonment appeared as minor in extent if not in degree. It was impossible to travel through the devastated towns of the Western zones without it seeming strange and horrible that we should sit in judgement on the Germans who had never succeeded in killing nearly so many civilians as we did, or in perpetrating worse atrocities than our obliteration bombing of whole cities. Were the German gas chambers really a greater crime against humanity than our attacks on such non-military objectives as Dresden. . . ?' As additional authority for this view she quotes the distinguished British soldier Major General J.F.C. Fuller, without mentioning that Fuller was also a top British fascist.

Her hatred of the Soviet Union scorches most of the pages. Stalin, she says, 'transformed Russia into a national socialist state' and was now 'wreaking a terrible vengeance on the whole German people for having followed its own National Socialist leaders instead of Russia's'. The USA and Britain went along with this, and 'the victors of World War II combined to despoil and enslave the Germans'. Stalin, she argues, was a far worse and more bloodthirsty dictator than Hitler. Hitler allowed many Jews to go abroad and tell the world about his atrocities. 'Hitler was a little less ruthless, or efficient, than Stalin in exterminating his enemies' – which (though she does not say this, or indeed mention her own experiences at all) must have contributed to her own sense of mission, as one of the few left alive to tell a first-hand tale of Stalin's atrocities.

Communists, Freda wrote, were now cynically using the Jews' hatred of Germany for their own ends, and manipulating Jewish opinion. Stalin was recruiting former Nazis for his secret police, 'welcomed into the ranks of their ideological brothers in the Communist Party'. She attacks, in the best McCarthyite style, 'the influential writers, radio commentators, professors and other moulders of public opinion who have allowed themselves to be influenced by the Communists, either because they are ignorant, or because they are ambitious, or because of the skill of the Communists in playing upon national and racial hatreds, and keeping alive the passions engendered by the recent war'.

The expulsion of millions of Germans from their homes was, she says, a crime against humanity, and 'the women and children who died of hunger and cold on the long trek from Silesia and the Sudetenland to what remained of the German Reich, may have thought that a quick death in a gas chamber would have been comparatively merciful'. This, perhaps, is the sentence which Deborah Lipstadt holds most strongly against her.

It's a remarkable book – detailed, passionate, the work of a top-class writer and researcher – yet, especially for those of us who know her story, in the end it tells us more about Freda herself than about public policy. And it narrowly fails to turn back at the border between criticising Allied policy towards Germany, and becoming an apologist for Nazi atrocities. It is the book of a woman whose soul was indelibly scarred by her own experiences in the Soviet Union.

As a journalist, she reported from China and denounced western policy for paving the way for communism, in work that was cited as authoritative in a 1948 report from McCarthy's House Un-American Activities Committee. In her later years she wrote an autobiography, *Odyssey of a Liberal*, and the *New York Times* review of it described her as 'thorny and indomitable . . . full of reproaches and resentments, possessed of acerbic wit, passionately didactic and remarkably readable'. (*Farnie*)

That book made it clear that she had transferred the bitter lessons she had learned in Moscow to other situations to which they were less obviously relevant. Thus she wrote: 'So many of those who now control the destiny of the newly independent states of Asia and Africa harbour the same illusions about socialism as I had in the twenties. Listening to Nehru in the fifties was like an echo of my own youth when I knew and understood as little about Communism as he did until the end of his life.'

She thought she understood communism's true nature because she had once been sufficiently committed to it to try living in the Soviet Union. People who stayed with communism had failed to put their beliefs to this ultimate test: 'it was precisely because they never fully committed themselves to the Communist cause that they continued to believe in it. Those of us who fully engage ourselves in the causes we believe in submit our ideals to the hard test of personal experience. By publicly professing our opinions, we risk being proved wrong, or being defeated, and having to take our punishment. But those who refrain from risking "their lives, their fortunes, and their sacred honour" in any cause . . . have no right to call themselves idealists or liberals.' (*Utley, Odyssey*)

She died in December 1978. Malcolm Muggeridge came from Britain to speak at her funeral. The son she had with Arcadi Berdichevsky, Jon Basil Utley, became a successful American businessman and was always close to her. In later years, as we shall find, his father's fate and his mother's convictions helped to bring him, too, to right-wing American politics.

* * *

So after 1956 Rose Cohen's friends knew she was dead, and Freda Utley knew that her beloved Arcadi was dead. They were not the only ones to learn the fate of their friends and lovers. As Khrushchev opened the doors, the truth came flooding out. It was a traumatic time for communists.

Phil Piratin, who had been the Communist MP for Mile End from 1945 until 1950, and in 1956 was a member of the party's Political Committee, remembered what happened in London in those years. Shortly before his death in the 1990s, Piratin told me: 'Sometimes at our political committee meetings after Stalin's death, Harry Pollitt would take from his pocket a piece of paper, and say that the Czech Ambassador or someone had given him the following names of people who had been – what was the word they used? Terrible word. Horrible word. Rehabilitated, that's it.' A terrible word, because if you had to be rehabilitated, you were generally dead. Many people did not know an old friend was dead until they heard that he or she had been rehabilitated.

Piratin remembered one of these occasions particularly vividly. He heard a Czech surname. 'I asked Harry to give us the full name. Harry just looked at me. My wife and I were friends with this man and his wife, they used to come to our house in Hampstead, we went to their flat in Kensington. Then in 1949, they were due to come over one night, and his wife phoned and said he'd been called away. A few weeks later my wife phoned the flat. There was a new voice, it said our friends had gone back to Prague. We never heard from them again. Now I knew why. They were not just comrades, they were friends. I was not sure whether to tell my wife. In the end I did tell her. Those things live with you, the look on my wife's face when I told her.'

Dozens of British idealists, perhaps hundreds, died or suffered in Russia at the hands of a regime which men like Harry Pollitt and Bill Rust defended to their last breath. Pollitt and Rust started their political life genuinely intending to make a better world, and ended up as apologists for a brutal dictator who tortured and murdered many millions, including some who were close friends of theirs. Yet to their dying day, neither of them ever lost their admiration for Stalin. Rust died in 1949, but for Pollitt, that meant holding on to his faith all the way to 1960, through all the Khrushchev revelations of 1956 and beyond. How can this be?

Maurice Cornforth, a young academic who had been at Cambridge with James Klugmann and the Cambridge spies Maclean, Burgess and Blunt, was on the party's Central Committee during the war. He took part in the impassioned debate about whether to follow the Comintern instruction to condemn the war now that Hitler and Stalin had cut a deal, and he voted for the Comintern resolution. He said: 'I believe that if one loses anything of that faith in the Soviet Union one is done for as a Communist and a Socialist.' (*King and Matthews*) Harry Pollitt believed that, too. At a meeting of Communist Party members in 1956 he was heckled, and shouted back from the platform: 'Defending the Soviet Union gives you a headache? You think I don't know that? All right – if it gives you a headache, take an aspirin.' (*Macleod*)

Pollitt had to swallow far more than just the treatment of the four women who are the main characters in this book. He knew of the deaths, and must have known of the torture, of dozens of people, of several nationalities, whom he had liked and admired, and he remained to his dying day an apologist for the man who was responsible for it all.

Pollitt, Bill Rust and the rest of their generation of communist leaders knew they had come desperately close to the terror – though Pollitt may never have known that he himself was, at the time of Rose Cohen's arrest, being fitted up for a place in the Lubyanka and a bullet. (Or did he know? Is that what Georgi Dimitrov told him in that private meeting in 1936, when Pollitt raised Rose's fate, when things were said which neither man ever revealed, but which Pollitt thought were so helpful?) The terror laid its hands on their lives in the 1930s and never let go. Pollitt's son Brian recalled for me a happy summer holiday at the home of a Czech friend of Harry's, Otto Sling. A year or more later, Brian, then sixteen, read in the newspaper that 'Uncle Otto' had been shot as a traitor. His father would tell him nothing about it, though we know now that he had gone despairingly to the Czech embassy to plead for Sling, just as he had pleaded for Max Petrovsky two decades earlier.

Petrovsky was far from being the only old friend of the British Communist Party to meet his end in the terror. His predecessor as the Comintern's man in London at the start of the 1920s had been Mikhail Borodin. Borodin, an old Jewish socialist, had survived prisons in Tsarist Russia and, during his time in Britain, had survived Glasgow's grim Birlinnie prison. But he was much older when he was sent to an Arctic concentration camp, and conditions there were too much for a man of seventy-seven.

In 1956, now aged twenty, Brian Pollitt went to Moscow with his father, and was there when a Soviet official told Harry that a British communist who had disappeared was now 'rehabilitated'.

'Rehabilitated?' said Pollitt. 'Is that all I am meant to tell his family?'

'What more can I say? That we are sorry?'

'That might help.'

But when a communist journalist came home from Czecho-slovakia and went to see Pollitt to tell him what he knew about the show trials, Pollitt looked heavily out of his office window for a long time, and then said: 'My advice to you is to forget all about it.' (*Beckett, Enemy Within*)

Pollitt at least felt visibly uncomfortable for a while after Khrushchev's speech. Not so Rajani Palme Dutt, the party's senior theoretician and often the only man in Britain apart from Bill Rust who was trusted in the Kremlin. Still editing the theoretical journal *Labour Monthly*, Dutt wrote of Stalin in April 1956, two months after Khrushchev's speech: 'That there should be spots on the sun would only startle an inveterate Mithras-worshipper. . . . To imagine that a great revolution can develop without a million cross-currents, hardships, injustices and excesses would be a delusion fit only for ivory-tower dwellers in fairyland who have still to learn that the thorny path of human advancement moves forward, not only through unexampled heroism, but also with accompanying baseness, with tears and blood.' It was a mark of changing times in the Communist Party that later in the year he was forced partially to withdraw this.

John Ross Campbell was one of Britain's top communists, the man whose leaflets aimed at British soldiers had triggered the events leading to the downfall of the first Labour government in 1924. He had taken over from Bill Rust as editor of the *Daily Worker* in 1931, and lost the job when, like Pollitt, he rebelled against the Comintern instruction to denounce Britain's war against Hitler. He became editor of the *Daily Worker* again after Bill Rust's death in 1949.

Campbell's oldest stepson William went to live in Moscow in the 1920s, and did not return to England until the 1970s. William's mother had five young children when her husband was killed in the First World War. After the war she married John Campbell, with whom she had three more children. She encouraged her oldest son to go to the Soviet Union and help build socialism, though, interestingly, John Campbell himself was not at all keen on the idea, saying that life was hard there.

So it proved; but William made his way in Russia, determined to show his stepfather that he could make it, and discovered that he had a talent as a circus clown, eventually performing with the Moscow State Circus as Villi the Clown. Then William Campbell did something that he afterwards called a 'mindless blunder': in 1939 he gave up British citizenship and applied to become a Soviet citizen. He was then banned for a while from appearing on stage because of his British origin. (*Campbell*)

He saw his closest friends disappearing into Moscow prisons and daily expected the same fate for himself. In fact, he did have a short spell in a Soviet jail, and it seems likely that John Campbell dashed to Moscow in 1952 and pleaded with Khrushchev, then an influential figure on the Central Committee but unknown outside the Soviet Union, to intervene and have him released. Oddly, William Campbell makes no mention of his imprisonment in his otherwise honest and comprehensive autobiography. John Campbell is thought to have privately lost his faith in the Soviet system some time during or after the Second World War. But with his stepson as a sort of hostage in the Soviet Union, he was not going to let anyone know of this.

When the storm of 1956 broke over the head of the Communist Party, John Campbell was still editing the *Daily Worker*, and it was his job to hold up the fast-shifting faith and morale of his journalists. He was hampered – so at least one of his staff, Alison Macleod, believed – by a gaping hole where his own faith had once been. He even found himself urging his younger and more enthusiastic colleagues not to minimise the injustices done to good revolutionary socialists, and perhaps he had Rose Cohen in mind when he said of William Gallacher: 'If Gallacher had been one of those unjustly condemned, I hope we'd have shed some tears for him.' When one of his journalists, Peter Fryer, told Campbell his faith had gone and he had to leave the paper, Campbell confessed to Fryer that he had been in Moscow during the purges and knew what was going on. But, he said, what could he do, when the war was on the way and the Soviet Union was certain to be attacked by Germany? This reasoning, of course, explains why the only time he and Harry Pollitt ever rebelled was when they were told to condemn the war against Hitler. The instruction made a mockery of their main reason for accepting the unacceptable. (*Macleod*)

William Campbell wrote in 1981 that, after 1956,

> for all his faults, Khrushchev did do something to ease the lot of the Russian people. At his initiative millions of political prisoners were released from the camps. At last we learned the fate of our many unfortunate friends and colleagues, those who had managed to survive and those who had gone to unknown graves. One after the other, the survivors, many of them famous, began to return. That splendid actress and singer, Ruth Kamenska, came back from exile in the Kazakhstan desert [we have some idea of what that must have been like from Rosa Rust's testimony]. The great folk singer and idol of the people, Lidia Ruslanova, was released from prison after five years. She rang us on the first morning of her arrival and spent the whole day with us. The news spread like wildfire and soon our room was packed with fellow artistes. . . . When she appeared on stage, dressed in her familiar Russian national costume, the audience rose to its feet and gave her an ovation lasting fifteen minutes. 'It's a protest' someone whispered. I thought grimly that not one person in the hall would have raised a finger to save Lidia from the horrible experience she had suffered. (*Campbell*)

A Communist icon from the 1930s, Len Wincott, suddenly reappeared in 1957. His story went back to 1931, when George Fles and Pearl Rimel were revelling in their first kiss beside the lake. That year, Able Seaman Wincott, a member of the crew of one of the British Navy's ships anchored in the Cromarty Firth, protested against a 25 per cent wage cut imposed by the government. He stood on the canteen table and told the others: 'We must strike, like the miners.' Wincott came from a poor family in Leicester. His father, a bricklayer, used to get drunk and beat his eight children, and there was seldom enough food in the house. Len Wincott grew up fearing life on the dole more than anything, and joining the navy seemed a way to avoid it. By the time of the so-called Invergordon Mutiny (Wincott always insisted it was not a mutiny but a strike) he had been in the navy for eight years.

The result of his speech was that sailors of the Atlantic Fleet agreed a strike resolution and several thousand men refused duty. The Admiralty acted swiftly: it reduced the size of the cuts, and it threw Wincott out of the navy. He joined the Communist Party. There were not many jobs around, and those that were available tended not to go to known communist troublemakers. So it looked as though his worst fears had been realised – he was condemned to life on the dole. But the Communist Party rescued him. He had a kind of heroic status among British communists, for the Invergordon Mutiny was seen as a brave but doomed revolutionary act. In 1934 the party sent him to the Soviet Union, where work was found for him in an international seamen's club in Leningrad, later at a bed-making factory, and then in a foreign languages college.

He was not caught up in the great purge of 1937–9 which saw the execution of Rose Cohen and Max Petrovsky. In 1941 when the Soviet Union entered the war, he was called up to be a private in the army and sent to Leningrad. So he endured the terrible German siege of Leningrad, and was awarded the Leningrad defence medal.

Then, on 14 April 1945, the secret police paid a call on him, and the next year he was sentenced to ten years' 'corrective labour'. Nine years later, on 18 December 1954, he was freed and sent into exile in Komi, in the frozen extreme north-east of Russia, where he worked in a coal mine. He was 'rehabilitated' and released in 1955, together with his Russian wife who had either been arrested with him, or whom he met in the camps – it is not clear which. They went to live in Moscow two years later. He had no permanent job, only occasional freelance work for the *Moscow News*, and was very short of money. (*RC 495/198/1321*)

But no one in Britain knew he had been released. Two years later John Campbell was in Moscow as head of a British Communist Party delegation, and according to his stepson William Campbell, 'he had been instructed to talk to no one at top level until he saw Len Wincott'. So 'he was informed that Len had been located and would be released'. (*Campbell*) Trotskyist Gerry Healy drew attention to Wincott's detention regularly. According to the often well-informed Trotskyist newspaper *The Newsletter*, published in Britain by Healy, British communist leaders were privately told in 1956 that Wincott had been released and to keep quiet about it. *The Newsletter* reported on 27 July and on 10 August 1957 that this was because 'rehabilitation of foreign communists was being done without publicity'. It claimed Wincott wrote to a London friend: 'What has been is to be forgotten. Besides books I don't need a thing so I have appealed to all my friends and well wishers in England to remember my address and that books come through without customs and other duties. My tastes range from "whodunnits" to Vergil.'

In London in April 1956, Soviet leader Nikita Khrushchev visited London, and was confronted by a demonstration, with banners reading 'Free Len Wincott'. This was the first most people in Britain knew of his disappearance. In his Moscow file there is this complaint: 'The bourgeois English press has published various slanderous articles, and not published Wincott's refutations.' To counter this, he was told to write an article for the *Daily Worker*. As a reward, he was given permission to visit England, as well as a permanent job with the Radio Committee to alleviate his considerable poverty. (*RC 495/198/1321*)

Wincott stayed in Russia with his Russian wife for the rest of his life, so he always had to be very careful what he said and wrote. His article in the *Daily Worker* of 12 September 1957 said:

I fell victim to the wave of suspicion of foreigners provoked by Beria. [Criticising Beria was safe; he had been shot.] I was secretly arrested and sent to prison on a trumped-up charge. Release and rehabilitation came for me when the power of Beria and his lot was broken, and the Communist Party and the Soviet government set about righting the wrongs that had been done.

I returned to Moscow, where I now live and work, mostly writing and teaching English. I know from my own experience that the comrades here over these past few years have been working might and main to help the innocent to make the return voyage to normal life. The steps which have been taken are, in my opinion, a firm guarantee in themselves that such things can never recur.

Of course, what happened when it happened, was hard to take. But I have no use for desertion, especially desertion under fire. Communism is my ship and she, and I with her, have not had an easy passage. But the harbour lights are shining brightly, the party is piloting us around the mole, and I am keeping right on to the end.

There are those in Britain today who want to use my experience as ammunition in the cold war as a means of whipping up anti-Communist feeling. To that I say, 'I abhor your crocodile tears and I greet your hypocrisy with the contempt it deserves.' To all good friends at home, I am glad to assure them, through the *Daily Worker*, that all is well, very well, with Len Wincott.

He was back in Britain again in 1974 to promote his book *Invergordon Mutineer*. He made it clear that he had nothing he wished to say about his life in the Soviet Union, and at a press conference to launch the book he warned that he would walk out if anyone asked about anything other than his life in Britain. (*Turner*) But he is said to have quietly told an old friend, Joe Jacobs, that no one knew the half of what had happened to him in Russia and that one day the story would come out. And, asked by a journalist if he regretted doing what he did at Invergordon, he said: 'When I got a little older I found out what Jesus Christ found out 2,000 years ago – that helping humanity is a farce.' (*Carew*)

A clearer picture emerges from William Campbell. 'He told me he had given up hope of ever leaving the coal mines. There were hundreds of thousands of prisoners and the one plane a day could only take about a dozen at a time. Suddenly he was awakened in the night by a bang on the door of his basement room and told to pack his belongings as a special plane had arrived to take him and his wife to Moscow.' Wincott said to Campbell: 'I should have signed the "confession" that I was the leader of an international spy organisation on the first day after my arrest. I had to sign it anyway, a year later, after they had systematically beaten hell out of me.' (*Campbell*) But if he had signed it, they would probably have shot him.

In the years after Patrick Breslin's death in a Soviet slave labour camp in Kazan in 1942, the daughter he never saw, Mairead Breslin-Kelly, has slowly learned the terrible details of what happened to him. Breslin, an Irishman born in 1907, firmly rejected the Catholicism of his parents and joined the Communist Party of Ireland at fifteen. The party sent him to the International Lenin School in Moscow, from which he was expelled in 1930 because he had become more interested in eastern philosophy than in communism, and because he rejected dialectical materialism. But he was invited to stay on as a translator for the school administration and, by now a fluent Russian speaker, he taught English for the Comintern and got some commissions to translate Russian literature. He also worked under Rose Cohen at the *Moscow Daily News*, and married a Russian woman, Katja, who worked in the Japanese section of the espionage department of the NKVD, with whom he had two children.

Katja was constantly confronted by her superiors at the NKVD with the nagging question: why did her husband not take Soviet citizenship? So in 1936, he did. But later the same year he left Katja, having fallen in love with Daisy McMacken, a Belfast Republican who was working in Moscow as a linguist. He married Daisy, she became pregnant and, rather like Pearl Rimel, went home in 1937 to give birth to Mairead.

Patrick tried to retrieve his British citizenship so that he could go back to Ireland and be with Daisy. But the British Consulate made difficulties about this, eventually telling him he could only have British citizenship back if the Soviet government permitted him to renounce Soviet citizenship. Then, early in 1938, Katja was arrested as part of an internal NKVD purge, and Patrick with help from Katja's parents looked after the two children. Patrick was arrested just before Christmas 1940 and underwent more than fifty nocturnal interrogations. He was sentenced to eight years in the Gulag. Already a sick man, he died soon after his arrival at the slave labour camp in Kazan. (*McLoughlin*)

Mairead has now been able to see transcripts of some of Patrick's interrogation; as the nearest living relative she was, like Thijs Berman, allowed access after much badgering. Like George Fles's, they make terrible reading.

Question: The investigation has precisely established that, living in the USSR, you were involved in espionage and received your tasks straight from foreign intelligence. Are you going to tell the truth?
Answer: I am telling the truth. I am not a spy and never received any tasks from any intelligence . . .
Question: Investigation has disclosed your connection with other Irish Parties [apart from the Communist Party of Ireland]. I suggest you give truthful statements.
Answer: I didn't have connections with other political parties. However, answering the previous question, I didn't state that I knew a member of the Irish bourgeois party Sinn Fein, Alex Lean.
Question: Is Sinn Fein a fascist party?
Answer: Sinn Fein is a bourgeois Irish party. I know nothing about Sinn Fein's programme after 1932 . . .
Question: You admit that your philosophical views are hostile to the materialist teaching of the Communist Party. Why then, being an ideological enemy of Marxism–Leninism, did you join the Communist Party?
Answer: I joined the Communist Party, being an ideological enemy of Marxism–Leninism, because due to my low ideological and political level of awareness, I didn't know that a materialist outlook is an inseparable basis of the programme . . .

Question: Do you admit that in September of this year you started singing loudly the English national anthem 'God Save the King' in the cocktail hall?

Answer: Yes, I admit. I was very drunk at the time.

Question: You know very well that the USSR has a friendly relationship with Germany, the enemy of England in the present war. Do you admit that your singing of the English national anthem in public under these conditions has a definite provocative meaning?

Answer: Objectively, yes. I admit that my singing of the English national anthem in public had a provocative character. But I didn't have provocative aims. I was drunk and didn't know what I was doing . . . (*Burke*)

George Hanna, another Briton, was arrested in the late 1940s and released in 1967. Hanna told his interrogators that Harry Pollitt would vouch for him. They looked up Pollitt in a little black book, and told him that Pollitt was a British Intelligence agent too. (*IoS 8/9/1992*) There were many more British victims of the Stalin terror. We do not know exactly how many.

* * *

Harry Pollitt never knew it, but 1956, and the Khrushchev revelations, marked the end of the party he had given his life to build. Later that year, Soviet tanks rolled into Budapest, and this seemed to confirm the impression of communism given by the Khrushchev revelations. The *Daily Worker* censored the reports of the invasion from its own man on the spot, Peter Fryer, because they were too accurate and made the Soviet invasion sound as brutal as it really was. The same year also, ironically, saw the British government's worst postwar crisis so far, Prime Minister Anthony Eden's foolish and botched invasion of Suez. In other circumstances this might have been an opportunity for communists. But then the invasion of Hungary and the revelations about Stalin ensured that it was in no position to take advantage of it. (*Macleod*)

Pollitt had worked so hard, and so successfully, to make it the only party on the left, and now, having stifled the Independent Labour Party to death and marginalised the Trotskyists, the Communist Party was consigned to long-term irrelevance. Seven thousand people left the party, more than a quarter of its membership. Its wealthy backers – mostly Jewish business leaders who saw it as a bulwark against anti-Semitism – deserted it as it became clear that Stalin's government had been, among many other things, brutally anti-Semitic.

The last word on 1956 goes to the two great new playwrights of the mid-1950s. In *Look Back in Anger*, John Osborne's hero Jimmy Porter describes how, as a boy, he watched his father die a lingering, painful death from wounds received while fighting for the Republicans in the Spanish Civil War, the Communist Party's finest hour, and shouts: 'There aren't any good, brave causes left.' The good, brave causes that communists had taken up in the 1920s and '30s – democracy in Spain was just one of them – had been tarred by the brutality of Stalin's regime, and the struggle between good and evil had become a struggle to distinguish good from evil. The legacy that the 1930s bequeathed to the 1950s was that nothing was simply a good, brave cause any more.

Arnold Wesker was brought up in a Jewish communist family in London's East End, with a mother and an aunt who had loyally supported the party through thick and thin, and who were the models for his first and greatest three plays, the Wesker Trilogy. The third of the trilogy, *Chicken Soup with Barley*, has the matriarch Sarah Kahn (modelled on Wesker's own mother) listening with horror to her daughter saying: 'How many friends has the party lost because of lousy, meaningless titles they gave to people. He was a bourgeois intellectual, he was a trotskyist, he was a reactionary social democrat. Whisht! Gone!' And a young man tells her: 'The whole committee of the Jewish Anti-Fascist League were shot! Shot, Sarah! In our land of socialism. That was our land – what a land that was for us. We didn't believe the stories then; it wasn't possible that it could happen in our one-sixth of the world.'

In 1956, then aged twenty-four, Wesker wrote his thoughts in a notebook, and unearthed them and sent them to me forty years later:

The Communist Parties of the world and especially of Britain suddenly found that Stalin and his policy which they once praised was now in disgrace; that the men they once criticised as reactionaries and traitors were not so; that the men whose deaths they once condoned were in fact innocent. There has been a fantastic spate of letters in the *Daily Worker* from Party members who are virtually in tears that they had ever been so lacking in courage. . . . It is as though they had all gone to a mass confessional and with terrible secrets in their heart now out in the open they feel new people . . .

But Leah, my mother . . . does not know what has happened, what to say or feel or think. She is at once defensive and doubtful. She does not know who is right. To her the people who once criticised the party and were called traitors are still traitors despite that the new attitude suggests this is not the case. And this is Leah. To her there was either black or white, communists or fascists. There were no shades . . .

If she admits that the party has been wrong, that Stalin committed grave offences, then she must admit that she has been wrong. All the people she so mistrusted and hated she must now have second thoughts about, and this she cannot do – because having bound her politics so closely to her personality she must then confess a weakness in her personality. You can admit the error of an idea but not the conduct of a whole life.

EIGHT

Rosa in Redcar

The year 1956 brought no obvious benefits for the Thornton family except to feed George and Rosa's growing certainty that the Communist Party was not the answer.

George could no longer hope for a career as an academic historian, though anyone who talked about history with him could tell that he would have been well suited to one. This was almost certainly the result of his early association with communism and with Rosa. Rosa herself had lost her job in 1951, the year her first child was born, because she worked for the Soviet news agency Tass, whose London office was closed by the Foreign Office in a bout of cold war hysteria.

Rosa's father Bill Rust was dead, and her mother Kay was not in a position to help them financially. For the Communist Party they were an embarrassment, a reminder not only of the working-class hero Bill Rust's peccadilloes but also of the terrible things that had happened in the Soviet Union. They were not on speaking terms with Bill's widow Tamara, who had tried so hard to airbrush them from history. (*Thornton*)

It looks as though Kay made an effort to get the party to help the family. She put up with the petty humiliations heaped on her because of the party's desire to forget all about her and to pretend that Bill Rust had only ever been married to Tamara Kravets. She changed her name, and was known for the rest of her life as Kath

159

Taylor, apparently to save the party and Bill Rust embarrassment. When the splendid new *Daily Worker* building in Farringdon Street which Bill had planned was finally opened, shortly after Bill's death, and named William Rust House, she was told firmly by the editor, John Campbell, that neither she nor Rosa would be welcome at the opening ceremony, since Tamara would be there as Bill's widow. It was a snub that she and Rosa felt very deeply.

In the wake of the revelations of 1956, she wrote to John Gollan, who had just taken over from Harry Pollitt as the party's general secretary. She began by emphasising her continuing loyalty: 'At the time when one reads of resignations of "leading" members of the party, as a very humble member of the party I want to re-affirm my belief and loyalty to the cause of Communism. What kind of Communists are they who fall before the first major onslaught. . . .'

Then she dwelt on her own 'personal tragedies caused by Party leaders both here and in the Soviet Union'. The 'murder of my husband' (the Russian Misha, whom she had married after Bill went off with Tamara, and who had become a victim of the purges) 'and his subsequent complete rehabilitation as a true Communist did not for one moment shake me in my belief'. But 'the in-humanity displayed towards my daughter and myself in connection with Bill Rust disgusted me beyond measure and I shall never forget or forgive that episode. . . . The one thing you all forgot was that Rosa was Bill's daughter and nothing could alter that fact, and she asked to be allowed to be present at the unveiling of his plaque at the *Daily Worker* and was told personally by Mr Campbell that "she was to stay away as she was not wanted – it was Tamara's wish". I could have told all of you that it certainly would not have been Bill's wish as he was very attached to his daughter. . . . It is seven years and more since Bill Rust died and I was subjected to a stupid attitude.'

Only one party leader, William Gallacher, had tried, unsuccessfully, to reason with Tamara about Kay's daughter, and he had been unsuccessful, so the party had turned its back on Rosa. 'The result has been, I feel, a certain guilt about Rosa and me.' She had not felt able to speak to Campbell, or Gollan, or Pollitt, since the incident. 'Perhaps it was not very important to you, but I can tell you that it shocked quite a number of people apart from myself and my daughter.'

But even this 'did not prevent Rosa and myself from remaining Communists . . .'. This was not quite true: Rosa at least had had enough of the Communist Party by then. 'The movement and the party cannot and will never be condemned by either of us simply because some of its present leaders fail in their personal attitudes towards people.'

The terrible events of that year – Khrushchev's revelations, the Soviet invasion of Hungary – did not shake her belief either, she claimed. 'It will be good riddance to the deserters', provided 'our leaders are true leaders and learn from the tragic mistakes which have caused the blood of thousands upon thousands of fine men and women to be shed.' And, she said, she was not convinced the party had leaders who could learn the lessons. 'Let it be the leaders who look into their own consciences and admit where they have gone wrong.'

She had not felt able to speak to the party's leaders for some time, but now she was making the effort to do so. 'We must not look too much on the past except to learn from it and avoid a repetition of its mistakes. . . . That is why I am writing this letter to you. It has cost me a great effort as you might appreciate. But at this moment when there are a number of defaulters I want to reaffirm my belief and loyalty.' She was probably trying to get some help for her daughter from the party which, though she did not say so, she blamed for the precarious situation in which Rosa found herself. If so, she was disappointed. Gollan passed it to someone else in the office with a despairing note on the top: 'What can I do about this?' The answer, presumably, was: nothing. (*Morgan*)

So Rosa did what hard-up young mothers sometimes have to do. After all the horrors she had suffered in the Soviet Union, she suffered the mundane misery of a hard-up wife and mother in Britain: she and her husband and baby went to live with her parents-in-law in Stockton, and George searched for work.

For a short time he had a job in Africa, which paid well, but he hated the job and hated being away from his family, and the egalitarian socialist in him was revolted by the way the company treated its African staff. One day he intervened when a more senior employee was whipping an African; the situation turned ugly, and George was fired and had to pay for his own flight home.

From George's parents' Stockton home George and Rosa moved to a rented flat in Saltburn, where David went to school, then to Middlesbrough, and finally to Redcar. They had three more children. George worked as a laboratory technician for ICI before, in middle age, becoming a civil servant in the Department of Social Security, where he was made responsible for investigating social security fraud. A less suitable job for this gentle, sensitive socialist it would be hard to imagine, and his working life ended in a nervous breakdown after he got into trouble at work because his conviction rate was slipping badly. This enabled him to get early retirement on medical grounds, after which he studied for and took A-levels in English and Russian.

George and Rosa's passion was drama. With different breaks, Rosa could have made a fine professional actor. She knew it, too. Once, in her fifties, she decided to try to change their lives, and travelled to London to enrol in the E17 drama school to train for the stage; but the cost of staying in London eventually drove her back to the north-east. For twenty years they were the mainstays of their local drama group, where, according to their son David, they were considered 'talented but weird'. (*Thornton*)

When I met George and Rosa in 1995, they talked with excitement and passion about the productions they took to the Edinburgh Festival: their *Antigone* which had the drama critic of the *Scotsman* in tears, their *Schweik*, their *Midsummer Night's Dream*, which was packed out every night and in which they played Oberon and Titania and David played Bottom. They also performed *A Midsummer Night's Dream* in the grounds of Guisborough Hall. Rosa brought a great passion to this scheme, saying to the others: 'We must do this.'

She could still get just as animated about it years later. '"So is mine eye enthralled to thy shape, And thy fair virtue's force perforce doth move me" – that's very hard for a foreigner to say, you know',

Rosa told me in her strong clear voice, her Russian accent adding to rather than detracting from the effect of Shakespeare's words. For a foreigner is what she always was, and how she always thought of herself: a woman whose formative experiences all took place in Russia; who learned to speak English when she was already almost grown up; whose great, strong, multi-layered voice always had more feeling and variation in it than the average English person thinks is quite proper; and whose grandchildren called her Babu, short for babushka, the Russian for grandmother.

George, by contrast, seemed, on the cold autumn day when I visited them in 1995, to be quintessentially English: a retired civil servant with a quiet voice and a neat moustache discreetly covering the nakedness of his upper lip.

By then they had lived in or near the small seaside town of Redcar for three decades. When not reciting poetry, they played the music they both loved, and walked by the sea, and talked of cricket and of their four grown-up children and five grandchildren: George in his light, dry, quietly humorous voice, Rosa with great, gay Russian-sounding gusts of poetry and laughter. Music bound George and Rosa together, especially the music of Brahms, Mozart and Beethoven, and they taught their children their own love of poetry, and very early on the whole family could laugh at the work of Ogden Nash:

> Children aren't happy with nothing to ignore,
> And that's what parents were created for.

Or:

> Weep not for little Leonie
> Abducted by a French Marquis.
> Though loss of honour was a wrench
> Just think how it's improved her French.

In the summer, in their retirement, they sometimes took a cheap package holiday to Bulgaria, where Rosa could speak Russian. She would have loved to show George St Petersburg, but their pension, diminished by George's early retirement, never stretched to it.

On one of these holidays, in 1984 during the British miners' strike, she traced a man she had been at school with, and with whom she shared a love of music. 'It was as though we had never parted', she told me. 'As children we used to play duets together, and he took me to his flat and about five minutes after we were playing duets together. He said he was gobbled up by the Bulgarian Communist Party, his life was arranged, he never married. There was the confirmation that my life before England did happen, did exist.' George said quietly: 'I found out who she was', and smiled his charming, understated, English smile. She and her friend went on Bulgarian radio together. The announcer asked: 'Have you any message for the Bulgarian people?' Rosa said: 'Yes, why are you allowing your coal to cross National Union of Mineworkers picket lines?' (*Rust*)

But in all those years stretching to decades, they had no contact with their old British communist friends. When, in the early 1990s, I was working on my history of British communism, I talked to the archivists who were preparing the party's papers for the scrutiny of posterity, to historians working on the papers, and to elderly communists who remembered Bill Rust. None of them knew anything about Rosa, apart from vague rumours from a long time ago. Many of them thought Bill Rust only ever had one wife, the Russian Tamara Kravets.

In 1967 George and Rosa's oldest son David, then sixteen, ran away from school one day, went to London, and found his way to William Rust House, the splendid *Daily Worker* office in Farringdon Road which his grandfather had had built with money from the Soviet Union. He marched into the newsroom. 'I'm Bill Rust's grandson', he told the bemused reporters. Eventually they believed him. 'How's Tamara?' they asked. Angrily, the teenage boy told them he had never met Tamara and never wished to. He knew exactly what his mother thought of Tamara.

'I always saw Bill Rust as a working-class hero', says David. 'I did not blame him for being a Stalinist. He practised the politics of the time.' Disgusted by what he knew of the Communist Party but equally by what he saw of poverty in the north-east, David joined a Trotskyist sect, the International Socialists, now known as the Socialist Workers' Party. George talked to him about that. He said that, even though the Communist Party was not what he had hoped for, Trotskyist organisations were not to be trusted – they had a hidden agenda. But how many of us take political advice from our fathers? David told George that Trotskyism was the original socialist flame, which had been perverted by the Communist Party. George, says David, was more of a political thinker than Rosa. His mother was anti-fascist and anti-racist but generally against governments and bureaucracies. David went to Essex University in 1970, attracted there by its radical reputation, to study modern literature, and he now works as a sub-editor on the features desk at the *Daily Mirror*. (*Thornton*)

Until I turned up on her doorstep late in 1995, Rosa had almost forgotten that she had a history worth telling. So complete was her disappearance that what remained of the British Communist Party (it had formally dissolved in 1991 amid bitter ideological disputes) had forgotten about her – even though the shadow of the Communist Party and the British Foreign Office hung over George and Rosa throughout their married life together.

Earlier that year I had published my book about British communism, which included such brief, sketchy information about her as I had been able to assemble without knowing where she was, or even whether she was alive. But soon after the book came out, I received some exciting news.

Alison Macleod had worked on the *Daily Worker* in the 1950s, and had left the Communist Party after 1956. In her eighties, she wrote a remarkable book describing the day-to-day events and discussions in the *Daily Worker* office as the appalling events of 1956 unfolded. She had kindly lent me the manuscript while I worked on my book. It has since been published, and is one of the most lucid and exciting descriptions ever written of the lethal mixture of idealism and cynicism that went to make up British communism. (*Macleod*)

165

Alison was determined to track Rosa down, and she had at last succeeded. She had an address in Redcar to give me. I spent a happy day in George and Rosa's small flat in the run-down north-east seaside town, drinking wine while George and I listened to Rosa: to her extraordinary life, to her deep, clear voice full of huge, happy, Russian-sounding gusts of poetry and laughter, to her natural mimicry and the way she could re-create a long dead human being before your eyes. I could happily have listened to her for days. Afterwards I wrote an article about her for the *Independent on Sunday*, and the actress Anna Calder-Marshall read it and got in touch with Rosa. She too made the pilgrimage to Redcar; she too was captivated, convinced that the world had lost a great actress with wonderful stage presence, and she toyed with the idea of creating a one-woman play for herself about Rosa's life, but feels now that 'no one could play Rosa except Rosa herself'.

I never saw Rosa again. Once I planned to look in on my way from London to Scotland, but ran out of time. Once she and George were in London staying with their son David, and had promised to come to Sunday lunch, to which I had invited a Russian-speaking friend – I pretended that was for Rosa's benefit, but the truth was that I wanted very much to hear Rosa speaking Russian. That weekend, her mother Kay, then living in Ireland and in her nineties, died, and Rosa had to cancel lunch and go to Ireland. She promised to come next time she was in London.

Early in 2000 I came home to hear a message on my answering machine. A shaky, tearful voice introduced the speaker as 'George Thornton, from Redcar – perhaps you remember my wife Rosa' as though it was possible to forget Rosa. Then he burst into tears, and just about managed to tell my unresponsive answering machine the terrible news.

Rosa died on 2 April 2000, a few days before her seventy-fifth birthday. George, who had seemed perfectly fit until then, outlived her by just two years. They had shared their passions for justice and music, socialism and cricket, racial equality and Shakespeare, through hardship and a persecution no less intense because it could not be proved or identified, for fifty-one years.

NINE

Shadows in a World after Communism

In 1991 the Moscow correspondent for Dutch radio, Thijs Berman, was covering one of the key events of the twentieth century, the fall of the Soviet Union. He saw the unsuccessful coup against Soviet leader Mikhail Gorbachev in August, and Gorbachev's resignation on Christmas Day, which marked the end of the Soviet Union.

But he also spent some time in Georgia, and there he found himself investigating the history of the regime which in Moscow had been dying before his eyes. Like the other former Soviet republics, Georgia – Stalin's own homeland – was breaking away from the loose-knit federation which had succeeded the Soviet Union. But this brought with it some vicious ethnic conflicts, and it was these that brought Berman to the Georgian capital, Tbilisi.

Like Rose Cohen sixty years earlier, he was surprised at how much alcohol the Georgians seemed able to drink, and how well it greased their social life. In the restaurant of his hotel, men drank at least two bottles of Georgian white wine each during dinner, then sang, in tune, standing around the table. Those who could not stand up straight any more would sing from their chairs, or fall asleep with their heads on their arms amid the dirty plates and empty bottles and glasses.

Berman took the opportunity to go to the KGB building in Tbilisi and try to clear up a mystery that he knew had troubled his grandmother all her life. What had happened to her baby brother,

George Fles, in this grim building nearly sixty years ago? The huge electric steel door clanged shut behind Berman and his interpreter. He told the KGB archivist about his grandmother's brother:

He was an idealist, a Dutch communist who came to the Soviet Union at the beginning of the thirties to help set up the socialist system. The family never knew exactly what happened to him, but at some point in 1936 George was arrested here in Tbilisi. We don't know why. They sent parcels from the Netherlands to the prison in Smolensk where he served his time. There was always a confirmation of receipt with his signature, until one day a parcel came back with a note that the addressee was no longer in that prison. Then his parents assumed that he was dead. That was in 1938 and nobody has heard anything of or from him ever since. He had an English wife with whom he had lived here in Tbilisi. She became pregnant and travelled to London to give birth. He was going to follow her later, but before he could leave he was arrested. The baby, a boy, never met his father. We would like to finalise this history now, not to be able to accuse anyone, but just to know the whole story and to understand what happened to him.

The archivist looked at him with sad, frightened eyes. A Dutchman you say, your grandmother's brother? And he went down due to the repression? Yes, horrible things happened back then. Every day people drop by to ask about relatives. Please give me his name and call me tomorrow, then I can tell you if there is anything about him in the files.

The next day, Berman acquired a powerful ally. In his professional capacity, he had been granted an interview with the then Georgian president, Zviad Gamsakhurdia, and afterwards, as he turned off his tape recorder and stood up to leave, he asked Gamsakhurdia if he was going to open the KGB files. Yes, said the president, but with precautions, because the files contained dangerous information. 'People could kill each other because of it.' Berman asked if Gamsakhurdia could see to it that he had access to the files of his

Dutch great-uncle? The grim Georgian leader thawed, for the first time in the interview, and a tired smile appeared on his face: 'Yes, I can. Give me his name and other details.' Perhaps Gamsakhurdia remembered that, back in the late 1970s, he had himself seen the inside of Georgian prisons as a result of 'anti-Soviet activities'. Berman got to him just in time: within months Gamsakhurdia had been ousted in a military coup and replaced by Eduard Shevardnadze, and in 1993 he was either killed or committed suicide when surrounded by Shevardnadze's soldiers.

Gamsakhurdia's intervention ensured that the file was quickly found, and Berman went back to the KGB building, past sound proofed doors, covered in artificial leather fastened by studs, along granite-floored corridors, until the archivist, David Chikhladze, opened one of the heavy doors and led him and his interpreter into a bare room containing a wooden desk, a table, four chairs, and a cupboard, which Chikhladze unlocked. It was empty except for three folders which he put on the table. The paper was thin, the blue covers were fading from age, and on the cover were the letters NKVD and the words 'To keep forever'. The three folders together were almost ten centimetres thick. As Chikhladze undid the ribbons, Berman felt as though he was opening a grave.

Berman was not allowed to photocopy the pages, but his interpreter was permitted to read them into Berman's tape recorder. Chikhladze tried to be helpful, but did not want to speak when he could be picked up on tape, so he gestured for the recorder to be turned off before he said: 'Initially there were two accusations against your forefather. He was suspected of espionage and of distributing Trotskyist literature among the Soviet population. The investigation was focused on these two accusations but they were never able to prove that he was a spy. That accusation therefore was not included in the file later on. In the end he was convicted for the distribution of Trotskyite literature.'

He told them that George Fles was regarded as a dangerous prisoner who had to be separated from the other prisoners, for they might tell him about others involved in the Trotskyist conspiracy which they thought they had discovered in Tbilisi.

In the second folder were two prison photos. Berman had never seen a picture of George. He wrote afterwards:

Now he suddenly looked me in the face with a striking similarity to my own father. A young man with a lively, tanned face. He looks seriously at the camera with a frown between his heavy eyebrows. He squeezes his dark eyes a little, because he is tired or maybe because of the lamp which stands next to the camera and is reflected in his eyes. He wears a knitted jersey with a closed zipper and a coarsely woven shirt. His thick dark hair is combed backwards in a mop and on his jaw grows a beard of a week. There is a hint of a cynical yet sad smile around his lips. He probably feels the look of his accusers in the camera and he looks back at them seriously and honestly as if he wants to convince them of his loyalty to the Soviet State. 'I have nothing to hide', those eyes say, but one can tell by his swollen eyelids he hasn't slept well for days. He has crossed his arms and his fingertips just fall within the frame. On the other picture he is in profile and looks calmer, more withdrawn. A bit hunched up.

The last page was a modern sheet of paper, a form, completed in ink and dated October 25 1989. It described George as a translator and literary editor, and it said: 'Fles, George Louievich, is entitled to article 1 of the decree of the praesidium of the Supreme Soviet of the USSR, dd. 16 January 1989 regarding additional settlements concerning rehabilitation of victims of the oppression which took place during the thirties, the forties and the fifties.'

They had rehabilitated George, along with 100,000 other victims of the Georgian NKVD, under a decree formulated by Mikhail Gorbachev in 1989.

The next day, Berman telephoned his grandmother in her old people's home in Groningen. He told her that he had seen George's file, and broadly what he had read in it. He tried to spare her feelings by making it sound normal and clinical. Doing this reminded him of the way his own father always talked of the

Holocaust, and of his relatives being 'taken away' by the Nazis – never 'sent to the death camps'.

She heard in silence what had happened to her little brother George, the late arrival who, in his family, was known by the pet name of Sjoppie. Berman, as he spoke, imagined her in her armchair, one hand on her lap and a book on the table next to her, and perhaps a cup of coffee with a lot of milk. *De Rotterdammer* would be there as well, folded open at the crossword. When he had told her what he knew, she thanked him. She said that although it was hard to hear the story, it was a relief that the uncertainty had ended.

But he only had the highlights from the mountain of papers about George. Eventually, after persistent badgering, the Georgian KGB gave Berman permission to photocopy the entire file. By then it was 1992, the Soviet Union had fallen apart, and Berman was busy in Moscow reporting for his radio station on this most unstable newly capitalist state. It was not until October that Berman could get away from Moscow and return to Tbilisi.

By then, his old contact President Gamsakhurdia had been driven out of Georgia and taken refuge in Chenya, after a short but furious civil war. Tbilisi was a smoking ruin. Berman rang the archivist David Chikhladze, who told him the files were still there, but told him to bring his own copier and paper.

He boarded an aeroplane, a copier at his feet, and in his rucksack, 2,000 sheets of paper. He also took a bag full of presents, in case he ran into bandits, for Georgia in 1991 was a dangerous place. But in war-torn Tbilisi, Thijs Berman learned that the archives had been completely destroyed in the civil war.

His journey was not wasted, though. He found out that George Fles's last employer, Yevgeny Kharadze, the director of the observatory where Fles had worked until his arrest, was still alive, aged eighty-five. He went to see him.

Kharadze was a distinguished Georgian academic, a powerful figure in Tbilisi University. They spoke in English. Kharadze said he remembered George Fles well. 'I am very grateful to him because he helped me a lot. I think it was 1936. You see, right at that time we were visited by a famous American astronomer, Professor Mentzel.

171

We organised a banquet for him and Mr Fles wrote a brilliant speech for me. I remember that he spoke English very well, which doesn't mean much on its own. It means more if you are able to write a beautiful speech. So I remember him very well.'

He fell silent, and at last he said: 'Then Mr. Fles disappeared suddenly and I don't recall the details of his disappearance. . . . Do you know what happened to him? Did he return to his home country? Do you know anything about it?'

Berman was sure the old man was lying. He said: 'Yes, I know where he went. He was arrested on August 26 1936 and died in 1939 in a camp near Smolensk.' This, Kharadze insisted, was news to him. 'He disappeared and we didn't know anything. It happened so often in those days. One day he worked for us, the next day he had disappeared and we didn't know anything, nothing at all.'

Kharadze is one of those men you find in leading positions throughout what was once the Soviet Union: one who has learned to keep his head down, to survive, to adapt to fast-changing political circumstances. They are the reason why there is a sort of continuity in Russian government. The Tsars fell in 1917, but their Kharadzes remained and embraced communism. Stalin died in 1953 and the Kharadzes adapted to a country that had lost its appetite for blood. The Soviet Union fell in 1991 and the Kharadzes became apostles of capitalism, in many cases staying in the same jobs. Vicars of Bray have their uses if you want an administrative structure to survive a revolution. And Kharadzes tend not to dwell on unpleasantness in the past.

'Mr Fles', he told Berman 'was an active, lively man. Very accurate. Very warm towards his colleagues. A very gentle, positive man. He was a good story-teller, always added something interesting to discussions. We were sorry he left, but we didn't know why and how.' Did Kharadze think he might be arrested himself? 'No, because you see, I was sure that all people who were arrested were guilty. So I remained calm. I was convinced I was innocent. Why would they arrest me?'

Berman went to the cell where George had been kept. On the dark blue metal doors of the cells, heavy locks were welded with irregular ironwork, giving them a medieval appearance. It was a large cell, with five bunk beds without mattresses, a tap and a tiny sink, and a hole in the floor for a toilet, from which an all-enveloping smell emerged. It was exactly the same as when George Fles occupied it. '*Nitchevo garochevo*', said one of the guards. 'Not very good. It is better to avoid this place.'

Berman went to London, to Pearl Rimel's sister Hetty Bower, to tell her all he knew, and see what she could tell him. He found Hetty in a middle-class North London suburb with her husband, Reg Bower: a left-wing Jewish family very like his Fles relatives in Amsterdam. They had stayed in the British Communist Party until it fell apart in 1991. They still had a strong sense of loyalty to it, and before telling Berman anything, they wanted to know his political purpose. Was he out to blacken the name of communism? He tried to reassure them that he was not. He wanted to show how idealists from the early twentieth century had fared, and to save a family member who died in vain from oblivion. Hetty said that books had political effects, and perhaps Thijs should have thought more about that.

But Hetty and Reg Bower warmed to Thijs Berman, and they helped him as far as they could. For years Hetty and Reg had not talked about George Fles. They never discussed him after the Fles family was told by the Soviet authorities to stop sending money or parcels, for then they were sure he was dead. Pearl, said Hetty, kept hoping that George was working somewhere in Siberia as a convict and would return one day. Every time an unexpected visitor rang her doorbell she half-expected it would be him.

And Berman took to the Bowers. He even envied them their innocence, the way they still believed in the coming of a better world. He told them that the interrogators stopped handing over Pearl's letters to George shortly before the birth of the baby. Hetty slowly shook her head: 'Why did they have to be so cruel?' And then – the words of a lifelong socialist – 'No wonder we have to start all over again now.'

He asked if they had ever thought George was a Trotskyist. 'Perhaps', said Reg, 'he had listened to their arguments. I would have done that, without agreeing with them at once. You want to know what they have to say. But . . .'

His wife interrupted, and told her husband: 'You actually said in those days: why did George leave the Netherlands, go to Germany; why did he join in with the Young Communists over there and later again in France and England? At first sight it was exactly what someone who wanted to spy would do.'

And then Reg said carefully: 'In my opinion the revolution was a continuing process and there were external attempts to interrupt that process. That is why I was prepared to accept much of what was happening or at least to understand a number of the reasons. Besides that the only information that we got was what they were willing to give us – I believed that they might have had something against George of which I was not aware. But I did not have any certainty.'

Hetty said: 'We never believed that he was a spy. We thought they had arrested him because he had been tactless to a party boss, that he had called some bigwig 'incompetent' or 'mad'. We knew he was capable of that, because tact wasn't his strongest feature and he wouldn't ask himself if he could say something like that. He was too honest for that – he was a very open and honest man. So we assumed that he had unwittingly offended someone.'

They felt guilty, too. They had been almost lifelong members of the Communist Party, they had supported the Soviet Union, they still held the ideals of their youth. They and Hetty's other older sisters had even introduced Pearl to left-wing politics. 'We felt guilty towards Pearl and her ruined life, because of what had happened, as if it was our fault', said Hetty. Berman showed them the prison photograph of George Fles and, unexpectedly, Hetty began to cry. Even Reg said: 'You wonder why it was all necessary.'

'It was the photograph that did it', said Hetty. 'It is coming so close in this way. As long as you look at it from the perspective of a historian and you keep a clear distance, it does not hurt you. And if you see this photograph you suddenly realise that he was a human being whose life was cut short without a reason.' She tried on herself the answers given her by a lifetime of communism: 'I know very well that it is the same for the Holocaust and for the children in

Cambodia, Angola and wherever.' Yet, perhaps for the first time, she found these answers inadequate. 'But this individual you knew. It is a much bigger blow.'

In Paris, his next posting, Thijs Berman talked to his own father, Peter Berman, who remembered little about his Uncle George, but knew that the resemblance between him and George was striking: older members of the family used to remark on it, and he had once seen a picture of George that confirmed it. George's disappearance had not destroyed his own communist faith. 'I pushed it away, the fact that you can go to a country with so much idealism and, despite your belief in all the positive sides of the country, still be destroyed by it. But it was not an argument for me to say that something was fundamentally wrong in the Soviet Union. I saw it as a tragic development. The Soviet Union was a heroic country to us after the great Soviet losses in the war and its enormous battle against fascism. . . . To my parents and me that country was an example, a land with a future.'

Despite what had happened to George? 'I thought that solidarity out of principle with the Soviet Union was so important, despite all the criticism against the Soviet Union. . . . I did not want to see the criticism and I definitely did not want to draw the conclusion that something was fundamentally wrong.'

All his father's political choices were determined by the idea of fighting fascism and anti-Semitism, and during the war the communists were to the fore in the Dutch resistance to the Nazis. In Holland, as in Britain, many Jews saw communists as the only political group prepared to stand up to the looming menace of anti-Semitism in the heart of Europe. 'I felt I would have liked George very much. But I never drew political conclusions.' He saw George's fate as a tragic mistake about which he should not talk too much.

George Fles's Jewish family suffered terribly after the Nazis invaded Holland. Most of George's brothers, sisters, nephews and nieces perished in the Holocaust, and his father and mother committed suicide rather than go to the death camps. Thijs Berman's father said that the family talked a lot about these losses: 'We talked about the memories, about the good things we remembered. But to me it was impossible to really go into it. And it was the same for your grandma. . . . All those uncles and aunts I had, that little cousin, my cousin Rudy, disappeared and murdered, just like that. I still dream about it. . . . To me it was a traumatic experience too, but by engaging in numerous things, by working hard, by trying to love people all the same and direct your energy to things that matter, it is all right.'

Belief in a better socialist future helped too, even though George's father was no longer the convinced communist he had been as a young man. He believed the Soviet Union was a criminal regime. And therefore, 'I regard Sjoppie's death differently from before.' (*Berman*)

In the USA, Pearl and George's son John Michael Fles led a strange life. The story of his father, even though his mother never told him the details, seems to have weighed on him and conflicted with his instinctively liberal and left-wing outlook, but he never knew quite what to do to cauterise the pain, and never tried to prise open the secrets of the Soviet prisons. He was a Californian beatnik in the 1960s, and a friend of Allen Ginsberg. The Rimels in England, with a very Jewish respect for steady careers, felt that he lived too much on his mother's limited financial resources, and always wanted him to settle down to something solid, but he never did.

He lived mostly with his mother until she died in 1983. A year after her death he contacted his aunt Hetty Bower and asked to come and stay with her. She said: 'You can come, you can stay, but I am not looking after you, John. I'm not as young as I was. There will be a room and a bed until someone else wants to come and stay.' She told me in 2003:

He had no – do you know any Yiddish? There's only a Yiddish word for it – no *zitsfleisch* [roughly, staying power]. He had lived off his mother for all his life. He opted out of doing an ordinary job because that would be supporting capitalism. He joined one of these bands that went round playing bars, then he learned to be a potter and was making pottery, then began to run a bookshop and café, but he got up late and opened the shop around eleven, so it didn't pay. This is what Pearl told me when she felt like confiding.

His uncle [George Fles's older brother Barthold, an American literary agent, whom we last met on his despairing trek round the Soviet Union trying to find George] helped him but he never kept a job for very long. He became a kind of impresario for a dance and music group. (*Bower interview*)

All this is probably a little over-censorious. He is now known as Michael Fles, and he has had three wives and, it's thought, about six children and several grandchildren. He spent a lot of time travelling, especially to South America, apparently inheriting his father's itchy feet. He learned to play many exotic instruments only known to small communities of indigenous people in Mexico, and studied music therapy in Vancouver, Canada.

The last record of him I can find has him playing his various instruments at Humboldt State University. The university's magazine, *Lumberjack*, reported in March 2002:

He said [when he moved to Mexico] he felt that it was time to move someplace new to be at peace with himself and his son. He decided to go to the state of Chiapas to play music with those he passionately referred to as the Indians living in the highlands. . . . Fles says he had dreams of setting up a scenario in which he could play music with the Indians. . . . 'I tried to do these workshops in a higher state of consciousness', Fles said, referring to his use of drugs prior to the performances. He said he found the use of mushrooms and peyote to be extremely beneficial in understanding the tiny nuances of the people. . . . The Indians usually made their own instruments and used an alcoholic beverage for stimulation.

Next stop, according to the magazine, was the Lancandon rainforest, from which the Zapatista Army for National Liberation sent their declaration of war on 1 January 1994, a declaration he enthusiastically supported.

Six months later the same magazine has him playing a variety of instruments at the university while dance teacher Jennifer Hawley does 'slow, belly-dancing type moves. Her shadow is used to contradict the other movements, Fles said.' He plays 'the bounty of instruments he has acquired over the years in foreign countries'. He is quoted as saying: 'The most unusual instrument the audience will hear is the monochord. It was custom-made and all of the strings play the same note. Each string reinforces the one before so that it sounds like a roar of thunder.' He has been a music therapist for twenty years, and has performed in Mexico, Europe and Israel.

He wrote in 2002 to a London relative, now a man in his late sixties, living in California, apparently happy but poor and jobless, saying he had a 'rich and fulfilling' life in which 'I can really devote myself to my music'.

* * *

When Freda Utley died in Washington on 22 December 1978, the Soviet Union was about to invade Afghanistan. Its strength seemed immense, despite everything she had tried to do to curtail it. No one knew that Afghanistan was to be the graveyard of Soviet power, and Freda Utley's writings were largely forgotten in the years immediately after her death. But the collapse of the Soviet Union in 1990–1 brought about a resurgence of interest in them. *KostspieligeRache* (1951), the translation of *The High Cost of Vengeance*, was reprinted in Germany in 1993. *The China Story* (1951) was translated into Japanese in 1993, and *Japan's Feet of Clay* (1936) in 1998. Her first book, *Lancashire and the Far East*, was reprinted in 1996. Her papers were deposited, appropriately for a dedicated McCarthyite, in the archives of the Hoover Institution in Stanford, California. (*Farnie*)

Her work was gaining currency at a time when its faults were more likely to be obvious, and they were angrily attacked, not only by Deborah Lipstadt. In 1966 Dr Carroll Quigley, Professor of Sociology and History at Georgetown University (who, as it happens, taught history both to Bill Clinton and Freda's son Jon Basil Utley), wrote:

178

The radical right version of these events as written up by John T. Flynn, Freda Utley, and others, was even more remote from the truth . . . although it had a tremendous impact on American opinion and American relations with other countries in the years 1947–1955. This radical right fairy tale, which is now an accepted folk myth in many groups in America, pictured the recent history of the United States, in regard to domestic reform and in foreign affairs, as a well-organised plot by extreme left wing elements, operating from the White House itself and controlling all the chief avenues of publicity in the United States, to destroy the American way of life, based on private enterprise, laissez-faire, and isolationism, on behalf of alien ideologies of Russian Socialism and British cosmopolitanism (or internationalism).

This plot, if we are to believe the myth, worked through such avenues of publicity as the *New York Times* and the *Herald Tribune*, the *Christian Science Monitor* and the *Washington Post*, the *Atlantic Monthly* and *Harper's Magazine* and had at its core the wild-eyed and bushy-haired theoreticians of Socialist Harvard and the London School of Economics. It was determined to bring the United States into World War II on the side of England (Roosevelt's first love) and Soviet Russia (his second love) in order to destroy every finer element of American life and, as part of this consciously planned scheme, invited Japan to attack Pearl Harbor, and destroyed Chiang Kai-shek, all the while undermining America's real strength by excessive spending and unbalanced budgets. (*Quigley*)

Jon Basil Utley has little clear memory of his father, Arcadi Berdichevsky. He does not remember the terrible night in 1936 when the secret police came for Arcadi, and Jon woke at 7 a.m. and was given breakfast while his parents tried to hide their terror from him. He does not remember wandering round the flat for weeks afterwards, looking behind the furniture for his father. But he knows about these things. As it did for his mother, it laid the foundations of a lifelong loathing of communism. 'I think of myself as a Conservative because I was always anti-Communist, like my mother', he told me. 'But my mother was also a compassionate person.' He joined the Young Republicans when he was eighteen and is still a prominent Republican.

He was close to his mother and learned much of his political philosophy from her. He told me: 'She was puritan in sex, not that sex was bad, but that it came last after work, duty, and so on. She enjoyed friends and parties and having a good time. She spent the little money she made, took life as it came. She maintained a female humanity or humanitarianism, something many right wingers lost, like Jeanne Kirkpatrick, Ayn Rand (I assume) and others.'

Jon Utley studied history at Georgetown University's School of Foreign Service, and studied languages in Germany, France and Cuba. He went into business, and in 1956 became a branch manager in Colombia for the insurance company American International Group. He stayed in South America for the next nineteen years, moving from Colombia to manage a mutual fund and insurance sales organisation in Ecuador and Peru. He was also a journalist there, founding Colombia's first English language newspaper and working as a foreign correspondent in South America for Knight Ridder Newspapers, a big group with local publications all over the USA, and for the *Journal of Commerce*.

Back in Washington after 1975, he was Associate Editor of the *Times of America* and wrote for a wide variety of publications – *Harvard Business Review, Washington Post* and *Washington Times*, among others. But he also worked in the oil business in Pennsylvania, and dabbled in real estate, buying up and renovating town houses in Washington, and made a good deal of money.

He was driven partly by the fact that his mother, though she mixed with wealthy people, never had much money herself, and everyone they knew was richer than they were. That, he says, motivated him to make some money. But another great benefit of having money, he says now, is that he can say what he likes. Today, when ambitious Republicans are rushing to join the Bush bandwagon, he is a Republican rebel, furiously opposing the Iraq war, condemning US policy in the Middle East. 'I'm anti-Empire and anti-Zionist. A lot of Republicans secretly agree with me but they dare not say so because their careers depend on the people round George W. Bush.'

Today, in his late sixties, Jon Basil Utley is the Robert A. Taft Fellow at the Ludwig von Mises Institute in Alabama. This institute calls itself 'the research and educational center of classical liberalism, libertarian political theory, and the Austrian school of economics'. It 'defends the market economy, private property, sound money, and peaceful international relations, while opposing government intervention as economically and socially destructive'. Its intellectual heroes include Margaret Thatcher's favourite thinker F.A. Hayek. It is, in short, a very right-wing US think tank. He is active in organisations like the Conservative Caucus, the Council for Inter-American Security, and Solidarity America, and writes for publications such as the *Conservative Digest*.

We tend to think of the Iraq war as an issue on which battle lines are clear, with the right in favour and the left against, but Jon Utley says: 'If you're against big government you're against war.' He's right, of course – wars always lead to a bigger role for government, because a government cannot prosecute a war efficiently unless it is in full control of the nation's resources. The Mises Institute's prospectus says: 'Government intervention is always destructive, whether through welfare, inflation, taxation, regulation, or war.'

So the Bushies, the people surrounding President Bush, are not real right-wing libertarians at all, according to Utley. 'Most of the Bush people know very little of the rest of the world', he says. He himself has spent much of his life abroad, mainly in South America, but also in Russia and Europe. 'The Neoconservatives are very insular and don't know much about the world.' A conservative who wants a job in government needs to support their line: 'I'm financially independent; most of them can't afford to criticise the war.' On an anti-war website he published an article headed 'Eight Washington Lies About Iraq'. (*Utley, Iraq*)

He distances himself from the conventional right over Israel, too, and some of what he contributes to anti-war newsletters and the publications of the Ludwig von Mises Institute could be taken by a casual observer as left wing, for he writes of 'Israel's expansion of settlements, the brutal occupation and consequent disruption in the whole Muslim world, contribution towards terrorism . . .'.

Europeans see Israel as the greatest threat to world peace, but 'What is not understood in Europe is the power of the religious right in Congress and how responsible it has become for Israel's policies, because it provides cover and money for everything that [Israeli Prime Minister] Sharon does. . . . The religious right is the real force making Bush cave in to Sharon at every meeting . . . and was also a main supporter of the attack on Iraq. Today its members are called Christian Zionists.' He told me that we should never underestimate its influence with the Bush administration.

It's possible to glimpse in all this a libertarian left winger failing to get out from under a powerful right-wing mother, which may be part of the truth, though it's too pat an explanation for this complex man with his complex history. He will still spring like a tiger to the defence of the things in which his mother believed. Another of his articles is headed 'Senator Joseph McCarthy's charges "now accepted as fact."' It begins: 'Although Joseph McCarthy was one of the most demonised American politicians of the last century, new information – including half-century-old FBI recordings of Soviet embassy conversations – are showing that McCarthy was right in nearly all his accusations.'

In particular the article insists that Owen Lattimore, against whom (though he does not mention this point) his mother had marshalled the evidence, was guilty. However, the case he builds against Lattimore seems a little thin, especially from a writer whose case against the Iraq war is so compelling. It consists mainly of saying that Lattimore's advice to Roosevelt was more pro-Soviet than Utley thinks it should have been. Lattimore was Roosevelt's adviser on China, and Utley says he 'supported Soviet policy at every turn, even declaring that the purge trials in Russia "sound like democracy to me".' Of course one can see how a man whose own father perished in the purges would find this hard to forgive, but it does not prove that Lattimore was guilty of anything more than a bad mistake which was shared by many other distinguished observers at the time.

The 'really important issue', writes Utley, is 'communist influence over American foreign policy'. Roosevelt adviser Harry Hopkins is charged with helping to 'bring about the disastrous Yalta and Potsdam agreements', the agreements between the USA, the USSR and Britain which brought down the curtain on the Second World War. He presumably thinks they are disastrous because of the large part of Europe which were consigned to Soviet hegemony, but I strongly suspect that his alternative – which, presumably, is to have confronted the Red Army – would have been far worse.

Utley is convinced, as his mother must have been, that McCarthy was murdered by the CIA while in Bethesda Naval Hospital, rather than simply dying of liver disease and alcoholism as the conventional story has it, because his anti-communism was inconvenient. (*Utley, McCarthy*)

But his past shines through Jon Utley's present most strongly in his work for an organisation called the Eurasia Center, which arranges for American families to adopt deprived Russian babies and give them a better life in the land of the free. Most of the babies come from Russian orphanages. He says it has never occurred to him that, had it not been for his mother's quick and practical thinking, he might have ended up in one of those orphanages, with no chance of adoption by well-heeled and well-meaning Americans. But I think at some level he must have realised that he might well have shared the fate of Alyosha Petrovsky, though he knew nothing of Alyosha or his story.

In 2003 he flew to Moscow to watch and report on the work. 'One couple told me their baby girl's father had been killed in Chechnya and that her mother, too poor to support her, had delivered the infant to an orphanage. There's little in the way of public assistance in Russia. . . . Most children are left until the age of sixteen and then put on the streets with little education, support or hope for the rest of their lives. And yet some 5,000 Russian kids came to America last year, to middle-class families, for lives unimaginable to those who are left behind.'

He admits that 'adopting can be politically sensitive for many Russians who don't like the idea of Americans taking away their children'. (*Utley, Eurasia*) That's putting it mildly. I was in Moscow in 2003 too, and read the angry stories in the English language paper the *Moscow News* about fury at rich Americans coming and buying Russian babies.

* * *

In 1994, while I was researching my book about Britain's communists, I turned up one evening for a lecture at the Marx Memorial Library, one of a series the library had organised on communist history. I do not remember what the subject was that evening, except that it had something to do with the relationship between British communists and the Soviet Union, but I do remember that as soon as it was time for questions, a short, late middle-aged woman whom no one seemed to know got to her feet and told a terrible story. She had an aunt, she said, a senior figure in the British Communist Party, who had gone to live in Moscow, and one night her aunt had been dragged from her bed by the secret police. Her young child had been torn from her arms and taken away to rot in an inhuman orphanage, and her aunt had been sent to the Lubyanka and shot.

As soon as the meeting ended, I went to speak to her, and that was the first time I heard the name Rose Cohen. In long meetings in Joyce Rathbone's big, comfortable, untidy Bayswater flat, she told me the story of her search for Rose, and dug through mountains of paper to find the letters which passed between Rose and her mother. It has to be said that Joyce did not seem to think much of Rose. She saw in her all the vanity that seems to have alienated Freda Utley, and none of the charm and wit that transfixed Harry Pollitt all his life. Joyce too was a communist for much of her life, and she too had tried not to let what she once saw as the mistakes and excesses of the Stalin era deprive her of her faith, but as she learned, bit by bit, the details of what had happened to her mother's sister, she too lost her faith.

Joyce's search, she told me, had ended at that meeting with Alyosha, Rose Cohen's son, which I have already described, in the flat of Alyosha's son Misha, where Alyosha cried over the mementoes of his mother that Joyce had brought with her from England, and assured her that it had all been a mistake – his parents were not really Trotskyists.

She never saw him again. A year or two after her visit to Moscow, Misha and his wife and daughter came to England. They stayed with Joyce, but somehow or other Joyce and Misha's wife fell out. 'It was an awful ten days. She was very rude. She was dreadful', was all Joyce told me. I have no idea what happened, but I did find that Joyce, though articulate and intelligent, takes offence rather easily, and it could be that Misha's wife was a little tactless.

She also had a low opinion of Rose's old Moscow friend Ivy Litvinov. Ivy and Maxim Litvinov somehow survived the purges even though Maxim fell out of favour with Stalin, and he died on the last day of 1951. If he had lived even a few months longer, then, old and ill though he was, he would have seen out his days in the camps, for not only had he fallen out of favour, but he was also a Jew, and these were the days of the Doctors' Plot, when Jewish doctors were imprisoned and tortured on a false charge of trying to kill top Kremlin officials, including Stalin.

Maxim Litvinov knew the danger he was in. This old Bolshevik, who had shared Lenin's exile in London, had long since lost his illusions, but he had also learned how to keep his thoughts to himself. Back in 1936, in England for the funeral of George V, he had secretly deposited £300 in an English bank, in case he or his wife should ever need to escape to her home.

He and Ivy had not always been happy together – they had both caused the other pain with their various lovers – but his last words were his best advice to her: 'Englishwoman, go home.' It took nine years for Ivy to get permission to visit England. She stayed in London and then Brighton for a year in 1960–1, and during that time she wrote out her memories of Rose, and of Rose's fate, from which I quoted in earlier chapters.

She seems to have made some effort to get in touch with Rose's relatives in England, but never managed to find Joyce Rathbone. She wrote at the time: 'He [Alyosha] has still got relations in England. I would love to get in touch with them and bring him news. But I don't know if I will ever be able to find him again.' (*Carswell*)

TEN

The Persecution Gene

Those who have studied Holocaust survivors say that the horrors of the concentration camps travel down the generations. In all sorts of unexpected ways, they change the lives of the next generation, and cast a shadow over the lives of men and women who were not even born during the Second World War. However hard the survivors, or their brothers, sisters, husbands and wives, tried to give their children a normal upbringing in a new country, their children's lives, and perhaps even their grandchildren's lives, are lived out in the shadow of what the Nazis did to their forebears.

So it is for Jon Basil Utley, carried out of the Soviet Union in his mother's arms at the age of two, forced to leave his father to a terrible fate. Although has no memory of searching for his father behind every bit of furniture in their Moscow flat, somewhere that memory is part of the man. So it is for John Michael Fles, whose mother, for years, never heard an unexpected ring at the doorbell without her heart leaping in the hope that it was her beloved George, finally released from a dreadful Siberian camp. So it certainly was for Alyosha Petrovsky in Moscow; while for Rosa Rust, her father's political decisions came to overshadow her life.

Jon Utley and Michael Fles are now in their late sixties. They both came to the United States when they were small children, and have made their lives there, Utley in Washington and Fles in Los Angeles. They were both brought up singlehandedly by their mothers in what seemed to both of them like rather straitened circumstances. They have both travelled widely. Oddly, both of them spent many years in South America, and both, in their very different ways, found themselves, learned who they were, by studying and working in South America. And the men they became owed something to what was done to their fathers.

Jon Utley is still, at sixty-nine, naturally a thinker and an activist, with interesting and often original ideas about politics, but he has to some extent been corralled by his family's past into a far-right laager where he defends and glorifies the memory of the seedy and illiberal Chairman of the House Un-American Activities Committee, Senator Joe McCarthy.

Michael Fles, now a man of sixty-seven, was told little about what had had happened to his father, but it seems to me that the unhappiness of it all, the betrayal of his parents' idealism, the useless and miserable death of the father he never knew, is a part of the man, and part of the reason for those characteristics which his aunts Anita Rimel and Hetty Bower and Hetty's husband Reg found less than acceptable.

Of course the effect was more direct for Rosa Rust, whose sufferings in Kazakhstan were the result of her father's political decisions. And it was more direct for Alyosha Petrovsky, who, if he is still alive, will now be seventy-four. He lost not one parent, but two. There was, as his mother realised in those last despairing days in the Lubyanka, no one left to get him out of the country, to give him a parent's love and a new life, and he has a tangible memory of the terror in the form of dreadful Soviet orphanages.

The poison of persecution trickles into the next generation, and spreads well beyond direct descendants. There was Anita Rimel, tortured in her last years by the fear she could never express, that her letters to George Fles, the magazines she sent him because she thought they would interest him, led directly to his lonely, miserable death. She refused to talk to Thijs Berman when he was researching George's story; perhaps she was frightened of what he might have to tell her.

So it was not just George and Pearl's idealism that was trampled and crushed in the purges. It was that of her sisters, Anita and Hetty,

188

and Reg Bower, and George's brother and sister Barthold Fles and Clara Berman, the only two out of six Fles children to come out of the Second World War alive. They all struggled to keep their belief intact. It is hard to imagine Anita Rimel's conflicting emotions as she told her sister not to write, in a death notice for Pearl, that George was a victim of the Stalin terror.

How hard the Rimels tried to keep their faith – even to the point of finding George guilty in their own minds. He was tactless, wasn't he, a man who didn't stop to think before he spoke? He'd been to all these countries and joined socialist parties in all of them – would not a spy do just that? He and Pearl went to the Soviet Union without a proper Marxist understanding. And if he was reading and distributing Trotskyist literature. . . . And so, the last anyone ever heard from George, whose only crime was to be young, and noisy, and brave, and entertaining, and irreverent, and adventurous, was the letter he wrote while crouched in some filthy little cell, almost certainly ill, the note to Pearl in Russian telling her that he would never get out and she was to marry again. It said nothing at all about Anita's magazines and his father's magazines, with articles by Trotsky, for what was the point of their knowing, now? But in the end, Anita knew, and so, I think, did Pearl.

The very last thing I did before completing this book was to go to see Hetty Bower again at the beginning of January 2004. I accompanied this extraordinary 98-year-old woman, whose mind is as clear and precise as it must have been when she was a young bookkeeper, whose political thinking is as sharp and focused as when she first joined the Communist Party in 1935, and whose idealism is as strong now as it was when she spent the Second World War years helping Eastern European refugees in London, on her morning walk through Highgate in north London, where she lives in an old people's home.

She had asked me to talk to her again before I sent this book to the publisher, because she had something to say to me. She set a brisk pace – she walks like a woman thirty years younger – but she slowed for a moment because she could see that I couldn't take notes and keep up with her at the same time, and she wanted me to get this right. This is what she wanted to say:

> Pearl felt angry with us because we stayed in the Communist Party after George was taken away. She was angry that the Communist Party did not leave the Third International [the Comintern] and angry that we were lied to. It makes me angry too. But it does not change my communist beliefs. What happened then and later was the loss of a great opportunity. If only the Communist Party had told the truth, about the Soviet Union then, and about Hungary and Czechoslovakia later. But a world dominated by the USA would be no better.

She believes, as she has always done, in a fairer society, free of the inequity and poverty under capitalism, and in socialism as the means to achieve it. She gave her life to this belief, and she has not stopped. In 2003 she was on all the marches against the Iraq war, almost certainly the oldest person there, walking the whole route among the noise and the placards.

To her, I think, Stalin's greatest crime, an even greater crime than the innocent men and women he murdered, was to disgrace socialism. He squandered all the good in the world that socialism could have done – and could still do, one day, but not in her lifetime, not now.

It seems likely that, somewhere in Pearl's heart, she never quite forgave her sisters for staying loyal to the Communist Party until the events of 1956 started to damage their faith irreparably. George's disappearance clearly placed a barrier between the sisters, even after Hetty and Anita left the party. When Pearl was with Hetty, and Harry Pollitt's name came up, Pearl would say in disgust: 'Don't talk to me about that man', but Hetty still admired Pollitt. Hetty was, I think, never close to Pearl again. Neither was Anita. There was a long period when Pearl and Anita were not on speaking terms: ostensibly because Anita criticised Pearl's son Michael Fles, but I suspect the rift went further back than that. The relationship between these sisters, and their peace of mind, is a small but tangible casualty of persecution nearly seven decades ago.

Alyosha Petrovsky's cousin, Joyce Rathbone, born in the same year as Alyosha, is another victim down the generations. Like the Rimels and the Rathbones, Rose's sister Nellie and her husband Hugo avoided talking about Rose after she disappeared. They, too, allowed themselves to wonder whether Rose and Max were quite what they seemed to be.

There had been some tension and jealousy between the sisters. Hugo, it's said, was among Rose's many male admirers. Rose had made enemies among the English community in Moscow, as she had in London. People who shine more brightly than those around them generally do, and Rose had brains and beauty and self-confidence – an unforgivable combination. The woman who had so many admirers when she was a rising star found precious few defenders in the end. Might there not be something in all this talk of her complacency, her standoffishness? Not that anyone was saying that she got what she deserved. But all the same . . .

For Joyce Rathbone, 'it was all so terrible at the time, we didn't talk about it'. Joyce seems to have felt comfortable talking about it in communist circles, as when I first met her after the lecture at the Marx Memorial Library. She was happy to talk to me about it, but became strangely unhappy when I wanted to write about it. I think, though she never put it this way, that she thought it was one of those things that should never be mentioned publicly. Poor Rose, and all that, but it only makes things worse . . . I wrote an article about Rose for *BBC History Magazine*, and, though Joyce knew it was being written, she was unaccountably furious when she saw it: unable to explain what it was she hated so much, but clearly deeply upset that it had been published. Sadly, she refused to cooperate with this book, or to let me print in it her lovely pictures of Rose and Alyosha, and all she would say by way of explanation was: 'My mother would be horrified. Horrified.'

For them, and for all of us, our parents' past, the mistakes they made, the injustices they suffered, are absorbed into our own make-up. I too had an inheritance from which I suspect I never quite escaped. My father was a fascist. I don't mean he held right-wing views. I mean he was a real fascist, an anti-Semite, an admirer of

Hitler who thought the Jews were at least partly responsible for having been persecuted.

John Beckett was born, like Rose Cohen, in 1894, and probably met Rose and Freda Utley in the 1920s, when they were all ardent young socialists in London, before – in a radically different way – his idealism, like theirs, was poisoned. He certainly met Hetty Bower in those days: she remembers it, as she remembers most of the events of her long life. But in the 1930s, when Rose, Freda and Pearl Rimel were travelling to Moscow in search of one dream, my father was searching for another, as propaganda chief for Sir Oswald Mosley's British fascists and editor of the fascist newspapers. He spent the years from 1940 to 1944 in prison, detained under wartime regulation 18B. I have told his story elsewhere. (*Beckett, Rebel*)

I was born after this part of his life was over, but today, surveying my own muddled past, I am sure that many of my decisions, which look inexplicable and irrational from a distance, probably go back, in one way or another, to this inheritance.

There's a real sense in which the crimes of Hitler and Stalin were committed against subsequent generations just as much as against the men and women they murdered. The traumas of each generation are passed to the next, and they become self-regenerating. When human beings do terrible things to each other, humanity literally never gets over it.

I am writing these closing words at the beginning of 2004. On the whole 2003 was a bad year. The Americans captured the dreadful Saddam Hussein, and we watched triumphalist American soldiers in Iraq 'kicking ass' as they would doubtless put it; we do not know how many Iraqi families will carry down the generations the memories of wicked deeds committed first by Saddam Hussein, then by his conquerors. We heard yet again, of Israeli soldiers wreaking terrible retribution on the Palestinian population for yet another suicide bombing. And a man called Ian Huntley received two life sentences for the murder of two ten-year-old girls in the Cambridgeshire village of Soham. Huntley's crimes will affect generations yet unborn in the families whose children he killed, in ways they will never fully understand. And monsters like Huntley do not just appear, fully formed, in our midst. They too are the products of generation upon generation of misdeeds.

George Fles understood how evil can damage the generation after the one that suffered it. His main concern, in those last few days in the prison in Tbilisi before they moved him to Moscow, was for the welfare of the son or daughter he knew must be being born in London while he stood in front of a KGB interrogator answering stupid questions over and over again. That, I think, is why the one message he managed to get to Pearl emphasised his wish for her to marry again while she was still young. He thought it might give his child a more normal life.

The four women at the centre of this book, Rosa Rust, Rose Cohen, Freda Utley and Pearl Rimel, were not just remarkable human beings themselves; they, too, were the products of their past. Rosa – strong, outgoing, with an immense talent which she never had the chance to use properly, and one of the most vibrantly alive people I have ever met – was set on her life's path by her father's decision to throw in his lot with the Comintern and Stalin; and this decision in turn had its root in the way Britain treated the poor at the start of the twentieth century.

Rose – happy, clever, beautiful, talented Rose, who might have achieved great things – must have carried with her, throughout her short life, the family memory of the Jewish pogroms from which her parents fled in the nineteenth century. Freda, with her fiercely powerful intellect, never forgot how, in her teens, her father was suddenly bankrupt and penniless, and was abandoned and left to die alone in pain and poverty, while Freda's own English private school suddenly wanted nothing to do with her when they found out that she was now the daughter of a poor man. And Pearl – loyal, loving, witty, practical and sensitive Pearl – Pearl, like Rose, came from a family which knew what it was like to be persecuted and pilloried for being a Jew.

It would be comforting to think that what destroyed their lives was the bitter ideological battles of a bygone era. But the sectarian spirit is still with us; it does not disappear simply because we live in a parliamentary democracy. It is just that, most of the time, we keep it in check. It's used to destroy careers, but not normally to take lives.

Stalin died in 1953, and the system that made Stalin died in 1991. And the *Moscow Times* of 30 December 2003 reported: 'In a major setback for the Federal Security Service, a Krasnoyarsk jury on Monday acquitted physicist Valentin Danilov on charges of spying for China while working on a commercial contract . . .'. It continued:

> Danilov's case is one of a series of high-profile espionage cases that have been brought against researchers and whistleblowers in the past few years by a security service whose deep suspicions of their contacts with foreigners seem little changed from Soviet times. Danilov's defence lawyers and human rights activists attribute the rare acquittal to his being granted a jury trial, still a novelty for the Russian judicial system.
>
> Prosecutor Sergei Kharin said the trial was tarnished by procedural violations and he would appeal the ruling to the Supreme Court. 'The evidence that the prosecution has collected over these four years is sufficient for the jurors to have made the opposite decision', he said.
>
> Another researcher accused of espionage, Igor Sutyagin, is having his case heard by a jury in Moscow. The trial opened in early November but has been repeatedly postponed. . . . An arms control expert at the respected USA and Canada Institute, Sutyagin is accused of passing military secrets to US intelligence through a British firm for which he did consulting work.

It would be nice to think it was confined to Russia, or to regimes like that of the now deposed Saddam Hussein, but we have no means at all of knowing how many of those in shackles in Guantanamo Bay are guilty of anything at all.

The evil that killed George Fles, and Rose and Max, and Arcadi Berdichevsky, trickles down the generations. It is not just the sins *of* the fathers which are visited on the children. Even more, the sins committed *against* the fathers are visited on their children.

Source References

(*Abramsky*): information given to the author by Professor Chimen Abramsky.

(*Beckett, Enemy Within*): *Enemy Within*, by Francis Beckett, John Murray, London, 1995, and Merlin Press, London, 1998.

(*Beckett, Rebel*): *The Rebel Who Lost his Cause*, by Francis Beckett, Allison and Busby, London, 1999.

(*Berman*): *Op zoek naar George Fles*, by Thijs Berman, Amsterdam, 1993, translated by Hanneke Klep.

(*Blagoyeva*): *Dimitrov*, by Stella D. Blagoyeva, University of Toronto Press, Toronto, 1970.

(*Bower autobiography*): unpublished fragments of autobiography by Hetty Bower.

(*Bower interview*): author's interview with Hetty Bower, 2003.

(*Burke*): information provided to the author by David Burke.

(*Campbell*): *Villi the Clown*, by William Campbell, Faber and Faber, London, 1981.

(*Carew*): information provided to Dr David Turner by Dr Tony Carew.

(*Carswell*): *The Exile, A Life of Ivy Litvinov*, by John Carswell, Faber and Faber, London, 1983.

(*Cohen and Morgan*): *Stalin's Sausage Machine – British Students at the International Lenin School 1926–1937* by Gidon Cohen (University of Salford) and Kevin Morgan (University of Manchester), Communist Party of Great Britain Biographical Project at the University of Manchester.

(*Cole*): *Growing up into Revolution*, by Margaret Cole, London, 1949.

(*Farnie*): 'Freda Utley, Crusader for Truth and Freedom', by Douglas Farnie, in *Japan Society Biographical Portraits*, London, 2002.

(*Flinn*): 'William Rust', by Andrew Flinn, in *Party People, Communist Lives*, eds John McIlroy, Kevin Morgan and Alan Campbell, Lawrence and Wishart, London, 2001.

195

(*Foot*): author's interview with Michael Foot, 1994.

(*Harvey*): *Comrades*, by Robert Harvey, John Murray, London, 2003.

(*Hyde*): *I Believed*, by Douglas Hyde, Heinemann, London, 1949.

(*IoS*): *Independent on Sunday*.

(*King and Matthews*): *About Turn: The Communist Party and the Outbreak of War, 1939*, by Francis King and George Matthews, Lawrence and Wishart, London, 1990.

(*Mcleod*): *The Death of Uncle Joe*, by Alison Mcleod, Merlin Press, London, 1997.

(*McConnell*): author's interview with Christina McConnell, 2001.

(*McLoughlin*): 'Visitors and Victims', by Barry McLoughlin, in *Party People, Communist Lives*, eds John McIlroy, Kevin Morgan and Alan Campbell, Lawrence and Wishart, London, 2001.

(*Manchester*): documents kept in the Labour Movement History Museum in Manchester.

(*Morgan*): information and documents provided to the author by Dr Kevin Morgan.

(*Morgan, Pollitt*): *Harry Pollitt*, by Kevin Morgan, Manchester University Press, Manchester, 1993.

(*Morgan, Rose Cohen*): entry in *Dictionary of Labour Biography* by Kevin Morgan.

(*Murphy*): *New Horizons*, by Jack Murphy, Bodley Head, London, 1941.

(*Pollitt*): *Serving My Time*, by Harry Pollitt, Lawrence and Wishart, London, 1940.

(*PRO*): file references from the Public Record Office, London.

(*Quigley*): *Tragedy and Hope*, by Carroll Quigley, Macmillan, New York, 1966.

(*Rathbone*): author's interviews with Joyce Rathbone, 1994 and 2002.

(*Rathbone collection*): letters in the personal collection of Joyce Rathbone.

(*RC*): Russian Centre for the Preservation of Documents.

(*Reckitt*): *As It Happened*, by Maurice Reckitt, London, 1941.

(*Rimel*): interviews with members of the Rimel family – Diana Rimel, Delia Scales, Mary Davis.

(*Rust*): author's interviews with Rosa Rust, 1995.

(*Thornton*): author's interview with David Thornton, 2003.

(*Thorpe*): *The British Communist Party and Moscow*, by Andrew Thorpe, Manchester Univerisity Press, Manchester, 2000.

(*Turner*): information provided to the author by Dr David Turner.

(*Utley, The Dream*): *The Dream We Lost: Soviet Russia Then and Now*, by Freda Utley, Chicago, 1940.

(*Utley, Eurasia*): article found on www.eurasiacenter.org/reports/ basilutley1.html.

(*Utley interview*): author's interview with Jon Basil Utley, 2003.

(*Utley, Iraq*): article on website of Americans Against World Empire, www.againstbombing.org.

(*Utley, McCarthy*): article found on www.biblebelievers.org.au.

(*Utley, Odyssey*): *Odyssey of a Liberal*, by Freda Utley, Chicago, 1970.

(*Utley, Lost Illusion*): *Lost Illusion*, by Freda Utley, London, 1949.

Further Reading

Note: All titles published in London unless otherwise stated

Applebaum, Anne, *Gulag: A History of the Soviet Camps*, Penguin, 2003.

Beckett, Francis, *Enemy Within*, John Murray, 1995; Merlin, 1998.

Berman, Thijs, *Op zoek naar George Fles*, Amsterdam, 1993.

Campbell, William, *Villi the Clown*, Faber and Faber, 1981.

Carswell, John, *The Exile, a Life of Ivy Litvinov*, Faber and Faber, 1983.

Conquest, Robert, *The Great Terror*, Oxford University Press, 1968.

Farnie, Douglas, 'Freda Utley, Crusader for Truth and Freedom', in *Japan Society Biographical Portraits*, 2002.

King, Francis and Matthews, George, *About Turn: the Communist Party and the Outbreak of War, 1939*, Lawrence and Wishart, 1990.

Lansbury, Violet, *An Englishwoman in the USSR*,

Mcleod, Alison, *The Death of Uncle Joe*, Merlin Press, 1997.

McLoughlin, Barry, 'Visitors and Victims', in *Party People, Communist Lives* (eds McIlroy, Morgan and Campbell), Lawrence and Wishart, 2001.

Morgan, Kevin, *Harry Pollitt*, Manchester University Press, 1993.

Murphy, Jack, *New Horizons*, 1941.

O'Clery, Conor, *Melting Snow*, Appletree Press, Belfast, 1991.

Reckitt, Maurice, *As It Happened*, 1941.

Thorpe, Andrew, *The British Communist Party and Moscow*, Manchester University Press, Manchester, 2000.

Utley, Freda, *Lost Illusion*, Heinemann, London, 1949.

Utley, Freda, *The High Cost of Vengeance*, Chicago, 1948.

Vaksberg, Arcadi, *Hotel Lux* (in French), Paris, 1993.

www.fredautley.com

Index

Abramovna, Anna, 89
Abramsky, Professor Chimen, xi
Academy of Sciences, 86–7
Adelphi Theatre, 2
American International Group, 180
Anderson, Irene, 98
Anglo-Soviet Friendship Society, 123
Antigone, 162
Arcos, 16, 29, 30
Atlantic Monthly, 179
Attlee, Clement, x, 124

Baldwin, Stanley, 1
Barlinnie Prison, 21, 148
BBC History Magazine, 191
Beaverbrook, Lord, 104
Beckett, John, 191–2
Bell, Tom J., 56, 60
Bennett, Arnold, 8
Berdichevsky, Arcadi, 25, 29–33, 52–4, 55, 66, 86, 87–9, 90,

91–2, 93, 138, 142, 145, 146, 179, 194
Berdichevsky, Vera, 31, 87, 88, 89, 90
Beria, Lavrenti, 74, 133, 153
Berman, Clara, 86, 170–1, 189
Berman, Peter, 175
Berman, Thijs, xi, 36–7, 38, 52, 74, 80, 83, 84, 86, 167–76, 188
Bernal, J.D., 141
Bethesda Naval Hospital, 183
Bird, Stephen, xi
Black Cat cigarette company, 34
Blunt, Anthony, 147
Borodin, Mikhail, 20, 148
Bower, Hetty, xi, 35, 36, 50–1, 80–1, 82–4, 138, 139–41, 173–5, 176–7, 188–90, 192
Bower, Reg, 50–1, 82, 83, 139, 140, 173–4, 188–9
Breslin, Katja, 154, 155
Breslin, Patrick, 154–6
Breslin-Kelly, Mairead, 154, 155

Brown, W.J., 91

Bukharin, Nikolai, 39, 40, 48, 49, 50, 97–8

Bulgarian Communist Party, 62, 164

Burdichev, 20

Burgess, Guy, 126, 147

Burke, David, x–xi

Bush, George W, 180–1, 182

Butirskaya Prison, 79, 88

Calder-Marshall, Anna, 9, 166

Cambridge University, 28–9

Campbell, John, 42, 67, 103, 148–50, 152, 160

Campbell, William, 149–50, 152, 154

Cardiff City, 2

Catherine the Great, 105–6

Chesterton, G.K., 17–18, 116–7

Chiang Kai-shek, 179

Chicken Soup with Barley, 157

Chikhladze, David, 169, 171

Chilston, Lord, 68–9, 81, 84, 90

China at War, 92

China Story, The, 178

Christian Science Monitor, 179

Churchill, Winston, 2, 124, 125–6, 134

Class against Class, 7, 36, 41, 120, 123

Clinton, Bill, 178

Cockburn, Claud, 5, 121, 125

Coen, Harry, xi

Cohen, Ada, 16

Cohen, Gidon, 15, 16

Cohen, Morris, 16

Cohen, Nellie, *see* Rathbone, Nellie

Cohen, Rose, vii, ix, xi, 16–19, 20–6, 27, 28, 29, 30, 31, 32, 37, 38, 39, 43, 49, 54–62, 63–6, 68–72, 74, 81–2, 86, 90, 94, 96, 97, 98, 99, 129–30, 134–5, 146, 147, 150, 151, 154, 167, 184, 191, 192, 193, 194

Cole, G.D.H., 21, 65

Cole, Margaret, 17–18, 65

Collier, Laurence, 69, 70, 71, 81

Collins, Tish, xi

Comedy Theatre, 2

Cominform, 125

Comintern (Communist International), 3, 5, 7, 8, 9, 15, 16, 19, 20–21, 22, 25, 30, 31, 33, 39–43, 45, 47, 55, 62, 66–7, 95, 97, 98, 102, 103, 111–12, 114, 122, 124, 125, 129, 154, 190, 193

Commissariat of Light Industry, 31

Communist Party of Great Britain, ix, x, 3, 5, 6, 7, 8, 11, 16, 17, 19, 20–1, 29, 30, 33, 38, 39–43, 45, 46, 47, 54, 55, 58, 59, 64, 66–7, 75, 81, 82, 90–2, 94, 95, 102, 103–4, 111, 115, 122, 123–5, 126, 137, 141, 148, 151, 156, 165, 173, 174, 184, 189–90

Communist Party of Ireland,154, 155

Communist Party of the Soviet Union, 23, 27, 32, 33, 40, 55, 67, 134–5, 153

Communist Youth International, 45

Conquest, Robert, viii–ix, 48
Conservative Caucus, 181
Conservative Digest, 181
Conservative Party, 124
Cook, Arthur, 4, 42
Cooper, Gladys, 2
Cornforth, Maurice, 147
Council for Inter-American Security, 181
Coward, Noel, 2
Cripps, Stafford, 46, 92, 134

Daily Herald, 3, 16
Daily Herald (US), 51, 59
Daily Mirror, 165
Daily Sketch, 72
Daily Worker, x, 5, 9–10, 22, 61–2, 67, 92, 94, 95, 97, 102, 103, 112, 115, 119, 121, 125, 127, 135, 149–50, 152–3, 156, 158, 160, 164
Danilov, Valentin, 194
David, Mary, xi
Death of Uncle Joe, The, x, 97
Denying the Holocaust, 142–4
De Rotterdammer, 171
Die Sammlung, 75, 76
Dimitrov, Georgi, 62–3, 64, 94, 111, 112, 114, 134, 147
Dolan, Margaret, xi
Doyle, Sir Arthur Conan, 2
Dream We Lost, The, 93
Dunedin, Lady, 2
Dunedin, Lord, 2

E17 Drama School, 162
East Midlands Allied Press, 34

Eden, Anthony, 156
Eikhe, Robert, 131–3
Enemy Within, ix
Essex University, 165
Eurasia Center, 183
Ewer, Monica, 24

Falkowski, Ed, 51, 84
Farnie, Professor Douglas, xi, 92
Fierlov, 75
First World War, 1
Fles, Barthold (Bap), 85, 86, 177, 189
Fles, Celine, 85
Fles, George, 34–8, 50–2, 55, 66, 73–80, 81–5, 88, 138, 139, 140, 151, 168–76, 187, 188–9, 190, 193, 194
Fles, Henriette, 85
Fles, John Michael, 84, 139, 140, 176–8, 187–8, 190
Fles, Louis, 34, 84–5
Fles, Mina, 85
Fles, Rosina, 86
Flinn, Andrew, 121–2
Flynn, John T., 179
Forward with Liberalism, 95
Franco, General Francisco, 36, 102
Francis, Ben, 98
Freedman, Sally, 25
Fryer, Peter, 150, 156
Fuchs, Klaus, 126
Fuller, Major General J.F.C., 143

Gallacher, Willie, 40, 41, 62–3, 66, 67, 150, 160
Gamsakhurdia, Zviad, 168–9, 171

Gardiner, Llew, 125
Gasviani, Lydia, 37–8, 55, 74, 76, 80
General strike, 4–5
George V, 185
Georgetown University, 178, 180
German Social Democratic Party, 35, 51
Gibbons, John, 112, 113
Ginsberg, Allen, 176–8
Glading, Percy, 97
Goering, Hermann, 63
Goldfarb, David, *see* Petrovsky, Max
Goldstone, Ray, 140
Gollan, John, 160, 161
Gomulka, Wladyslav, 16
Good Soldier Schweik, The, 162
Gorbachev, Mikhail, 167, 170
Gray, Olga, 97
Guantanamo Bay, 194
Guest, David, 127

Hadow, R.H., 68–9, 71
Halifax, Lord, 68
Hanna, George, 156
Hannah, 104–10, 113–14
Harpers Magazine, 179
Harvard Business Review, 180
Harvard University, 179
Harrods, 2–3
Hawley, Jennifer, 177–8
Healy, Gerry, 152
Heiser, Sadie, 18
Hennessy, Professor Peter, x
Herald Tribune, 73, 179

High Cost of Vengeance, The, 143, 178
Hitler, Adolf, 1, 47, 101, 103, 105, 114, 123–4, 133, 141, 144, 147, 192
Hobbs, Jack, 2
Holmes, Professor Colin, x
Honecker, Erich, 16
Hoover Institution, 178
Hopkins, Harry, 183
House Un-American Activities Committee, 140, 145
Hulton Press Agency, 6
Humboldt State University, 177
Huntley, Ian, 192–3
Hussein, Saddam, 192, 194
Hutt, Allen, 16, 25, 121, 125
Huxley, Julian, 22
Hyde, Douglas, 5, 95–6

Independent on Sunday, 166
Independent Labour Party, 4, 7, 29, 36, 42, 51, 75, 81, 82, 123, 157
Institute of World Economy and Politics, 31
International Socialists, 165
Invergordon Mutineer, 153
Invergordon Mutiny, 151
Iraq war, 181, 190, 192
Iris, 2
Israel, 181–2
Ivanovo-Vosnesensk, 12–13

Jacobs, Joe, 153
Japan's Feet of Clay, 30–1, 32, 89, 92, 178
Jewish Socialist Bund, 20

Johnstone, Monty, x
Journal of Commerce, 180
Journalist, The, 16

Kalmanovsky, 86
Kamenev, L.B., 23, 33, 47, 92, 98
Kamenska, Ruth, 150
Kaye, Alan, 17
Kayek, F.A., 181
Kerrigan, Peter, 60
Keynes, John Maynard, 53
Kharadze, Yevgeny, 171–2
Kharin, Sergei, 184
King, Dr Francis, x
Kings College London, 29, 120, 136
Kirkpatrick, Jeanne, 180
Kirov, Sergei, 47
Knight Ridder Newspapers, 180
Khrushchev, Nikita, viii–ix, x, 130–4, 135, 136, 139, 146, 148, 149, 150, 152, 156, 161
Kravets, Tamara, 8, 9, 11, 12, 99, 122, 159, 160, 164
Krestinsky, 47
Kun, Bela, 59, 60, 63

Labour History Museum, xi
Labour League of Youth, 34
Labour Monthly, 42, 54, 65, 91, 148
Labour Party, 3–4, 6, 7, 11, 36, 38–9, 40, 123, 124, 126
Labour Research Department, 16, 17, 20, 65
Lancandon rainforest, 177
Lancashire and the Far East, 178

Landau, Abraham, 45
Lansbury, George, 98
Lansbury, Violet, 98
Lascelles, 71
Laski, Harold, 90–1, 92
Lattimore, Owen, 142, 182
Lean, Alex, 155
Left Book Club, 67
Left-wing Communism: An Infantile Disorder, 11
Lenin School, 11, 15–16, 21, 122, 136, 154
Lenin, Vladimir, viii–ix, 3, 5, 6, 11, 20, 23, 26, 38–9, 40, 121, 125, 136, 185
Lipetz, David, *see* Petrovsky, Max
Lipstadt, Deborah, 142–4, 178
Litvinov, Ivy, 26–8, 56, 63, 136, 138, 185
Litvinov, Maxim, 26–7, 56, 71, 90, 93, 185
Litvinov, Tanya, 56
Lloyd George, David, 46
Lockheed, 86, 139
London County Council, 16
London School of Economics, 28, 29, 179
London University, 29
Look Back in Anger, 157
Lost Illusion, 93
Low, Ivy, *see* Litvinov, Ivy
Lubyanka, 79, 87, 147, 184, 188
Ludwig von Mises Institute, 181
Lumberjack, 177
Lux Hotel, 8, 15, 22, 31, 45, 59, 60, 100, 113
Luxemburg, Rosa, 1

McCarthy, Senator Joseph, 140,
142, 182, 183, 188
Macdonald, Ramsay, 124
Maclean, Donald, 126, 147
Macleod, Alison, x, 97, 115, 127,
150, 165
McMacken, Daisy, 154
McManus, Arthur, 46–7
McShane, Harry, 6
Manuilsky, Dimitri, 41, 134
Mao Tse-Tung, 13
Martin, Kingsley, 92
Marx, Karl, 53
Marx Memorial Library, xi, 184,
191
Maxton, James, 42
MCC, 2
Mentich, 53, 90
Mentzel, Professor, 171–2
Metro Vickers, 47
Midsummer Night's Dream, A, 162
Mikoyan, Anastas, 142
Miller, Bob, 51–2, 80
Miller, Jack, 80, 84, 85, 138
Miller, Jenny, 51
Moffat, Alec, 16
Molotov, V.M., 101
Monks, Pieta, x
Morgan, Kevin, x, 15, 16, 59, 135
Morning Star, 140–1
Moscow Daily News, 8, 12, 21–2,
24, 27, 37, 51, 56, 60, 99,
154
Moscow News, 152, 184
Moscow Times, 194
Mosley, Sir Oswald, 192
Muggeridge, Malcolm 145

Murphy, Jack, 8, 40, 45–6, 97–8,
141

Nash, Ogden, 163
National Union of Journalists, 16,
121
National Union of Mineworkers,
164
National Union of Railwaymen, 120
Nehru, Jawaharlal, 145
News Chronicle, 92
Newsletter, The, 152
New Statesman, 18, 64–5, 92
New York Times, 145, 179
Nikolayev, 132
Norman, 75

O'Donoghue, Kathleen, 3, 4, 5, 6, 7,
8, 10–12, 22, 99–100, 111,
113, 115, 116, 119–20, 121,
122–3, 159–61, 166
Odyssey of a Liberal, 145
O'Flaherty, Liam, 136
Osborne, John, 157

Page Arnot, Robin, 10–11, 55, 66,
91–2
Palme Dutt, Rajani, 9, 42–3, 90–1,
103, 125, 148
Parsons, Olive, 22
Parti Communiste Français, 35, 125
Paynter, Will, 16
Petrovna, Sophia, 100, 102
Petrovsky, Alyosha, 22, 23, 24, 25,
26, 56, 57, 98, 134, 135–6,
137–8, 183, 184–5, 187, 188,
191

Petrovsky, Max, xi, 20–22, 24, 25, 26, 27, 29, 32, 38, 39–41, 43, 49, 54–62, 66, 94, 134, 147–8, 151, 194
Petrovsky, Misha, 137, 184–5
Piatakov, 47
Piatnitsky, Osip, 60, 64
Pinero, Arthur, 2
Piratin, Phil, 146
Polish Communist Party, 50
Pollitt, Brian, 147, 148
Pollitt, Harry, x, 6, 9–11, 19–20, 22, 29, 39, 43, 45, 47, 55, 57, 59–61, 63–4, 65–6, 68, 81–2, 91–2, 94–8, 101, 103, 104, 123, 124, 125, 134–5, 138, 146–7, 148, 150, 156–7, 160, 184, 190
Popov, 76
POUM, 103
Practical Psychology Club, 2
Pravda, 134
Pritt, D.N., 126
Promexport, 31, 86
Pushkin, Aleksandr, 13, 116

Quigley, Dr Carroll, 178–9

Radek, Karl, 48
Rakosi, Matyas, 13
Rand, Ayn, 180
Rathbone, Hugo, 54, 136, 191
Rathbone, Joyce, xi, 57, 136, 137–8, 184–5, 191
Rathbone, Nellie, 22, 23, 24, 54, 55, 57–8, 90, 135–6, 191
Reckitt, Eva, 22, 23, 24

Reckitt, Maurice, 18, 23, 58, 64–5
Red International of Labour Unions, 15
Regent Street Polytechnic, 116
Regent Theatre, 2
Republican Party, 180
Riley, Dr Nick, 46
Rimel, Anita, 51, 75, 80–1, 84, 139, 140–1, 188–9, 190
Rimel, Diana, xi
Rimel, Hetty, *see* Bower, Hetty
Rimel, Pearl, vii, ix, x, xi, 33–8, 50–2, 58, 60, 73, 76, 80–4, 90, 138, 139–40, 151, 154, 173, 176, 187, 189, 190, 192, 193
Robeson, Paul, 123
Roosevelt, Franklin, 179, 182–3
Rothstein, Andrew, 42, 120, 126, 136–7
Rothstein, Theodore, xi, 136
Ruslanova, Lidia, 150
Russell, Bertrand, 29, 92, 93
Russian Centre for the Preservation of Documents, x
Russian Social Democratic Party, 20
Rust, Bill, 1, 2, 3, 4, 5–10, 11, 12, 13, 16, 22, 41, 45, 67, 99–100, 101, 102–3, 104, 110, 111–12, 113, 114, 115, 116, 119, 120, 121–3, 125, 146–7, 148, 159, 160, 164
Rust, Kathleen, *see* O'Donoghue, Kathleen
Rust, Rosa, vii, ix, x, xi, 1, 2, 3, 4, 5, 7–9, 12–13, 15, 16, 21, 31, 41, 99–102, 104–17, 119–121,

122–3, 126–7, 150, 159, 160–4, 165, 166, 187, 188, 193
Rykov, 47, 98

St Joan, 2
Scales, Delia, xi
Scotsman, 162
Section Française de l'Internationale Ouvrière, 35, 51
Sharon, Ariel, 182
Sheffield United, 2
Shelley, Percy Bysshe, 121
Sinn Fein, 155
Shevardnadze, Eduard, 169
Sling, Otto, 147
Smith, F.E., 17
Smolensk Prison, 80, 84
Socialist League, 46
Socialist Workers Party, 165
Society for Cultural Relations with the Soviet Union, 126
Soham murders, 192–3
Solidarity America, 181
Soviet Weekly, 119
Soviets in America, 75, 76
Spender, Stephen, 95
Stakhanovite movement, 77
Stalin, Joseph, vii, viii, x, 5, 10, 11, 19, 22–3, 33, 38, 39, 40, 43, 45, 46, 48, 49, 50, 59, 63, 66, 67, 70, 71, 74, 87, 95–6, 97–8, 101, 102, 103, 105–6, 115, 119, 123–4, 130–4, 135, 136, 141, 143–4, 147, 148, 157, 158, 167, 172, 184, 185, 190, 192, 193, 194
Stanislavsky, Constantin, 9

Strong, Anna Louise, 22
Supreme Soviet Economic Council, 22
Sutcliffe, Herbert, 2
Sutyagin, Igor, 194

Tass, 119, 127
Taylor, Kay, *see* O'Donoghue, Kathleen
Thatcher, Margaret, 100, 181
Thompson, Llewellyn, 142
Thornton, David, xi, 120, 127, 162, 164–5, 166
Thornton, George, xi, 120–1, 123, 126–7, 136, 159, 161–4, 165, 166
Thorpe, Andrew, 40
Times, The, 2
Times of America, 180
Tito, Josip, 13, 16, 119
Tivel, Alexander, 48, 49
Trotsky, Leon, 7, 23, 45, 46, 47, 58, 75, 76, 189
Tukachevsky, Marshal, 48
Turner, Dr David, x

Ushakov, Z., 132
Utley, Freda, vii, ix, xi, 25, 28–33, 37, 52–4, 55, 58, 60, 86–93, 94, 140, 141–5, 146, 178–9, 184, 187, 192, 193
Utley, Jon Basil, xi, 52–4, 87, 88, 89, 93, 138, 141, 145, 178, 179–84, 187–8

Vasiliev, 74–8, 79
Vereker, Gordon, 69, 70

Villi the Clown, *see* Campbell, William

Volga Germans, 105–6, 122

Von Hindenberg, Field Marshal, 1

Vortex, The, 2

Washington Post, 179, 180

Washington Times, 180

Webb, Beatrice, 16–17, 23, 65, 134

Webb, Sidney, 16–17, 23, 65, 134

Wedgwood, Josiah, 70, 71

Wesker, Arnold, 157–8

Wesker, Leah, 157–8

Wesker Trilogy, 157

Wheeldon, Hetty, 46

Wheeldon, William, 46

Whistler, James, 3

Wincott, Len, 151–4

Workers Educational Association, 16, 28

Workers' News, 21, 22, 24

Yezhov, N.I., 48, 74, 87

Young Communist League, 1, 6, 11, 67, 120

Zapatista Army for National Liberation, 177

Zinoviev, Grigori, 23, 33, 47, 92, 97–8

Zurich University, 29